PAKISTAN
THE POLITICAL ECONOMY
OF LAWLESSNESS

PAKISTAN

THE POLITICAL ECONOMY
OF LAWLESSNESS

Azhar Hassan Nadeem

OXFORD
UNIVERSITY PRESS

OXFORD

UNIVERSITY PRESS

Great Clarendon Street, Oxford OX2 6DP

Oxford University Press is a department of the University of Oxford.
It furthers the University's objective of excellence in research, scholarship,
and education by publishing worldwide in

Oxford New York

Auckland Cape Town Dar es Salaam Hong Kong Karachi
Kuala Lumpur Madrid Melbourne Mexico City Nairobi
New Delhi Shanghai Taipei Toronto

With offices in

Argentina Austria Brazil Chile Czech Republic France Greece
Guatemala Hungary Italy Japan Poland Portugal Singapore
South Korea Switzerland Turkey Ukraine Vietnam

Oxford is a registered trademark of Oxford University Press
in the UK and in certain other countries

ISBN 978-0-19-579621-6

Fourth Impression 2011

Typeset in Times
Printed in Pakistan by
Mehran Printers, Karachi.
Published by
Ameena Saiyid, Oxford University Press
No. 38, Sector 15, Korangi Industrial Area, PO Box 8214,
Karachi-74900, Pakistan.

For my late father
Syed Safdar Hussain Shah
to whom I owe everything
and
For my soul mate and wife, Tasneem;
sons, Hassan, Haseeb, Haider and Hannan.
They made the world
and life worthwhile for me.

CONTENTS

CONTENTS

PREFACE

During the past few decades the law and order situation in Pakistan deteriorated significantly. Not only was there a general concern about the rising crime, sectarian and ethnic violence, terrorism, drug-related offences, kidnapping for ransom and robberies but also about widespread corruption, financial mismanagement and political chaos. All these factors had their impact on economic performance. Generally targets relating to GDP, investment, savings, fiscal deficit, inflation, poverty alleviation and physical and social infrastructure remained unachieved.

As an economist turned police officer, I always had a simultaneous interest in Pakistan's economy as well as law and order. The worsening situation on the law enforcement front and unsatisfactory economic performance made me think about the possible lacuna in our economic management. Though the prevailing milieu of lawlessness had its obvious impact on the pace and quality of economic development in Pakistan, in all plans and policies, law enforcement and criminal justice administration were not given the priority they deserved. Actually no effort was made to allocate resources commensurate with the importance for law enforcement. Indeed successive governments continued to ignore law and order notwithstanding the fact that the maintenance of order was their primary duty.

During my posting as the Deputy Inspector General of Police of Gujranwala Range (from 3 August 1991 to 1 August 1993) the success story of community policing in combating crime and its impact, particularly on the confidence of the business community in the law enforcing machinery, made me think about evolving a model, measuring in concrete terms, the impact of lawlessness on economic development. The anguish and pain on the neglect of the most important vehicle of economic development, i.e. the system of criminal justice administration in general and the police in particular, were instrumental in making me undertake this research. In this connection first hand knowledge of problems relating to lawlessness and a background of the strategies of economic development adopted in Pakistan from time to time were a great help. The idea was to search for the lilt and the lift that might inspire policy-makers, economic planners, administrators, and police officers.

All said and done, the fact remains that this study is only the first of its kind which establishes linkages in quantitative terms between lawlessness and economic development with reference to Pakistan during the period from 1969 to 1996. It is, therefore, at best, an attempt to provide guidelines for further research and clarification of issues.

At the end, it will be in the fitness of things to mention that I alone remain responsible for all I have done with the data and information collected from a variety of sources and also for the views expressed herein.

ACKNOWLEDGEMENTS

Many people have helped make this book possible. To Mr Sardar Muhammad Chaudhry, former Inspector General of Police, Punjab, I am indebted for having so generously given me time to discuss various dimensions of law and order. He encouraged me to undertake this book and helped in many ways; he shared the manuscript of his book with me, and his own cogent ideas, and handed over to me many papers prepared by him in his capacity as the Inspector General of Police, Punjab. To Dr Aqdas Ali Kazmi, Joint Chief Economist, Planning Commission, Government of Pakistan, Islamabad: I am equally indebted for his generous assistance in collecting material regarding theoretical and conceptual framework. I gratefully acknowledge his help in clarifying and refining various techniques of analysing economic data. I thank Dr A. R. Kemal, Director, Pakistan Institute of Development Economics and former Chief Economist, Planning Commission of Pakistan, for critically reviewing the manuscript and giving useful suggestions.

My colleague, Deputy Inspector General of Police Mr Zamir Alam (late), helped by inviting me to participate in 'The Joint Seminar on Contemporary Issues, Concerning Criminal Justice—A Comparative Perspective' held under the auspices of the United Nations Asia and Far East Institute for the Prevention of Crime and the Treatment of Offenders (UNAFEI) and The National Police Academy, Islamabad, from 12 to 16 March 1995. Warmest thanks to my fellow participants in the 61st National Management Course of Pakistan Administrative Staff College, Lahore, and police officers posted in the central police offices and crime branches of Lahore, Peshawar, Quetta, and Karachi for assisting me in collecting accurate crime figures. I thank Mr Vaqar Ahmad, former Member Directing Staff of Pakistan Administrative Staff College, Lahore, for providing me information on various publications relevant to this book. I am grateful to Mr Ralph Lazar of Baring Securities International Ltd., America Square, London, for providing me a copy of their report on Pakistan's economy.

My old friend, Mr Asghar Ali Bukhari, assisted me in preparing graphs for which I am grateful to him. My continuing gratitude and appreciation to Mr Mazhar Sethi, Incharge Computer Bureau of the Punjab Police, Mr Vaqar Ahmad and Mr Muhammad Riaz Hussain, Computer Operators of my office for their co-operation in sorting out computer-related problems. Mr Vaqar Ahmad not only typed the final manuscript but was also singularly helpful in steering me towards new material.

For this book I have interviewed a great number of economists, industrialists, traders, dealers in stock exchange markets, criminologists, and police officers in Pakistan and Great Britain; and although there is not enough space to mention each by name, I wish to thank them all for helping me to better understand ideas, concepts and realities relevant to this book. I am particularly indebted to Dr Michael Levi, Professor in Criminology, University of Wales, Cardiff. He most warmly encouraged me to write this book and helped me by way of sharing with me his own cogent articles. I am grateful to Mr Sher Afgan, former Librarian of the Quaid-i-Azam Library, Lahore, and staff of the Pakistan Administrative Staff College Library and American Centre, Lahore, for their help in microfilming and photostatting relevant papers for me. To Ms Aquila Ismail, Associate Professor, NED University of Engineering and Technology, Karachi, I owe my thanks for editing this manuscript and rearranging it methodically. Thanks are also due to the office bearers of the Pakistan Federation of Chambers of Commerce and Industry, Karachi, and Secretaries Karachi and Lahore Chambers of Commerce and Industry for providing the relevant data.

It was an honour and a privilege for me to have been attached with a learned authority in Economics, Dr Rafique Ahmad, Professor Emeritus and former Vice Chancellor of the University of the Punjab, who acted as my guide, friend and philosopher.

For his guidance, advice and useful comments I am indebted. For inspiration and generous criticism my warmest thanks are due to him. The memories of my association with him I will cherish for the rest of my life.

I am indebted to my mother not only for her care and affection but also for constantly persuading me to concentrate my energies on completing this book as soon as possible. I especially thank Hassan, Haseeb, Haider and Hannan for providing me great moments of love and parental pride, which enabled me to spare time and energy for this book. As for my dearest wife, Tasneem, who had nurtured, sustained, and inspired me and my works throughout the past twenty years, I confess that no good things I have ever done or written would have been possible without her co-authorship.

Azhar Hassan Nadeem

1

ISSUES IN LAWLESSNESS AND DEVELOPMENT

Since no society can make any progress in a state of chaos and disorder, it is axiomatic to postulate that the conditions of law and order must have direct and significant bearing on the pace and pattern of economic development of a country. Despite the fact that lawlessness has a significant impact on economic development, a rigorous analysis of the linkages between the two remains conspicuous by its absence in the general economic literature. The only redeeming feature of the literature concerned with the identification of sources of economic growth is that during the last half of the century, empirical research has come to focus on the relationship between political instability (one obvious manifestation of law and order situation) and economic growth. A few interesting studies, reviewed later in this chapter, have appeared in recent years, which have explored the impact of political instability on growth of the specific countries and specific regions. Paradoxically, however, the issue of the linkage between law and order and economic development has generally remained neglected both in theoretical and empirical literature concerned with the identification of sources of development.

This book attempts at filling in the existing gap by presenting a quantitative measurement of the impact of lawlessness on Pakistan's economic development with special reference to the years 1969–1996, though other critical periods have also been touched upon. A quantitative measurement of the impact of lawlessness on Pakistan's economic development is yet to be effectively established. The disturbances and crimes which took place between the years 1969 and 1996 are representative of the malaise for two reasons. First, in terms of frequency, intensity, and violence of disorders and crimes, this has been the most disturbed period of Pakistan's history. Second, it has also been a period of lost opportunities of development for Pakistan. The decade of the 1980s saw the emergence of liberalized markets in the world, which helped many developing countries, particularly those lying around the Pacific Rim, to attain faster rates of growth. Pakistan could not reap benefits from global economic linkage possibly because of its internal political turmoil and strikes. Unfortunately this situation continues to persist even today. No in-depth and systematic study of the impact of lawlessness on Pakistan's economy has been undertaken so far. Stray articles have appeared in newspapers and magazines highlighting the adverse impact of disturbances on local trades and industries but the problem has not been examined in any coherent way from the standpoint of national economy as a whole.

The prevention of crimes in the context of economic development has increasingly become a matter of universal concern. The Milan Plan of Action adopted by the Seventh United Nations Congress on the Prevention of Crime and the Treatment of Offenders held in Milan in 1985 issued the following statement:

> Crime is a major problem of national and, in some cases, international dimensions. Certain forms of crime can hamper the political, economic, social and cultural development of peoples and threaten human rights, fundamental freedoms, and peace, stability and security. In certain cases it demands a concerted response from the community of nations in reducing the opportunities to commit crime and address the relevant socio-economic factors, such as poverty, inequality and unemployment. The universal forum of the United Nations has a significant role to play and its contribution to multilateral co-operation in this field should be made more effective.
>
> Interested Governments should co-operate, bilaterally and multilaterally, to the fullest extent possible, with a view to

strengthening crime prevention measures and the criminal justice process by undertaking action-oriented programmes and projects.

Crime prevention and criminal justice should be considered in the context of economic development, political systems, social and cultural values and social change, as well as in the context of the new international economic order. The criminal justice system should be fully responsive to the diversity of political, economic and social systems and to the constantly evolving conditions of society.

The above statements refer to main impediments in the way of achieving goals of effective international co-operation in the prevention of crime. Such impediments arise because of variations in legal system, differences in the stage of economic development, change in social environment, and newly emerging forms of crimes. There are many reasons behind the need for adoption of concerted effort to curb crime, the basic factor being the threat posed by organized crime and terrorism. The complexity and seriousness of this threat is on the increase as a result of the following developments:

• Unlike traditional criminal activity, which largely involved individual responsibility for individual acts, criminal and terrorist associations of persons are now typified by extremely complex organizational structures, frequently using structural models of legitimate industrial and commercial world. Similarities between terrorist and normal industrial organizations include value placed on money or power, capacity to self-finance, allocation of duties, division of sectors of activity, and the tendency to reinvest profits. The organizational structure of terrorist or crime bodies is indeed their strength, and the multidisciplinary approach necessary to combat them is not a part of the traditional law enforcement culture. Actually a combination of traditional law enforcement personnel, companies and securities regulators, and financial and scientific experts are necessary to identify individual members of organized crime structures.

• Advances in communications and technology are such that national boundaries have, in many cases, ceased to provide any impediment to unlawful activities. The growth of multinational corporations, including financial institutions, has provided even greater means of shifting moneys and obfuscating the evidentiary trail. Differences in stages of development also create scope for organized crime. Developing countries, who for their own protection and development, impose currency and exchange controls, are likely to find their financial systems targeted by organized fiscal crime. As a result of organizational structure and concomitant pooling of talent, organized crime and terrorism have become more innovative. If one area of activity is curbed, new and equally profitable areas of unlawful activity are quickly found. A good example is provided by the activities of organized crime in the United States both before and after the repeal of the 'prohibition' laws relating to alcohol.

The above mentioned factors make it obvious that crime is a complex and multidimensional phenomenon that requires systematic strategies and approaches by the criminal justice system, in accordance with existing human rights standards. Apart from its national dimensions, the problem of crime now has serious international dimensions. Crime prevention, being a global phenomenon, should not be confined to common criminality but should also deal with nationally harmful crimes, including economic crimes, environmental offences, illegal drug trafficking, terrorism, apartheid, and other unlawful activities that affect development.

The following crimes are inimical not only to peace and order but also to the overall development of a country:

Organized/Syndicated Crimes

Organized/syndicated crime groups are engaged in various crimes such as robberies, hold-ups, car-snatchings, gambling, and other such activities for the purpose of accumulating wealth and power. Illicit drug trafficking is another widespread problem. The money earned from this activity threatens to undermine legitimate business, particularly in the newly emerging financial markets.

The UN Conference on Crimes held at Cairo in early May 1995 paid special attention to the harmful financial implications of the way illegal money was circulating in the world. In this connection the following observations were made at the Conference:

Illicit drug money strengthens the economic power of criminals and gives them the power to corrupt political systems. Organized crime syndicates, including Italian and Russian mafia, Japanese yakuza, Chinese triads and Colombian drug cartels, all laundered money through deposits in unregulated banks or by buying up real estate and companies. Because the money is coming from crime it gives to criminal organization's businesses a competitive advantage against legitimate businesses. So the legitimate economy is definitely threatened by organized crime. No one really knows how much money is being laundered. A figure I think plausible is $300 billion a year.[1] We think it goes on in virtually every country in the world. The Financial Action Task Force (FATF), focused on the need for legislation to curb money laundering by criminal syndicates in Russia and Eastern Europe. Russia, where between 2,000 to 3,500 criminal syndicates operate, faces particular problems after the collapse of communist rule and an explosion of banks which authorities have been unable to regulate. We fear a sizeable number of Russian banks are either controlled or infiltrated by organized crime.[2] A country's need for capital may perhaps lead it to take the short sighted view that money has no smell, that it doesn't matter what the origin of the money is, and that it's all coming in for investment and it's all to the good. We stress that taking action against money laundering as part of financial reform is essential. You can't open up your economy without taking measures to protect it from criminal money.[3]

Criminology expert Professor Ernesto Savona, in a report prepared for the Conference, said that other criminal syndicates, many with decades of sophisticated money laundering experience behind them, were recycling money all over the world. He added that Colombian cartels, enriched by drug trafficking on an industrial scale, marketed their dirty money anywhere they were able to avoid the control system and could get the best interest rate on investment.[4]

Economic Crimes

Economic crimes and their social consequences dwarf those of inter-personal violence and crimes against property in as much as they entail losses of millions of rupees to the government and also because they often lead to murder, destruction of property or other grave allied offences. Included under this category are smuggling and bank fraud. Economic crimes also include trafficking, counterfeiting, black marketing, or mass movement of local or foreign currency in violation of existing laws, sale of prime commodities in violation of price control law, tax evasion, bank swindling, violation of land reform laws and regulations, illegal recruitment when committed by a syndicate on a large scale, fraud in securities transactions and housing. This list is by no means exhaustive. Other categories of crime may be added depending on their definition in various penal codes.

Terrorism and Insurgency

Organized threat groups in various countries including Pakistan have managed to derail development through destabilization manoeuvres. For example, Japanese gas attacks, Oklahoma bombing and South Korean gas blast and occasional bomb explosions in Pakistan have underscored the awesome power of saboteurs. A well-known American writer Clavey has defined the terrorist activity thus:

> War is a political act. Terrorism is a form of low intensity war, and therefore terrorism is also a political act. The object of the terrorist is not to overthrow the government of a country, but rather to

change the political calculus of that country. We need to remember what the enemy is. A terrorist is not a soldier, not a revolutionary, not a freedom fighter. In a country like America where every body has civil rights and the right to petition the government, a terrorist is nothing more than a common criminal. To think of such people in any other way means losing something else.[5]

While considering the significance of lawlessness in impeding economic development and finding its solution, it is pertinent to point out that no development can take place without the protection of life, liberty and property. For providing this protection it is necessary to adhere to the rule of law. In this connection an analysis of various theories of the economic impact of law and order will not be out of place.

Theories of the Economic Impact of Law and Order

The two terms, law and order and economic development, which are of critical significance in our discussion, have to be defined before we proceed with our analysis. By 'law and order' we mean the continuation of the basic norms and structures of the existing socio-legal framework ensuring stability and continuity to the prevalent modes of production and distribution. Analogously, all those conditions, which create fissures and interruptions in this framework, reflect what we call the 'law and order situation'. This is a comprehensive term, which incorporates the main factors that bring about breakdown of social order in a country. These factors can broadly be identified as:
• External aggression, i.e. wars.
• Internal political upheavals leading to political instability.
• Labour union action, involving strikes, lockouts, and other similar actions.
• Ethnic, regional or sectarian disharmonies leading to internecine conflict and disorder.

In the international and cross-country framework, the relative weight and significance of these factors can show perceptible variations and fluctuations. In many circumstances, the initiation of one particular source of law and order situation can trigger off other forces, thus exacerbating the chaotic and disorderly conditions putting immense pressures on legal, administrative and executive resources of the country.

The term 'law and order condition' can be used in juxtaposition to the aforementioned term 'law and order situation'. The 'law and order condition' is supposed to prevail when the basic socio-economic framework of the country is intact and is not facing a breakdown on account of any factors leading to a law and order situation with the result that economic growth continues without any hindrance or interruption. Hence a society which experiences law and order situation would be one which fails to meet the law and order condition. In brief, law and order situation and law and order condition, in the context of our discussion, represent mutually exclusive social structures and phenomena. Social, cultural, religious and political values and institutions that enshrine those values and make them operational in day to day business and dealings between the main agents of a particular society determine the conditions of law and order.

The second key term is economic development. This term is used to refer to 'a process whereby an economy's real national income increases over a long period of time'.[6] A popular and acceptable indicator of economic development is a gradual increase in the per capita real income of a country over a defined period of time. The path and process of economic development of a country is also affected by the interaction of a large number of socio-economic, legal and cultural factors or different combinations of such factors.

In addition to these specific 'economic' objectives, there is now a new emphasis on 'non-material' needs that cannot be dispensed, but, in addition to being valued in their own right, may be the conditions for meeting 'material' needs, like self-determination, self-reliance, political freedom and security, participation in making the decisions that affect workers and citizens, national and cultural identity, and a sense of purpose in life and work. This has been accompanied by attempts to evolve human and social indicators of development that would reflect the extent to which some of these needs are met.

Law and Order in Selected Growth Theories

The relationship between law and order and economic development, though generally absent or implicit in earlier theories of economic development, did find explicit mention in relatively recent growth theories. The relevant literature can be reviewed with reference to the following classification:
– Classical and Neo-Classical Approaches
– The Value System Theory of Growth
– Security, Welfare and Constitutional Order Approach
– Institutional Setting Theory
– Human Development Doctrine

Classical and Neo-Classical Approaches

An overview of both Classical and the Neo-Classical Growth Theories indicates that in the process of economic growth, law and order was assumed as a given factor and therefore its significance was recognized implicitly. Law and order as a determinant of economic development was spelled out in explicit terms only in the theories of growth advanced by the later day economists and economic historians such as J.J. Spengler and W. W. Rostow.

The classical landscape of economic growth presents something like a kaleidoscope composed of diversified strands such as Adam Smith's identification of growth with efficient use of the basic factors of production (namely: land, labour and capital), division of labour, stock of savings and capital accumulation; Malthus's stress on geometric rate of population growth outstanding the growth in food production, and capital growth outstripping the growth in food production, and the effect of subsistence wage; Ricardo's doctrine of economic growth as a race between increases in population and the capital stock; and J.S. Mill's emphasis on the stimulus provided by universal education, liberation of women through abolition of legal and social disabilities imposed on them and population control.

Within the classical tradition comes Karl Marx's extension of the Ricardian theory of value, emergence of 'industrial reserve army of the unemployed', exploitation of workers and their polarization against capitalists, constant elaboration of labour-displacing machinery, appearance of business crises, and finally the stage when 'the expropriated expropriate the expropriators'. Then we have Schumpeter's identification of economic change with the dynamism of individual entrepreneurs, technological innovations, inventions and demise of bureaucratized corporations.

The Value System Theory of Growth

Subsequently, attempts were made by economists to present comprehensive analysis of the phenomenon of economic change and development, which is seen as the function of a multitude of factors and determinants, affecting social behaviour and economic outcomes. For example, J.J. Spengler, in his *Theories of Socio-economic Growth: Problems in the Study of Economic Growth*, published by the National Bureau of Economic Research in July 1949, identified seventeen determinants of economic growth, out of which the first four determinants refer directly or indirectly to what we would call as 'law and order conditions'. Spengler assigned immense importance to the values and institutions relevant to the maintenance of law and order in a country. These four determinants (or law and order conditions) are as follows:

i) Makeup of the prevailing value system, in particular the values of socio-economic leaders and the values which significantly affect economic creativity and the disposition of man to put forth economically productive effort.

ii) Dominant character of the politico-economic system. Is it free enterprise, mixed, social-democratic, or totalitarian in character?

iii) Effectiveness and stability of the rules, institutions, and legal arrangements designed to preserve economic, political, and civil order.

iv) Degree of co-operation and amity obtaining between groups and classes composing the population.[7]

The structure of the prevalent value system of a community can reasonably be considered as an important condition of law and order, because the value system defines the basic norms and ethos of human conduct. For example, if the value system of a society is predominated by sectarian or ethnic dispensations, then such a society would be continuously ridden by law and order problems, thus putting frequent twists and turns to the process of economic growth.

The other conditions of law and order from (ii) to (iv) above, identified by Spengler as determinants of economic development are self-explanatory.

Security, Welfare and Constitutional Order Approach

The multi-factorial approach to economic change has been effectively extended and incorporated by W.W. Rostow in his now well-known scheme of development embodied in five stages of growth, namely, traditional society, transitional society, take-off stage, drive to maturity, and mass consumption. Rostow thus interprets economic progress as an outcome of interaction between numerous factors, sociological, economic, psychological, and political. The mechanism and linkages through which these factors influence development are provided by the following six propensities:

i) The propensity to develop fundamental sciences (physical and social).
ii) The propensity to apply science to economic ends.
iii) The propensity to accept innovations.
iv) The propensity to seek material advance.
v) The propensity to consume.
vi) The propensity to have children.

These propensities, according to Rostow, summarize 'the effective response of a society to its environment, at any period of time, acting through its existing institutions and leading social groups; and they reflect the underlying value system effective within that society'.[8]

When a society suffers from a law and order situation, the basic propensities such as to develop fundamental science, to apply science to economic ends or to accept innovations, are completely blunted and the society is deprived of the important stimuli and catalysts of growth, which have greater effectiveness and impact in the long-term perspective.

In his *Politics and the Stages of Growth* published in 1971, W.W. Rostow extends the themes of stages, 'propensities' and their linkages to the role of political factors, institutions and the law and order framework in determining the pattern of economic growth. The primary tasks of any legal government are defined as the (a) provision of security, (b) welfare and growth, and (c) constitutional order, as briefly described below.

Security: To protect the society's territorial integrity or, more generally, to secure or advance the nation's interests in the international arena of sovereign powers, as those interests are defined by those who wield effective power.

Welfare and growth: To provide for the general welfare (including, where relevant, growth).

Constitutional order: To preserve the constitutional order or adjust it by the means the constitutional order prescribes; that is, to provide justice, maintain public constraint and individual freedom of action and expression of opinion. The constitutional order—explicitly or implicitly—also defines who shall wield effective power and how he shall do it.[9]

Using Montesquieu's terms, W.W. Rostow argues that the political liberty of the subject is a tranquillity of mind arising from the opinion each person has of his safety. In order to have this liberty, it is requisite the government be so constituted as one man need not be afraid of another. According to Rostow, in Freud's terms the constitutional outcome is similar. The end-result would be a state of law to which all—that is, all who are capable of uniting—have contributed by making some sacrifice of their own desires, and which leaves none, again with the same exception, at the mercy of brute force.

There is a double balancing built into this view of the art of politics. It is not only likely that the imperatives of security, welfare, and constitutional order will clash among themselves, but each involves potential conflict and choice: war versus the possible costs of not fighting; welfare versus growth; (including individual freedom) versus order.

Rostow then concludes:

> The pursuit by government of these tasks raises immediately a kind of economic or, even, input-output problem. The execution of security, welfare, and constitutional tasks requires resources. Resources are inherently scarce and must be drawn away from private consumption and private investment. Once mobilized by government, resources must be allocated among uses that rarely converge and usually conflict. Lionel Robbins' classic definition of economics is relevant to a great deal of government and politics: 'Economics is the science, which studies human behaviour as a relationship between ends and scarce means which have alternative uses.'[10]

Institutional Setting Theory

The Nobel Laureate Douglas North of Washington University at St. Louis has formulated a more recent perception about the role of law and order.[11] He has examined the question as to why similar strategies fail to produce similar results in different countries. One of the key reasons for this failure is that too often structural economic reforms have been implemented without corresponding changes in social and political institutions. Douglas North has written extensively about this phenomenon. His studies of economic development in various parts of the world provide important answers to the dilemmas economic reformers and policy-makers face in developing countries. He has also underscored the critical role that the rule of law and equitable enforcement of legislation play in effecting lasting economic reforms and building democratic institutions in various countries. The circumstances he mentions in different countries are not different from those in Pakistan and the economists working for economic development here would learn much from the new branch of economic thought which he calls New Institutional Economics.

Professor North recognizes that standard textbook neo-classical economics, though useful and thorough in many ways, cannot explain why many nations with abundant natural resources have failed to grow wealthy, while resource-poor countries have become rich. From his research, North realized that differences in development outcomes could not be simply explained by 'bad' economic systems. Instead, he found that economies function within a broad institutional setting in which culture and ideology can help or hinder the economic growth of a nation over time. In his words: 'History demonstrates that ideas, ideologies, myths, dogmas and prejudices matter.' North has therefore focused on the role which institutional settings play in determining the character of economic performance.

From North's perspective, it is not surprising that contemporary identical reform packages often succeed in one place and fail in another. The reasons lie in variations in countries' institutional setting. North defines institutions as 'the rules of the game' which take two forms: formal law such as constitution that confides the rules under which a society and an economy function, and informal codes of conduct and behaviour. A society, however, is also affected by other established codes of conduct and norms that govern behaviour in all interactions. While economies can and have functioned without formal laws, they are bound by established informal codes. Subsistence agricultural villages have persisted effectively for centuries without laws but they have always had definite standards of social conduct. These are enforced by the conscience of the people and also by communal sanctions such as ostracism.

Informal codes may, in fact, have a more powerful hold on behaviour than formal laws. A law can be enacted to grant rights, say over property, to an individual, but it will be meaningless if it is at odds with norms of group ownership or it may be enforced only very slowly as beliefs about what is legitimate evolve. Similarly, passing laws establishing private banking will be ineffective if the surrounding culture or environment frowns on it. As North cautions, 'While the (formal) rules may be changed overnight, the informal rules usually change only ever so gradually.'

North also stresses how crucial enforcement is to the effectiveness of both informal and formal rules. Two governments may enact identical economic reform laws but the outcome will be very different from one country to the next depending on how they are enforced. If the first government reliably and impartially upholds all legislation and the new law is in accord with social values there is a good chance it will achieve its intended purpose. But in another setting the same law may not be enforced or may be enforced only selectively resulting in different behaviour and economic results. This is why in North's view 'economies that adopt the formal rules of another will have very different performance characteristics'.

A critical tenet of the New Institutional Economics is how institutions, involving a nation's rules of the game, create a powerful incentive system for a society. In North's words, 'institutions are not necessarily or even usually created to be socially effective; rather they, or at least the formal rules are created to serve the interests of those with the bargaining power to create new rules. Rules constrain people in some ways and open opportunities in others.' If a country's system rewards piracy, to use one of North's favourite examples, its people will have incentives to become pirates, indeed to become the best pirates possible. Piratical organizations will emerge and prosper. In North's framework, where institutions are the rules of the game, organizations are the players. Organizations such as the political parties, companies, trade unions, and bureaucracies may have different objectives; some will try to reap profits, others power and still others prestige. Both have in common the desire to survive and benefit in a given institutional setting. That means they will want to acquire the kind of skills and knowledge that will let them survive and will also invest in trying to change the rules to increase the benefits they receive from the system.

Human Development Doctrine

At the Eleventh Annual General Meeting of PIDE (Pakistan Institute of Development Economics), held in Islamabad from 18 to 21 April 1995, Prof. Paul P. Streeten, a leading development economist of our times, in his Quaid-i-Azam lecture, provided an excellent critical survey of the evolution of thinking on development since the early 1950s.[12] Starting with the GNP and its growth, a highly abstract and unspecified conglomerate of goods and services, irrespective of what and for whom, development thinking then turned to employment, a somewhat more specific goal. It then moved on to the concept of basic needs. The basic needs approach appealed to members of the national and international community and was therefore capable of mobilizing resources. As the basic needs concept entered the North-South dialogue, serious misconception grew around it. Developing countries viewed it as an excuse to reduce development aid and to put up protection measures, or to divert attention from the need to reform the international economic system. The result was that the concept faded away although it still has many adherents.

At the same time new concerns were incorporated in the development dialogue. They naively related economic development to the role of women (and children), physical environment, population, habitation, human rights, political freedom and governance, military expenditure and culture.

Prof. Streeten explained that the new trend in development thinking was characterized by its focus on human development, which, as defined in UNDP's Human Development Reports, implied enlargement of the range of people's choices. To elaborate it further, a human development strategy stresses the importance of institutions for improving the human conditions. Among these are, first, the central and local governments, which are expected to make markets work efficiently, to step in where they fail, and to correct maldistribution where they succeed at the expense of human needs. Secondly, there is the market; thirdly, the civil society; and fourthly, global institutions. It is in the interaction between the State and the civil society that the conditions for the good life should be found. It includes, of course, maintenance of the rule of law and protection of life, liberty and property. Prof. Streeten admits that the concept of human development cannot be caught in a single index like the one used in UNDP's Human Development Reports (1990, 1991, 1992, 1993, and 1994). Such an index, notwithstanding its limitations, has however its utility in so far as it focuses attention on important issues and presents the problem in a simplified manner. It emphasizes the need for a perception of relative security for the continuation of gainful economic activity.

Whereas classical and neo-classical economists referred to political instability as a variable affecting economic development and Rostow and J.J. Spengler explained this relationship in a little more detail, the real emphasis on the importance of human attitudes, social institutions, and political power structures has been laid by Professor Douglas North and Paul P. Streeten. Notwithstanding the complexity of the process of growth, law and order situation has always been a critical factor in determining the course of economic development.

During the past five decades there has been extensive debate as to what development is all about. Is it the relentless pursuit of a higher Gross National Product (GNP)? Is it the acquisition of the status symbols of development like sleek jets, towering skyscrapers, five star hotels, and state of the art electronic gadgetry? Or does development consist of life's three core values, life sustenance: the availability of basic necessities; self-esteem: the ability to be a person in one's own right; and freedom from servitude: the right to choose? These are all valid issues. The problems of development, however, have proved to be too complicated and multidimensional to permit an easy solution. According to Ahmad:

> Both external and internal pressures are weighing down developing countries. Externally, increasing debt burdens, shrinking resource flows, deteriorating terms of trade, and rising protectionism are creating difficulties. Internally, demographic pressures, resource inadequacies, income inequalities, social inequities, unemployment, and downward trends in output are generating socio-economic instabilities.[13]

It has to be concerned with basic human needs and the quality of life. Professor Naqvi has identified areas of weakness in the heritage of development economics. Some of these are:
  (i)   too much growth expectation from the savings rate.
  (ii) the negligence of the crucial role of technology,
  (iii) the indifference towards human capital formation,
  (iv) the under-estimation of the growth potentialities of agriculture, and
  (v)   the inadequate attention to the problems of equity and distributive justice.[14]

One need not agree with the above conclusions but there can hardly be two opinions about the important role of the government, economically and socially, in lifting up those who are below or near the poverty-line. As Ahmad has pointed out, 'Market forces will never deliver the goods to the non-privileged classes, which still form the bulk of the underdeveloped world.'[15] Education and health, particularly, are among those areas where the operation of the principles of pareto-optimality or profit-maximization can only play havoc with an already fragile social framework.

The government being an indivisible entity, its developmental and administrative roles cannot be separated. Although opinions differ about the nature and extent of governmental intervention in economic affairs, it is now being widely recognized that without maintaining rule of law and creating conditions of peace, no developmental activity can take place in either the public or private sector.

Seen in the context of above observations, during the last few decades, particularly from the years 1988–89 to 1998–99, Pakistan has faced an intertwined crisis of a collapsing economy and a deteriorating law and order situation. Erosion of business and investor confidence, instability of the macroeconomic framework, a very narrow tax base, declining exports, multiplicity of non-essential imports, a fluctuating exchange rate, low national savings, woefully inadequate human development indicators, a classic debt-trap (public debt exceeding 95 per cent of the Gross Domestic Product and 600 per cent of annual revenues),[16] a large segment of population, particularly the poor, bearing the greater burden of the cost of governance, falling revenues, poor quality of public resource use, a high rate of inflation and a low industrialization trap were the main characteristics of Pakistan's economic performance.

These economic indicators were accompanied by a kalashnikov culture resulting in ethnic and sectarian terrorism, kidnapping for ransom, bank robberies/dacoities, drug offences, emergence of organized crime of dangerous proportions, and a mushroom growth of armed militant groups as rival powers to that of the State within its formal territorial domain. Added to such crimes were corruption, loan defaults, non-payment of utility dues, a sizeable black economy, and inconsistent policies of successive governments creating problems like disputes with independent power producers. A natural outcome of this dual crisis of the economy and the deviation from the rule of law was the erosion of many of the institutions of the State through which effective governance is exercised. This book seeks to establish the causal relationship between these two developments, which have been taking place, more or less, simultaneously.[17]

Conclusion

This chapter reviews economic literature with reference to the impact of lawlessness on the pace and pattern of economic development. The interconnection between the two has found place in economic theories either implicitly or explicitly. Whereas classical and neo-classical economists referred to political instability as a variable affecting economic development and Rostow and J.J. Spengler explained this relationship in a little more detail; the real emphasis on the importance of human attitudes, social institutions, and political power structures has been laid by Professor Douglas North and Paul P. Streeten. Notwithstanding the complexity of the process of growth, law and order situation has always been a critical factor in determining the course of economic development. This has been particularly true in case of Pakistan where economic imblance and lawlessness have been taking place simultaneously. This book attempts to show in concrete terms the economic impact of lawlessness in Pakistan.

This study, though comprehensive, is by no means exhaustive. Collection of data regarding the exact impact of various types of crimes on economic performance was a Herculean task. Though capital flight in the wake of disturbances in Karachi was a well-known fact yet its quantum and magnitude were difficult to ascertain. Similarly the size of black economy was anybody's guess. There were claims and counter claims from various quarters depending on their interests. Whereas the industrial and commercial circles painted a very grim picture of the impact of virtual anarchy in Karachi in particular and other parts of the country in general, the official circles were taking pains to give the impression that the trouble was confined only to a part of Karachi and economic activity had not been much affected by these disturbances. It was, therefore, very difficult to arrive at the correct magnitude of the impact of lawlessness on Pakistan's economic performance. However, relying on independent sources, I have tried to present the actual impact of law and order situation on the economic development of Pakistan.

Similarly crime data was to be collected from all the four provincial police forces which, on account of a sizeable dark figure of crime, presented various problems. There being no reliable crime record for tribal areas the study had to be confined to crime data and law and order incidents recorded by the provincial police forces. Regarding white collar crime only official data was available in a scattered form. The figures regarding key economic variables too were to be checked and counter checked with reference to independent sources in view of the doubtful credibility of official data. I had to interpret the data collected from various sources with reference to the relationship between lawlessness and economic development. Causes of peculiar economic performance, other than those resulting from a law and order situation, were carefully analysed and ruled out. It was extremely difficult and was to be done under obvious limitations.

The remedies proposed, too, point towards a viable system of criminal justice administration commensurate with the dictates of economic development. However, there does exist room for further research on the subject. Actually this is the need of the hour and modern economicsts should pay sufficient attention towards it. In the context of Pakistan, this subject assumes pivotal importance because of the fact that the preservation of a smooth law and order condition is a prerequisite for achieving the goal of sustainable economic development.

NOTES

1. Griffiths, D. (1995), 'Monitoring International Money Laundering', The UN Conference on Crime, 9 May, Cairo.
2. Ibid.
3. Ibid.

4. Savona, E. (1995) 'Criminal Syndicates', The UN Conference on Crime, 9 May, Cairo.
5. Clavey, T. (1995), *Terrorism*, Article published in the *Los Angeles Times*, reproduced in the daily *News International*, 20 April 1995, Lahore.
6. Meier, G.M. and Baldwin, R. (1972), *Economic Development—Theory, History, Policy*, Charles E. Tuttle Company, Tokyo. Asia Edition.
7. Spengler, J. (1949), *Theories of Socio-economic Growth: Problems in the Study of Economic Growth*, National Bureau of Economic Research, July 1949.
8. Rostow, W. (1971), *Politics and the Stages of Growth*, Cambridge University Press.
9. Ibid.
10. Ibid
11. North, Douglas, C. (1991), *Institutions, Institutional Change and Economic Performance*, Cambridge University Press.
12. Streeten, P. (1995), *Development Ideas in Historical Perspective—The New Interest in Development*, Quaid-e-Azam Lecture at the Eleventh Annual General Meeting of Pakistan Institute of Development Economics, 18–21 April, Islamabad.
13. Ahmad, R. (1993), Book Review of *Development Economics—A New Paradigm*, Pakistan Banker, Magazine of the Punjab Bank, July–December 1993.
14. Naqvi, N. H. (1993), *Modern Development Thinking Areas of Global Consensus*, Pakistan Banker, Magazine of the Bank of Punjab; January–June 1993, Lahore, p. 47.
15. Ahmad, R. (1993), Book Review of *Development Economics—A New Paradigm*, Pakistan Banker, Magazine of the Punjab Bank, July–December 1993, Lahore, p. 124.
16. Hassan, O. (1999), 'Pakistan's Debt Problem: Its Changing Nature and Growing Gravity', Paper presented at the 15th Annual Conference of the Pakistan Society of Development Economists. 6 November, Islamabad.
17. The relationship between law and order and economic development has been explained in Appendix-I with reference to Computable General Equilibrium Model. It mentions real and nominal flows pertaining to various indicators like production, investment, and markets of products, labour and capital, value of output, expenditure and a host of factors related to consumption and investment demand. It establishes logical relationships with regard to endogenous and exogenous variables. They are, by and large, affected by the prevailing law and order situation. Upon that basis a law and order computable general equlibrium model has been developed for the present study. I have designated it as Modified Structualist CGE Model of Linkages between Law and Order and Economic Development.

2

SOCIO-ECONOMIC DEVELOPMENTS AND CRIMES

This chapter refers to indicators of economic and social changes, i.e. urbanization, housing, unemployment, juvenile delinquency and health care and shows that economic development is not necessarily an unmixed blessing. It lends to all-round changes in the socio-economic setup and its own pattern is also affected by such changes. There is thus a close and mutually interdependent linkage between the processes of economic and social changes which, if not properly handled, breeds anti-law activities related to crimes.

Urbanization

At a macro level, there is general agreement that the question of urban development and the sociology of the city must be discussed in the context of the overall political economy in which the urbanization is taking place.[1] From this perspective vulnerability to urban crime is seen as related to rapid unplanned growth with insufficient long-term concern for housing, employment, educational, medical and social services for recreation and the use of leisure.

At a micro level the concern is for avoidance of factors, which may force co-option into crime. In the experience of some eastern European countries, careful social planning at the city level might avoid increased criminality in circumstances of rapid urbanization. In developing nations, increase in criminality in the cities is seen not as a direct result of urbanization, but as sudden and unplanned urban expansion (economic colonialism). From the criminological perspective, the discussion on 'urban criminality shows a dearth of information and analytical insight with respect to many issues of criminality in the city'.[2]

The criminological perspective in relation to cities has been much too influenced by questions of law and order neglecting other important issues such as the examination of interrelations between various aspects of city life and crime. To overcome present inadequacies of systematic knowledge in the area, what is needed is an integrative, interdisciplinary perspective resulting from the participation of urban planners, urban sociologists and economists, educators, population and manpower experts and health and housing planners.

Contemporary urbanization in developing countries differs significantly from patterns of former periods. In developed nations urbanization took many decades while the process in developing nations is taking place far more rapidly. Between 1950 and 1975 the urban areas of developing countries involved an enormous number of people, about 400 million. Between 1975 and 2000 the increase will be close to one billion people.

The number of large cities in the developing world is expanding rapidly: in 1950 only one city in South America had a population of over 5 million while five in the industrialized world were of this size. By the year 2000, forty cities in the developing world have the same or larger size, compared with only twelve in developed nations. Eighteen cities in the developing world are expected to have more than 10 million inhabitants and one at least, Mexico City, is expected to triple this number. The characteristics of urbanization among developing nations vary according to broad regional groups. Notwithstanding the difference in patterns, in all of them, urbanization is excessively rapid, concentrated and costly, and this brings concentrations of poverty and inefficiency (especially in relation to housing and public service), congestion and pollution. In contrast to these trends, mention is often made of economic opportunities. Urbanization provides for increases in productivity and income, and reduction in the incidence of poverty.

Though rural to urban migration is frequently mentioned as the primary factor of urbanization, population growth appears to be equally crucial, particularly in some countries of Latin America and the African region. Migrants move mainly in relation to forces that determine the location of occupational opportunities, and perception of chances to improve the overall quality of life. The nature and patterns of industrialization, the structure of agricultural activities, the growth of transportation and communications and improved educational opportunities also have a differential impact on migration.[3]

Urbanization is a psychological, social, political and economic reality. It connotes all types of changes, in patterns of population distribution and displacement, work habits, housing, greater complexity of life, urban unemployment and under-employment, urban poverty, impersonality of relationships, conflicting socialization processes and increased opportunities for crime.

In some Latin American countries, it has been reported that urbanization in relation to juvenile delinquency signals the transition from the individual offender to collective forms of crime perpetration.[4] Delinquency and crime are not unduly concentrated in the urban areas of any country, but in larger cities. In the developing countries, such cities as Mumbai, Kolkata, Bangkok, Curacao, Bogota, Mexico City, Cairo, Lagos, Accra, Abidjan, Kampala, and Nairobi have a much larger share of the delinquency and crime than their percentage of the population would warrant. Migration to cities results in a highly heterogeneous population. In one African city, the population make consists of as many as twenty to thirty tribal groups with varied cultural backgrounds. Tens of thousands of youth in a Central American country migrate from the countryside to a city, which is an internationally known tourist sea resort. In this city, youth engage in various forms of crime and are often victims of crime, both individual and organized.

The dynamics of human settlements at the micro and macro levels require creative, interpretative thinking and application to provide in urban settings conditions for human and social space, reinforcing basic values of safety, co-operation, peace and opportunities for meaningful interpersonal and community interaction. While long range preventive action requires institutional change, some direct safety measures can be taken to reduce occasions for the perpetration of crime. More structured efforts involve remodelling of old structures, low cost housing schemes with adequate security, designs that will foster in residents strong territorial identification with their environment and the preservation of privacy as an essential human right.[5]

Modern high-rise complexes with their anonymity as well as squatter settlements are both counter to a balanced perspective of personal space. But, in developing areas, the shortage of housing is an alarming factor affecting the quality of life. In Africa, for instance, it has been estimated that on the average for each housing unit built in the city, ten new families were immigrating from rural areas.[6] This mass migration facing the lack of housing adds to the emergence of squatter settlements in which the quality of life has been so much impaired that crime can emerge as a concomitant phenomenon.

In the case of Pakistan the process of urbanization can be explained with reference to Karachi which is the largest metropolitan city of Pakistan. It is the industrial and commercial and trade centre of the country, and has a well-developed economy that continues to show growth rates in excess of 6 per cent of Pakistan's total population and 24 per cent of the urban population. The population growth rate is estimated to be around 5.6 per cent per annum, of which 3 per cent is Karachi's natural growth and between 2 and 3 per cent is due to migration. Karachi provides one-quarter of the country's federal revenues and 23.2 per cent of its GDP. Not surpassingly, since it is the industrial and financial capital of Pakistan, more than half of the country's bank deposits lie in banks in Karachi and almost three-quarters of all issued capital is raised in the city.[7] In addition, 32.9 per cent of the national value—added in manufacturing, 26.4 per cent in trade, 61.6 per cent in banking and insurance, and 37.3 per cent in services, is generated by the city.'[8]

Karachi has a high per capita income—$900 in May 1993—almost two-and-a-half times Pakistan's GDP per capita. Estimates show that more than 30 per cent of income accrues to the relatively affluent households in the city—those who earn as much as ten times the country's GDP per capita.[9] Other indicators also clearly show Karachi's dominance in the economic and social sphere: the male literacy rate for Karachi is 20 per cent higher than the male urban literacy rate for Pakistan as a whole, while the female literacy rate for Karachi is almost twice as high as for the rest of the urbanized country. Although only 8 per cent of Pakistan's population lives in Karachi, it owns about 35 per cent of all television sets in the country, and almost half of the cars registered in Pakistan are registered in Karachi.[10]

Almost all economic and social indicators show that Karachi is still way ahead of the rest of the country in terms of development, despite the fact that other areas, notably central Punjab, have benefited from changes in Pakistan's economic, social, and political fabric.[11] Nevertheless, the richest and largest settlement in the country, which supplies a large amount of revenue to the exchequer, has been confronted with serious problems that have hampered further development and progress. While the collapse and failure of government institutions has been all pervasive, Karachi's difficulties may have been compounded by the uniqueness of the city's political developments. Violence and carnage dominated Karachi's landscape for much of the 1990s and exacerbated the problems typically associated with a large and fast-growing metropolis.

The formal sector and the government planning machinery have failed to develop and provide affordable and appropriate land, housing and/or credit for the lower-income groups and the poor in Karachi; instead, the informal sector fulfils this need.[12] Due to poor planning at a city level, poverty in terms of poor housing and social services has actually been created by government institutions.[13] The macro economy impacts heavily on the incidence of poverty across Pakistan, where higher GDP growth and other related factors affect the livelihood and living standards of the people. In Karachi, because of its linkage with the rest of the economy, especially in industry, manufacturing, and the export sector, a poor performance of the overall economy affects a larger number of people, thus contributing to more unemployment and poverty.[14]

Since the early 1990s, the IMF and World Bank structural adjustment programmes have had a major impact on the country's economy. Because of their austerity drives, privatization, cutbacks in subsidies, reductions in development expenditure, and cuts in the fiscal deficit, they have helped to maintain, if not create, poverty. Clearly, these policies do not play a poverty alleviation role.[15]

Mapping poverty is difficult in a city like Karachi, where different sets of indicators are used to capture the extent of poverty. Saying that half of the city's population lives in *katchi abadis* (squatter settlements) need not imply that half the population is poor; katchi abadis, particularly in Karachi, maintain a standard of living well ahead of most areas of the country and possibly even better than many households living in planned areas; the provision of services in unplanned areas and katchi abadis, due to the active role of the informal sector, may in fact be far better than that of the planned settlements.[16]

The process of settlement by the nonofficial sector can be explained with reference to the Orangi Pilot Project. Orangi Township consists for the most part of katchi abadis. It covers an area of over 8000 acres and has a population of about one million living in 94,122 houses. The population is mixed, consisting of mohajirs (immigrants from India), Biharis (immigrants from Bangladesh), Pathan and Punjabi immigrants, and local Sindhis and Balochis. The majority of them belong to the working classes. They are day-labourers, skilled workers, artisans, small shopkeepers, pedlars, and low-income white-collar workers. The settlement began in 1965. Land colonization, house building, development of income-generating activities, were all undertaken by local residents with help from the informal sector and without any assistance from government agencies.[17] Writing about the energy and initiative of the people of Orangi, Akhtar Hameed Khan says,

Familiarity with Orangi reveals that a town larger than Colombo or Gujranwala receives scanty services from official agencies The people of Orangi depend mainly on 'informal' sources. Land is obtained through *dallals* (middle-men); credit, materials, and advice for housing is obtained from *thallewalas* (block manufacturers). Self-supporting schools teach their children. Quacks (physical and spiritual) treat their ailments. They continuously resort to the black market or the bribe market for business facilities or welfare amenities or peace from harassment. That this informal sector and its black market is many times the size of the official sector indicates the weakness of government planning for the poor. At the same time it indicates the vitality of the poor and their skill in the art of survival. Besides, their vitality is demonstrated by the presence everywhere of *anjumans* (associations) which lobby intensely all the time, presenting claims and guarding gains. It is further demonstrated by the growing consciousness, specially among the younger generation, of their collective vote power and street power.[18] However, this informal sector, in spite of its vitality and energy, cannot effectively overcome the technical and managerial problems that its involvement in development has forced upon it, as it has no access to relevant research or qualified professional expertise.[19]

Improvements in the legal and registration systems, in the judicious relaxation of land regulations and controls, in the adequate provision of essential services to land used for housing, and in long-term loans and moderate interest rates, will certainly contribute to the alleviation of this dramatic problem in developing countries.

In some countries, the benefits of these steps, when combining the efforts of the public and private sectors have reached large numbers of the urban poor. The conditions faced by overcrowding and dilapidated housing contribute seriously to health hazards for the urban poor, and negatively affect the socialization pattern of children and youth in developing nations. Various policy bases concerning industrialization have heightened the rapid process of urbanization. Industries tend to locate themselves in urban areas to benefit from easy access to capital and labour, and to financial, legal and technical support infrastructures.

In addition, mention should be made of the fact that sometimes preferential treatment in foreign exchange policies, tariffs and industrial incentives are given to cities than to rural areas, as well as lower energy prices and transportation. Furthermore, easy access to central government authorities and the pace of agricultural developments have further fostered these processes. The elimination of these biases is perhaps a preliminary precondition for a more balanced and equitable development, combined with strong efforts to provide the countryside with an adequate infrastructure for industrialization, including educational and social service components. A policy of effective decentralization should be carefully planned, including assessment of proposed alternative.

In devising strategies to cope with urban problems, it is important to mention the need to focus on the inadequacy of basic urban services: water, health, housing, education and transportation, and the urgency to provide remunerative employment to the unskilled and the migrant. These efforts should be combined with a systematic strategy for accelerated rural development viewed in an integrated perspective.

Housing

In many cities of developing nations more than half of the population lives in slums and squatter settlements; between one-fourth and one-third of the urban population have no access to water supply and have no facilities for the disposal of human waste.[20] This is, indeed, one of the more urgent problems facing developing societies. Housing strategies in developing countries have to counter the fact that the urban poor are particularly affected in secure adequate shelters, due to their incapacity to compete for scarce housing supplies. Since they are not able by themselves to remove institutional and economic barriers affecting their access to the housing market, they engage sometimes in land invasion, illegal land deals or illegal developments. Here is where public policy concerning supply of land services and finance is particularly pertinent. Pakistan has been no exception to this process.

There are 19.7 million households in Pakistan (13.5 million in the rural and 6.2 million in the urban areas), accommodating a total population of 131.5 million. The household size has marginally declined from 6.7 persons in 1981 to 6.6 persons in 1998 which is overcrowded by international standard. The present estimated backlog of housing is 4 million units, including 52 per cent to deal with overcrowding plus 48 per cent substandard dilapidated houses, requiring immediate re-construction. About 35 per cent of the total urban population lives in the katchi abadis and slums. Most of the rural houses are *katcha* and devoid of water supply and sanitation facilities. Safe water supply is available to 58 per cent of the total population and sewerage/sanitation facilities to only 32 per cent. The corresponding figures in the urban areas are 80 per cent and 50 per cent, while in the rural areas, these are 48 per cent and 23 per cent, respectively.[21]

As far as the provision of low-income housing is concerned, attempts in the past have failed to address the needs of this community, as government policy has been incompatible with the economics and sociology of the poor. The cost of development and/or lease has been inaffordable for this target group, and in most cases members of the middle class have bought low-income houses. The demand for housing by the poor is immediate and they cannot wait for the long-drawn-out development process to be completed and for possession to be taken; often this process takes years. The poor in Pakistan, whether in rural areas or in cities, have no representation in framing policies. Most of the 'technocrats who give physical shape to political thinking have also been from the middle classes and have not only a very poor understanding of the urban poor, but look upon them with suspicion and hostility. Thus, government policies have invariably catered to the needs of the middle and upper classes at the expense of the poor.'[22] This consistent failure in formal/government attempts to provide for housing and basic urban services, such as land, credit, water, sanitation, transport, employment, health, and education, has given rise to the burgeoning informal sector.

Despite the huge success of projects like the Orangi Pilot Project and smaller groups, which have significantly altered the lives of many thousands of the poor in Karachi, NGOs are not the sole solution to the problems of the low-income groups in Karachi. NGOs cannot replace government at a city level; however, they can play a useful role working either with the government or in areas where government has failed to deliver services. Nor can government be replaced by the private sector through an indiscriminate process of privatizing state-owned and state-run concern.[23] While it is clear that government and its institutions have been a failure in the context of Karachi, the knee-jerk response of privatization is inappropriate.

Unemployment

In 1977, there were close to 40 million persons openly unemployed in the world, 12 million were in Africa, 22 million in Asia (excluding China and other Asian countries with planned economies), and 6 million in Latin America. There is an increase in the number of unemployed in the world from 1975 to 1977. In effect, unemployment rates have increased from 3.9 per cent to 4.3 per cent in Asia, from 7.1 to 8.1 in Africa and from 5.1 to 5.6 in Latin America.[24]

In the majority of Latin American countries the minimum unemployment rate of the decade falls either in 1972 or 1973 and the maximum either in 1976 or 1978. In developing countries under-employment is a more preoccupying phenomenon than open unemployment. In Latin America unemployment is the lot of the secondary labour force constituted by women and young people who belong to the labour market. In most cases, it is under-employment, which causes poverty.[25]

Economic Survey of Pakistan (1998–99) defines unemployment as all persons of ten years of age and above who during the period under reference were: (a) without work, i.e. were not having paid employment or self-employment; (b) currently available for work, i.e. were available for paid employment or self-employment; and (c) seeking work, i.e. had taken specific steps in a specified period to seek paid employment or self-employment.[26] According to this definition, about 2.4 million persons of labour force were estimated as unemployed in 1999.[27]

The unemployment rate is only one of the indicators of the unemployment situation in a society and needs to be complemented by other indicators, especially the frequency and duration of unemployment. Pakistan witnessed a ban on recruitment in government offices and a slowdown of economic activity for a long time during the period from 1989–90 to 1998–99. This resulted in increased numbers of suicides and a mushroom growth of young militants who were exploited by extreme sectarian outfits. The culture of violence flourished under these conditions.

Poverty

The profile of poverty in the world varies with its definition. The World Bank defines poor as he/she whose income is not sufficient to satisfy his/her minimum food requirement; ILO adds basic nutrition requirements resulting in higher poverty lines. It has been said that: 'Half of the mankind was below the poverty line in 1974 and more than one-third will be still poor in 1982.'[28] The impact of the present recession has been quite severe both in relation to unemployment and poverty. Contrary to the hypothesis that recession and stabilization policies have had no impact on the degree of equality and integration of the societies, which have implemented them, the available data indicates that, on the average, they have worsened the employment situation and the income distribution pattern.[29] The reduction in public expenditures associated with the impact of the recession has also affected employment directly, especially public employment. Data on wages and salaries would indicate that their purchasing power has decreased in the aftermath of the implementation of stabilization policies.[30] A reduction in the income of the households of the informal sector has been very likely a result of the recession and stabilization policies. This has resulted in increases in the proportion of under-nourished children and malnutrition in general, when families are pushed below the poverty line.[31]

In synthesis, the results of recession and stabilization policies have worsened income distribution patterns and the poverty of the population. This, in turn, has affected the structure and functions of the family and its multi-varied functions. Prevalent among these changes are the result of the recession in the participation of women in the economic structure of societies, and as a result, changes in fertility ratios and nuptiality.

Seen in the context of Pakistan, much of the research done on poverty, prior to 1990–91, indicates an impressive downturn in its incidence in Pakistan. A number of studies show that decline in the incidence of consumption based poverty in Pakistan has been consistent and substantial throughout the decade of the 1980s.[32] The head count ratio of the poor in 1984–85, which was as high as 46 per cent, declined continuously to 37.4 per cent in 1987–88 and further still to 34 per cent in 1990–91. Pakistan's fall in poverty took place at a time when poverty actually increased in Latin America, the Middle East, and North Africa. However, the fall in poverty between 1984 and 1991 was far greater in faster-growing, more dynamic countries like China, Indonesia, Korea, Malaysia, the Philippines, and Thailand.[33] And as we will show below, herein lies the key to the poverty question in Pakistan and in Karachi.

Since no data of a comparable level for a pre- and post-1991 period exists, the analysis conducted by Sayeed and Ghaus[34] uses an indirect approach. After identifying the causes of the fall in incidence in the first place, they look at these factors in the post-1991 period, taking a macro perspective. The reasons that are given for the fall in poverty prior to the 1990s are the high overall GDP growth, impact of remittances of workers in the Middle East, the role of safety nets in protecting individuals and households from falling below a particular minimum level, and the contribution that fiscal policy and government expenditure have made to the economy and to a large number of beneficiaries.

The analysis of poverty in Pakistan suggests that poverty returned to Pakistan in the 1990s, as the growth rate of the economy had fallen, remittance declined, food subsidies have cut, and inflation increased, affecting the poorest the most. Government curtailment of spending on development expenditure only makes things worse. Public sector employment, historically an important anti-poverty measure, has fallen, while wages have decreased in real terms: real wages, which increased by 0.7 per cent between 1980 and 1991, fell by 2 per cent between 1991 and 1995,[35] public sector employment is estimated to have fallen by 10 per cent between 1990 and 1993, and 43.2 per cent of workers previously employed in public enterprises were laid off by their new employers.[36] Providing statistical evidence for these figures, Kemal has shown that the share of wages in national income fell from 32.3 per cent in 1987–88 to 30 per cent in 1990–91, and personal income distribution, which improved between 1979 and 1988, worsened considerably between 1987 and 1991, with the overall Gini coefficient increasing from 0.35 in 1987 to 0.41 in 1991; in rural areas, the Gini coefficient increased from 0.307 to 0.41 in the same period.[37] In addition, not only was there a cut in food subsidies of 22.4 per cent between 1991 and 1995,[38] but also the 'rationalized' tax structure resulted in more indirect taxes, with a decline of 4.3 per cent in the tax burden on the rich, and an increase of 10.3 per cent in the tax burden on the poor.[39]

The return of poverty to Pakistan in the 1990s needs to be seen in the context of the imposition of the structural adjustment programmes of the IMF and the World Bank, which were initiated in 1988.[40] Research by Khan and Aftab[41] shows that 'structural adjustment conditionalities are proving to be detrimental to the socio-economic well being of the poor.'[42] While the causality of the growing incidence of poverty in

Pakistan with the involvement of the IMF and World Bank in its economy may be debated, one thing is clear: research suggests that the increase in poverty is closely related to the poor performance of the economy at an overall macro level. There are many factors, which are generating and aggravating the poverty situation in Pakistan. Unjust distribution of resources, monopolization of power, corruption, stratification of society into groups, classes and vested interests, all are responsible for the deplorable situation that confronts us in Pakistan.[43]

These changes are also reflected in family socialization pattern, especially the behaviour of children and youth. The psycho-social impact of these changes and its increasing pressure in given population sectors, to depart from conforming legal norms and values and to engage in criminal and/or deviant activities, cannot be underestimated.

Juvenile Delinquency

The school has always been mentioned in relation to the complex aetiology of crime in developing societies. A revitalization of education as a force for development and social cohesion is urgently needed. This implies the need for educational models suited to the practical priorities of natural growth and conditions of rapid social change.

Most of the juveniles in conflict with the law have experienced the effect of educational problems in the context of a varied aetiological phenomenology. It has been said that instruction and formal education imparted at school, rather than promoting basic values common to all sectors of given nations in development, has accentuated cultural cleavages and heightened discriminatory policies against ethnically and culturally disadvantaged groups. The school could be used to transmit and build a socialization process oriented towards social justice, co-operation, solidarity and respect for others and the environment. The educational process could greatly help in the prevention of crime and the rehabilitation of the offender.

As a result of educational efforts, the proportion of illiterate adults in the world declined from 44 per cent in 1950 to 39 per cent in 1960 and 34 per cent in 1970. It was estimated that by 1977, about 800 million people—one-third of the world's population—were still illiterate. Africa, Latin America, and to a lesser extent, South Asia, remain the most affected regions.[44]

Financial constraints and economic problems combined with a questioning of the efficiency of educational systems are, however, restraining the move towards developing areas or the expansion of secondary and higher levels of education in other developing countries. There are some 800 million adult illiterates in developing countries. In practice, nearly all children who do not complete several years of primary school remain illiterate. Nearly a third of the children of primary school age in developing countries are not in school. A small percentage of rural children complete four or five years of primary school.[45]

No precise figures pertaining to juvenile delinquency in Pakistan are available. However, on 31 March 1999 the total population of juvenile offenders in the prisons of Pakistan stood at 3780 including 3378 under trial, 340 convicted and 62 condemned young prisoners.[46] Traditional factors like money, land, women, *ghairat* (honour), old enmity, and water disputes are the main factors causing juvenile delinquency in Pakistan. Added to these factors is the recent phenomenon of the emergence of *deeni madaris* (institutions of religious education) which impart instruction in militancy and sectarian hatred to young persons below eighteen years of age. According to a recent survey conducted by the Special Branch of the Punjab Police, the number of such insitutions in the Punajb stood at 3080 in the beginning of the year 1999.[47] Raw minds with indoctrination to kill persons belonging to the sect other than their own add to the number of juvenile delinquents involved in serious offences. A recent trend of chatting on the Internet by young boys and girls, often using filthy language, has a tendency to cause gang wars. It is thus a contributory factor to juvenile delinquency in Pakistan.

Health Hazards

In relation to nutrition, low-income countries had, on the average, 35 per cent of their population suffering from malnutrition. They would need to increase the number of physicians nearly tenfold and the number of hospital beds by almost two and a half times in order to reach the level of other developed countries whose modest capital income ranges from $400 to $1000. About one billion people in the developing areas are at risk of contracting one of six tropical diseases: malaria, shistosomiasis, planasis, tpyanosomiasis, leischmamiasis, and leprosy.[48] These conditions contribute to the social victimization of millions in the under-developed areas. Without appropriate cross-sector planning, legal victimization, in the form of criminal sanctions are prone to further aggravate these massive problems.

Like its literacy and education statistics, Pakistan's health statistics are extremely poor. Life expectancy is only 60 years; the IMR 80 per 1000, and the MMR 340; 55 per cent of the population have access to health services (a proportion higher than for countries at similar levels of development), 70 per cent to safe water, and 47 per cent to adequate sanitation; and 40 per cent of children are classified as malnourished.[49&50]

The effects of malnutrition and ill-health in children seriously impairs school performance and working habits, and this pattern of imposed failures is prone to emerge in the form of criminal behaviour as an alternative way to cope with distressing life conditions. The causes of delinquency are multifarious and could not be asserted that either economic conditions or malnutrition or satisfaction of all basic needs were invariably and directly associated with delinquency—although all of these factors played certain roles. The best that could be asserted was, that in all probability, a social policy, which aimed at keeping primary social groups intact, had the chance of success in delinquency prevention.

Life expectancy at birth in low-income developing countries averages 50 years. In middle-income developing countries, it averages 60 years, and in industrialized countries, 74 years. Of the some 120 million infants born in 1977, 10 per cent still died before reaching their first birthday (giving an infant mortality rate of 100) and another 4 per cent before their fifth birthday. In many developing countries, the rate is of the order of 200, in industrialized countries, it averages fourteen.[51]

In a city of Asia like Kolkata, the incidence of infant mortality, tuberculosis, gastro-enteritis, malnutrition, and anaemia is two to eight times as high in squatter areas as in non-squatter areas. In a big metropolitan centre, like Brasilia, in South America, infant mortality is rising and there is resurgence of malaria and of the bubonic plague. Greater emphasis on basic education, functional training, relevant curricula to reflect more accurately objective assessment of occupational programmes for pregnant women, lactating mothers and infants, health education, availability of medical and paramedical and health personnel, is important among many other programmes to improve education and health in developing societies. Life expectancy at birth continues to range from forty-two years of life in some African countries to seventy-three in developed countries, e.g., in Europe. Similarly, infant mortality is still five to six times higher in developing than in developed regions.[52]

Some 100 million children under five years of age are suffering from protein-energy malnutrition, and some 10 million from severe protein-energy malnutrition, usually fatal if untreated. An average of only 20 to 25 per cent of the population in developing countries have access to any health services. Only 28 per cent of the population in low-income developing countries have access to safe water, compared with 59 per cent in middle-income developing countries. More than 1200 million people of developing countries have no safe water supply and more than 1400 million have no sanitary waste disposal facilities.[53]

Pakistan's health care system is typical of many post-colonial underdeveloped countries, although it has some particularities, which are not found in other countries. For the most part, the health care model has changed little from the time of the British. It is essentially doctor-oriented, it has a curative rather than a preventive emphasis, it is urban biased in terms of resources and personnel, and with the now dominant role of private sector over public sector health facilities, it is highly inequitable, with ability to pay rather than need determining access to health care.[54]

The burden of structural adjustment under the structural adjustment programme initiated in 1988 and of the changed health system is likely to fall unevenly on different groups. Not surprisingly, the poor will suffer the most as the economic situation worsens and low growth results in fewer employment possibilities. Higher inflation and lower food subsidies will make life even more difficult for this section of the population, and private health care will be beyond their reach. Hence, they will be not only more vulnerable to disease, but also less able to acquire health care. In addition, if utilities like water and sewerage are privatized, they may not be available to those who cannot afford the higher prices. Women usually bear the brunt of austerity before men; this suggests that, while all the population will be affected, women, and especially those from lower income groups, will be affected more adversely. In terms of food intake and access to health care, women and girls come last; now, with greater austerity, it is probable that their already dismal health status will worsen further.[55]

Conclusion

A high rate of growth of population, rapid urbanization, complexity in productively absorbing the increasing labour force, unemployment, poverty, slums, food shortages, inadequate health coverage, squatter settlements and acute housing shortages explain in part the pattern of crimes and law and order situation prevailing in a country. Many social and urban problems are closely related to the overall rate of economic growth and have become increasingly relevant not only to development but also to a meaningful strategy of crime prevention. The interrelations between poverty, urbanization, housing, unemployment, health hazards, juvenile delinquency and crime, crime prevention and criminal justice issues are obvious though complex.

NOTES

1. McClintock, D., General Report on the Criminological Aspects, pp. 17 and 19, in *Cities and Criminality*, 10th International Congress of Social Defence.
2. Ibid.
3. David, P. (1981), *The World of the Undocumented Migrant*, with M. Lucero Palma, Universidad Autonoma Ciudad Juarez, Juarez, Mexico, 1981 (in press).
4. David, P. (1979), *Sociologia Criminal Juvenil*. Edit. Depalma, Buenos Aires, 1979, p. 139.
5. Oscar, N. (1972), *Defensible Space: Crime Prevention Through Urban Design*, New York, Macmillan, 1972.
6. J.N. (1978), *Report on the World Social Situation*, p. 35.
7. Zaidi, S.A. (1999), *The New Development Paradigm: Papers on Institutions, NGOs, Gender and Local Government*, Oxford University Press, Karachi, pp. 81–2.
8. Ibid.
9. Ibid.
10. Ibid.
11. Ibid.
12. Ibid., p. 105.
13. Ibid.
14. Ibid.
15. Ibid., p. 106.
16. Ibid.
17. Hasan, A. (1998), Introduction in *Orangi Pilot Project: Reminiscences and Reflections* by Dr Akhtar Hameed Khan, Oxford University Press, Karachi.
18. Khan, A.H. (1998), *Orangi Pilot Project: Reminiscences and Reflections*, Oxford University Press, Karachi, pp. xix–xx.
19. Ibid.

20. World Bank (1979), *World Development Report, 1979*, p. 81.
21. Government of Pakistan (1998–99), *Economic Survey, 1998–99*. Finance Division, Economic Adviser's Wing, Islamabad.
22. Hasan, A. (1992), Seven Reports on Housing, OPP-RTI, Karachi, p. 17.
23. Ercelawn, Aly and Nauman, M. (1996), 'Restructuring Water and Sewerage Services in Karachi: Citizens' Consent or Coercion', paper presented at the seminar on *Citizens' Role in the Governance of Karachi*, 20–30 November 1996.
24. World Bank (1978), *World Development Report, 1978*.
25. Preale (1979), *The Employment Problem in Latin America: Facts, Outlooks and Policies,* Santiago, 1976. *Growth, Employment and Basic Needs in Latin America and the Caribbean*, Report of the Director General to the 11th Conference of American States, Geneva, ILO, 1979, p. 6.
26. Government of Pakistan (1998–99), *Economic Survey, 1998–99*. Finance Division, Economic Adviser's Wing, Islamabad, p. 137.
27. Ibid.
28. CESDHA (1982), 'The Social Impact of Major Development Measures on Specific Population Groups', pp. 37, 47, 54 and 56, Draft Paper.
29. Ibid.
30. Ibid
31. Ibid.
32. Sayeed, Asad and Ghaus, A. (1996), 'Has Poverty Returned to Pakistan?' mimeo, Social Policy and Development Centre, Karachi, 1996.
33. Ibid., p. 2
34. Ibid.
35. Ibid.
36. Kemal, A. R. (1994), Structural Adjustment, Employment, Income Distribution and Poverty, in *Pakistan Development Review*, Vol. 33, No.□4, 1994.
37. Ibid.
38. Sayeed, Asad and Ghaus, A. (1996), 'Has Poverty Returned to Pakistan?' mimeo, Social Policy and Development Centre, Karachi, 1996.
39. Kemal, A. R. (1994), 'Structural Adjustment, Employment, Income Distribution and Poverty', in *Pakistan Development Review*, Vol. 33, No.□4, 1994.
40. Zaman, A. (1995), 'The Government's Present Agreement with the IMF: Mis-government or Folly?' in *Pakistan Journal of Applied Economics*, Vol. 11, No.□1 and 2, 1995.
41. Khan, Shahrukh, R. and Aftab, S. (1996), 'Structural Adjustment, Labour and the Poor in Pakistan', mimeo, Pakistan Institute of Labour Education and Research, Karachi, 1996.
42. Ibid., p. 18.

43. Sahibzada, M.H. (1997), *Poverty Alleviation in Pakistan: Present Scenario and Future Strategy*, Institute of Policy Studies and Friedrich Ebert Stiftung, Karachi.
44. CESDHA (1982), 'The Social Impact of Major Development Measures on Specific Population Groups', pp. 37, 47, 54 and 56, Draft Paper.
45. Ibid.
46. Auolakh, A.M.A. (1999), *Prison Administration in Pakistan*, S and S Publishers, 22 Urdu Bazar, Lahore. pp. 245–6.
47. Special Branch (1999), District/Sect-wise Details of Deeni Madaris, Directorate of Research and Reference, Special Branch, Punjab Police, Lahore, February 1999.
48. United Nations (1978), *Report on the World Social Situation*, p. 33.
49. Haq, M. (1997), *Human Development in South Asia, 1997*, Oxford University Press, Karachi.
50. UNDP (1997), *Human Development Report*, Oxford University Press, New York.
51. United Nations (1978), *Report on the World Social Situation*.
52. Ibid.
53. Ibid.
54. Zaidi, S.A. (1999), *The New Development Paradigm: Papers on Institutions, NGOs, Gender and Local Government*, Oxford University Press, Karachi, pp. 269–70.
55. Zaidi, S.A. (1996), 'Gender Perspectives and the Quality of Care in Underdeveloped Countries. Disease, Gender and Contextuality', in *Social Science and Medicine*, Vol. 43, No. 5, 1996.

3

A REVIEW OF SOCIO-ECONOMIC
SITUATION IN PAKISTAN

Many social and urban problems are closely related to the overall
rate of economic growth and have become increasingly relevant
not only to development but also to a meaningful strategy of
crime prevention. In fact, poverty is multifaceted and often self-
perpetuating. The poor lack education, adequate health care,
access to credit, and such basic assets as land. Many of these
problems are linked to each other and to both gaps in knowledge
and imperfections in information, which force the poor into
economic relationships that limit their productivity. Low levels
of human development signify disempowerment of the masses
who do not have understanding of even the basic system and
laws. Lack of access to information and knowledge in
conjunction with non-availability of resources creates a
dichotomy. The poor, the indigent and the unprivileged are not
fully aware either of their rights and obligations or institutions
and policies. Being unable to fully participate in the development
process on account of their deprivation in terms of education,
health and other facilities, the masses tend to be carried away
by high sounding promises and slogans of the unscrupulous
elite with the result that a culture of corruption starts thriving.
This is borne out by the simultaneous existence of poverty and
corruption in a number of countries. For example, as is evident
from figure 3.1, the world's poor are concentrated in East and
South Asia.[1]

FIGURE 3.1
Poverty by Developing Region

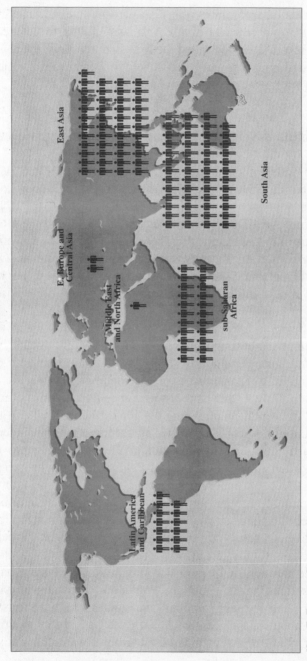

Key: E. Europe - Eastern Europe.
Note: Each figure represents 10 million persons living on $1 a day or less at 1985 international prices.
Source: *World Bank Report 1998/99*.

Incidentally, according to the Transparency International Survey, Pakistan and India in South Asia were found to be the most dishonest. Indonesia headed the list as the most corrupt country.[2] All these countries have low levels of human development as well.

Pakistan's Selected Human Development Indicators

Since independence, population census have been held in Pakistan in 1951, 1961, 1972, 1981, and 1998. Data on housing has been recorded by the Housing Census in 1960, the Housing, Economic and Demographic Survey in 1973, and the Housing Census of Pakistan in 1980. These studies revealed that housing was growing significantly slower than the population. On the basis of the 1980 housing census figure of 6.7 persons per house, about nine million additional dwellings would be required by the year 2000.[3]

Population growth has resulted in higher density in family dwellings increasing from 5.5 persons per house in 1960, to 6.7 in 1980, and an estimated 7.0 in 1987. More than half of the housing in Pakistan consists of one room with an average of six persons. Only 13 per cent of the homes have interior plumbing and 8 per cent have plumbing outside the house. In 1973 just 18 per cent of households had electricity, while the remainder used primarily kerosene oil for lighting. The situation improved by 1980 when about 30 per cent of Pakistani houses had access to electricity, 54 per cent of urban and 5 per cent of rural households. In the period 1973–80 an equal number of households had electricity in both rural and urban areas. However, in terms of percentages this represented 71 per cent of urban and only 15 per cent of rural houses.[4]

The availability of pure drinking water has been a nagging and serious health problem. Population demands on potable water have reduced supplies and aggravated health risks. In 1973 about 17 per cent of households had access to drinking water, while the remainder used ground water for daily use.

Although in 1980, 20 per cent of households had access to drinking water, this did not match population growth. In urban areas 58 per cent of the households had access to drinking water in 1980, in rural areas only 5 per cent. At the present rate of growth, it seems unlikely that potable water will be provided to a majority of Pakistanis in the foreseeable future.[5]

In 1973 only 4 per cent of households had flushing toilets, 30 per cent had non-flushing toilets, and 66 per cent were without toilets of any kind. Only 24 per cent of households that year had any bathing facilities (50 per cent of urban and 15 per cent of rural households), and by 1980 there had been little improvement in urban areas. Households with baths had increased from 50 per cent to 54 per cent in the period 1973–80, but population growth and rapid urbanization had kept the percentage of increase modest.[6]

The pattern of internal migration indicates that 88 per cent of the migrants originated from rural areas; about half (51 per cent) settled in urban areas and half (49 per cent) in other rural areas. Of the 12 per cent of the migrants originating from urban areas, 27 per cent settled in rural areas and 73 per cent in other urban areas. Of all domestic migration reflected in the 1981 census, Sindh received 60 per cent of the migrants, Punjab 20 per cent, NWFP 10 per cent, Balochistan 5 per cent, and Islamabad 5 per cent.[7]

During the years 1988–93 Pakistan was in the category of Low Human Development. Not only was the majority of the population poor, in bad health and uneducated (Table 3.1 and 3.2 and Figures 3.2 and 3.3) but the situation was becoming increasingly difficult in other respects as well. In many areas of Pakistan the maintenance of law and order was no longer assured, violence and corruption were virtually out of control while the judicial settlement of disputes became increasingly difficult. Under these conditions, illegal activity grew, while moral and civic values had been threatened and development policies became increasingly difficult to pursue across a wide front.

TABLE 3.1
Human Development Indicators Relating to Children

	Pakistan	Low human development group	All developing countries[5]	Industrial countries
Infant mortality rate[1]	106.0	99.0	76.0	–
Under five mortality rate[1]	162.0	155.0	116.0	18.0
Females % of males[2]	104.5	92.9	92.3	81.8
Malnourished children[3]	53.0	41.0	33.0	–
Primary school enrolment				
N Total[4]	40.0	86.0	105.0	103.0
N Female[4]	28.0	75.0	97.0	103.0

Source: *World Bank Report, 1991.*
Notes: (1) Per 100 live births, 1989.
     (2) 1989 data source: World Bank, *World Development Report 1991.*
     (3) Children under five who are significantly underweight 1980–88.
     (4) Percentage of age group enrolled in 1988.
     (5) Low-income group (excluding China).

FIGURE 3.2
Human Development Indicators Relating to Children

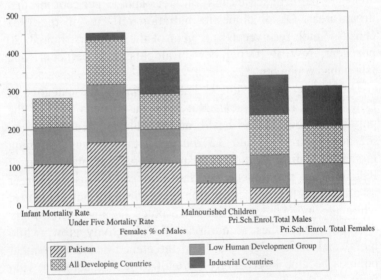

Source: Developed by the author with reference to the data in Table 3.1.

TABLE 3.2
Human Development Indicators (1990–1993)

	Pakistan	Low human development group[5]	All developing countries	Industrial countries
Life expectancy at birth[1]				
Total	57.7	55.0	65.0	74.5
Females as % of males	100.0	103.0	104.0	110.1
Adult literacy rates[2]	31.0	47.0	60.0	–
Male	43.0	59.0	70.0	–
Female	18.0	34.0	49.0	–
Purchasing power of real GDP per capita in $[3]	1790.0	1080.0	2170.0	14350.0
% of population with access to				
Health services[4]	55.0	56.0	63.0	–
Safe water[5]	45.0	50.0	62.0	–
Sanitation[5]	20.0	29.0	46.0	–
Daily calorie supply as % of requirements[6]	97.0	99.0	107.0	132.0

Source: *World Development Report, 1993.*
Notes: (1) Life expectancy at Birth 1991.
   (2) Adult Literacy rates 1990.
   (3) GDP per capita in $ 1991.
   (4) Health services 1990.
   (5) Safe water 1990; Sanitation 1990.
   (6) Daily calorie supply as % of requirements, 1990.

The *Human Development Report 1999* describes Pakistan's human development challenges as 'pressing'. Though Pakistan was ranked 138 among 174 countries on the basis of the Human Development Index and moved from the category Low to Medium Human Development Countries, yet this change was not due to any sudden and spectacular improvement but because of methodological changes in Human Development Index calculations. After eight five-year plans and completion of the first phase of a separately launched Social Action Programme, Pakistan's human development indicators are woeful. Over 34 per cent of Pakistan's total population lives below the poverty line, 62 per cent adults are illiterate, twenty out of every hundred

FIGURE 3.3

Human Development Indicators

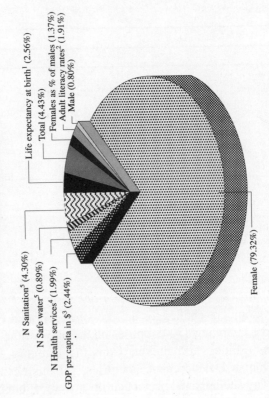

Life expectancy at birth[1] (2.56%)

Total (4.43%)

Females as % of males (1.37%)

Adult literacy rates[2] (1.91%)

Male (0.80%)

N Sanitation[5] (4.30%)

N Safe water[5] (0.89%)

N Health services[4] (1.99%)

GDP per capita in $[3] (2.44%)

Female (79.32%)

Source: Developed by the author with reference to the data in Table 3.2.

do not have access to safe drinking water and forty-five to health facilities. Among children, 38 per cent under the age of five years are underweight. Income disparities have persisted and may worsen with the continued increase in the country's population. By and large, these statistics have remained unchanged. The *Human Development Report 1999*, the last of the century, finds Pakistan making no breakthrough in improving these indicators.[8]

Despite the above mentioned dismal state of affairs the allocation made for general administration, law and order, community services, social and economic services hardly remain 15 per cent of the total expenditure. It is only the 17.50 per cent of total expenditure, which can be restricted and reallocated. To check their legitimacy take education, which has been receiving step-motherly treatment so far. The literacy rate of Pakistan is at the lowest among the observed countries. In spite of having concern towards this end, Pakistan's allocation to education is at bottom. To foster growth of the education sector, increased allocation in this field seems a must. This is so because education plays an important role in giving voice to the poor. As the poor learn, they become more aware of their own circumstances and compare them against possible alternatives. They also discover ways to overcome the obstacles they face. With this awareness comes the ability to articulate concerns and desires, to make suggestions, to voice complaints. For example, in China, where concern is mounting over deteriorating environmental conditions, complaints about air pollution are much more frequent in provinces with higher literacy rates.[9] Researchers estimate that an increase in a province's literacy rate from 60 per cent to 84 per cent would almost double the number of complaints, from 7.5 to 13.9 per 100,000 people.[10]

Similarly, the allocation made by Pakistan to the health sector is desperately low too. Bangladesh, with a population of 111 million spends 4.8 per cent of its total expenditure on health. Indonesia, having a population of 181 million, spends 2.4 per cent and even India, which has eight times more population than Pakistan, exceeds Pakistan so far its expenses on health facilities are concerned, that is 1.6 per cent.[11] Like education, Pakistan is at the lowest level in health sector with a meagre allocation of 1 per cent only, hence, Pakistan has been at bottom among these countries in its health and education allocations. It remains low even to the minimum level prescribed by the UN for developing countries. So both sectors, education and health, need their allocation raised instead of cutting it further down. India and Bangladesh have bigger health budget allocations than that of Pakistan. Turkey which is considered among middle-income economies matches Pakistan in allocation for the health sector, the reason being its small population size which is below half that of Pakistan's.

TABLE 3.3

Distribution of Total Expenditure

(As percentage of total expenditures)

Low-income economies	Defence	Education	Health	Housing Amenities Soc. Security and Welfare	Economic services	Debt-servicing	Law and Order
India	17.0	2.5	1.6	6.9	20.8	51.2	2.56
Bangladesh	10.1	11.2	4.8	8.0	34.4	31.5	7.1
Pakistan	27.9	1.6	1.0	3.4	11.6	54.6	3.62
Indonesia	8.2	9.1	2.4	1.8	27.1	51.5	1.54
Middle-income economies							
Philippines	10.9	16.1	4.2	3.7	24.7	40.3	1.96
Thailand	17.1	20	0.2	7.4	5.9	24.3	6.75
Turkey	10.4	17.6	3.0	3.3	25.2	40.5	29.11
Upper-middle-income economies							
Argentina	9.9	9.9	3.0	39.4	16.0	21.7	5.51
Brazil	3.5	3.1	6.7	25.5	3.2	57.9	1.42
Mexico	2.4	13.9	1.9	13.0	13.4	55.5	0.46
South Korea	22.2	15.8	2.0	11.3	19.2	29.5	10.58

Source: (1) *World Development Report, 1993.*

(2) *The Europa World Year Book 1995*, Vol. I and II (the percentage of expenditure on Law and Order has been calculated by me on the basis of absolute figures obtained from *The Europa World Year Book 1995*).

FIGURE 3.4

Distribution of Total Expenditure

(As percentage of total expenditure)

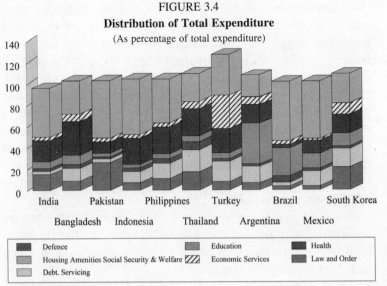

Source: Developed by the author with reference to the data in Table 3.3.

Like Turkey, the Southeast Asian economy of Philippines, allocates 3.7 per cent to this head but its reasons look compatible with those of Turkey, that is, small size of population. Except these three countries, all other surveyed economies have a remarkable edge on Pakistan. It is pertinent to take into consideration with reference to Pakistan the fact that a strategy of economic development which brings about high growth rates may result in political instability if the general perception is that incomes generated through high growth rates have not been equitably distributed.

Political Instability

The importance of labour intensity provides one reason why rapid growth can be accompanied or followed by serious political difficulties for the government in power. If the growth is capital intensive then majority of the poor are unlikely to benefit. Rapid growth with stagnant income for the poor obviously means that the not poor are getting richer at a great rate. When there is a general air of prosperity, and especially when that results in conspicuous consumption by the upper income groups, while the majority sees no improvement, it would be surprising if that did not make them very angry indeed. But it is possible to have political instability even when the poor are benefiting from rapid growth, as was the case in Pakistan in the 1960s. First there are usually non-economic factors in political troubles. Government can lose elections or face riots because of ethnic conflicts, widespread corruption or lost wars. Economic policy and economic factors may just play a large role in some political events.

However, in many other cases, it seems that economic factors precipitated political problems despite a longer-term improvement in the well-being of the poor. Pakistan (then including the present Bangladesh) in the 1960s is an excellent example. Income distribution over the decade improved and real wages of unskilled workers rose substantially. But, according to Papanek, in 1966–67, what he describes as the 'Index of Perceived Poverty', increased dramatically. There are four elements that increase the index:

- A decline in the income of the poor. True, over the 1960s as a whole their income increased, but in the short-term it suffered a sharp decline in 1966–67 (based on wage data). Short-term declines in income even during longer-term periods of prosperity occur frequently as a result of bad harvests, or an increase in the international price of a country's imported staple food, or a decline in the price of its principal export. For instance, in Pakistan, in the period 1966–68, a bad domestic harvest and a temporary interruption in food aid combined to sharply drive up the prices of wheat, rice and other food grains with a consequent decline in the real income of the poor, who spent a high proportion of their income on these staple foods.
- Such a decline in income is especially hard to accept if it comes after a long period of improvement when continued betterment becomes widely expected. Disappointed expectations can be especially devastating. Wages in Pakistan had substantially and

consistently been rising from 1959 to 1965. A sharp drop was, therefore, quite unexpected and disappointing.

- A decline in the income of the majority has particularly serious political consequences if it is accompanied by unchanged or rising conspicuous consumption. In Pakistan, as the result of the liberalization of luxury imports under the Export Bonus Voucher Scheme, the mid-1960s were, indeed, a period when conspicuous consumption (e.g. of cars) was on the rise.

- If government then gives the impression of not caring, of being indifferent to the suffering of the poor majority, rather than providing hope that it is doing all it can to ameliorate the situation, anger can turn against the government. There was some evidence of that as well in Pakistan in the late 1960s.[12]

In short, medium-term improvement in the situation of the poor, as part of rapid growth, may not be enough for political stability. There will inevitably be short-term setbacks, which can result in a dramatic short-term decline in the income of the poor, even in the context of medium-term improvement. If then there is the perception that the wealthier groups are living very well, even flaunting their wealth, and that the government does not care, trouble can result.

Conclusion

Pakistan has not done well in terms of some important health and education indicators. For instance, life expectancy is one of the lowest while infant mortality is one of the highest in the Asian region. A large number of our children are anaemic. The literacy rate and other indicators of education too, place Pakistan very low in relation to other developing countries of a comparable level of economic growth. This state of affairs coincides with the prevalence of organized violent crime and a culture of corruption. The perception of inequality in the distribution of income resulted in the separation of the eastern wing of Pakistan in 1971. Furthermore, there is a serious distortion in the ratio of resources allocated to social sectors and defence. Even resources allocated for criminal justice administration are extremely inadequate. It appears that scant attention was paid to long-term planning of social sectors as well as the law enforcement machinery.

NOTES

1. World Bank (1998/99), *World Development Report*, p. 118.
2. *India Today* (1995), The Transparency International Survey, quoted in the 15 July issue of *India Today*.
3. *Asian Survey* Vol. XXX, No. 5, May 1990.
4. Ibid.
5. Ibid.
6. Ibid.
7. Ibid.
8. UNDP (1999), *Human Development Report 1999*, launched at the UN Information Centre, Islamabad, on 16 July 1999.
9. World Bank (1998/99), *World Development Report*, p. 119.
10. Ibid.
11. World Bank (1993), *World Development Report*.
12. Papanek, Gustav F. (1987), *Lectures on Growth, Equity and the Political Process: Lessons from Southern Asia*, Pakistan Institute for Development Economics (PIDE), Islamabad.

4

NATURE OF VIOLENT CRIME

Culture shapes the conditions under which we attribute responsibility and blame to individuals whose acts result in harmful consequences, even though there may be high agreement across different cultures and over time. This chapter depicts various contours of violent crime including socio-cultural dimensions, behaviour of individual criminals, and political offences with reference to research conducted on the subject and judicial interpretation given to political offences by the Tokyo High Court in the context of hijacking.

Socio-cultural Dimensions

The conceptual issue of what acts count as violence does not cause too many difficulties for criminologists in practice because they usually ignore it. Almost all the literature on explaining violent crime focuses exclusively on violence as conventionally delimited, at the most drawing analogies between violent crime and rape (which may be considered as a form of violent crime, even though it would be wrong to argue that there is nothing sexual about it).

Gartner has conducted some cross-national research in developed countries to see what factors best account for variations in homicide rates. She concludes that more micro-level research is required, but observes that nations with greater material deprivation, more cultural heterogeneity, more family dissolution, higher female labour force participation, and greater exposure to official violence generally have higher homicide rates.[1] Braithwaite likewise focuses on economic inequality as a primary predictor of homicide rates. Links between unemployment and criminality are stronger for property crime than for violent crime, but more sophisticated sociological accounts might separate out the unemployed into those who are psychologically integrated into 'straight society' and those who see themselves as part of an 'underclass' (and are policed as if they were).[2]

Burgess and Draper examine family violence in evolutionary terms, arguing that under certain conditions child maltreatment has a benefit in helping the fittest to survive; moreover, hostility towards stepchildren, for example, may be explicable in terms of our being prepared to act in a more hostile way towards people who share none of our genes, while greater rates of violence against poor and 'physically challenged' children are understandable in relation to competition for scarce resources and optimizing future individual reproductive potential.[3]

One of the earliest attempts at a comprehensive explanation of violence was the 'subculture of violence' theory.[4] While not providing a plausible account of why the supposed subcultures developed in the first place the authors showed that many acts of violence arise from incidents that are trivial in origin—an insult, a curse, or a jostle—whose significance is blown out of all proportion in poor neighbourhoods where self-esteem is low. A more micro-sociological successor to their approach is the 'lifestyle' theoretical paradigm, based on victimization survey research, which shows that offenders and victims of street violence not only are the same 'sort of people'—for example, two-thirds of those who attacked sixteen 24-year-olds were in the same age group.[5]

Feminist theories of male violence against women stress the social construction of masculinity, violence, and sexuality in patriarchal society, whose object is to reproduce and maintain the relative status and authority of men over women.[6]

Comments from senior police officers and politicians, and media reports of violent incidents, sometimes depict violent outcomes as the result of interactive social processes, but they normally have little difficulty in blaming the public (or rather, some 'hooligan' section of the public, which is hostile to the police). By contrast, in the specific area of violence in which police are hurt, early American research by Toch observed that many police victims of assault become so because they are personally insecure and wish to prove to themselves and others that they are 'real men' by daring others to defy them.[7] (In societies such as the USA with ready recourse to fatal weapons this desperate search for challenges can be very dangerous.)

A focus on the police contribution to their own victimization—which Levi labels as the 'public-excusing' theory would therefore follow the lines of a general or force or area or shift police subculture in which aggressive policing was encouraged or, at least, was not actively discouraged.[8] Adherents to this 'Dirty Harry' subculture believe—along with detectives who 'strengthen' evidence against those they 'know' to be guilty that unless they act firmly 'things will get out of hand', and that they must especially clamp down on 'known troublemakers' in their area who set a bad example to others by demonstrating 'contempt of cop'. How do they know who the troublemakers are? Every police officer who joins an area in the police station is out on the beat. Other prime candidates are young 'ethnic', bikers, and other potential 'rowdies'. So, the 'public-excusing' theory would have us believe that the police pick on those who either are labelled for them by prior personal or subculture-derived prejudicial stereotypes, or in some other way fail to show the right attitude to police control over the area or to the seriousness of their offence.

To the extent that assaults against the police have been increasing in recent years, this may also be because police legitimacy in the eyes of the public has diminished—something which the police acknowledge has happened but do not usually attribute to a general deterioration in police behaviour and/or because the police have become less skilful in the handling of relations with the public.[9] The process of de-subordination to authority is a generalized feature which is implicated in assaults against a variety of personnel—police, prisoners, social workers, teachers—all of whom pose a threat to the desire for autonomy. This may be extended to others who threaten or are expected, reasonably or unreasonably, to threaten in the future the self-gratification of the offender. Looked at in this way, what may look like individual paranoia may be understood to have some socio-cultural roots.

Toch's view that the way the police approach the public such as appearing to pick on them, making them face humiliation in front of their friends or their girlfriends to whom they wish to present a tough image, or standing physically very close, thereby (a) winding them up psychologically, and (b) bringing themselves within ready head-butting range is an important dimension in understanding assaults against the police. Bernard likewise concludes that a subculture of angry aggression arises under conditions when serious social disadvantage is continued with individual social isolation.[10]

At the level of individual incidents and area/class rates of violence, police attitudes towards the public and public attitudes towards the police, the general violence-using styles of citizens, and lifestyles which expose people to differential risks of negative encounters with the police are all salient. Beyond this, however, it remains easier to disentangle and demystify the police than to explain why some people commit it when they do. This applies to most forms of violent crime. It seems undeniable that some people obtain powerful reinforcement from the pleasure of causing pain, and it may be simply chance or, more likely sub-culturally approved or at least ambiguous values, which determines whether rape or armed robbery or overseas war or all three represent the venue within which that 'high' is obtained and reinforced. Peer activity routines, once established, are likely to account for the immense social class and status group and gender variations in the prevalence of all these different forms of violence.

Let us now turn to what research indicates about individual involvement in violence.

Behaviour of Individual Criminals

Even given a conventional view of what constitutes 'violent crime',[11] controversy rages about the role of genetic factors. Some people behave violently for a long time in a variety of settings; although the manifestations of aggression vary, a child who is top of the distribution for aggression at age eight is likely to be near the top, twenty years later. Psychological research has tended to focus upon the role of 'temperament', which is obscure in origin but seems to be a relatively stable phenomenon. Children who are extremely inhibited or uninhibited at twenty-one months are likely to be similarly classified at age seven and a half. Farrington has argued that when they are children, violent offenders tend to be high on hyperactivity impulsivity attention deficit and tend to be restless and lacking in concentration, lack empathy (the ability to identify with others' feelings), and find it difficult to defer gratification. This may look like a caricature of the 'feckless poor' but is an infra-class discriminator of aggression levels.[12] American research suggests that violent offenders have longer criminal careers and are less likely to stop in the early stages of their offending than are property criminals.[13] Nearly all London offenders studied by Farrington were convicted of non-violent as well as violent crimes, and only a quarter of their crimes were violent.[14]

Toch has usefully distinguished several types of violent offenders; the 'self-image demonstrator', who uses violence to demonstrate toughness which he believes will be admired by his peers; the 'self-image defender' who tends to feel easily slighted or disparaged and will react to defend his ego; and the 'reputation defender', who acts as a member of a group to defend the values of the group when he believes them to be threatened. All these involve various methods of coping with fragile self-concepts; this fragility may be linked to class or status-group, in so far as those who are used to commanding social resources and respect may be less prone than poor whites or people of colour to having their self-image undermined. On the other hand, some high-status people expect respect and may react aggressively—for example, by firing staff or 'freezing' partners—when contradicted or thwarted; whether this ever comes to be defined as 'violence' or 'violent crime' depends upon what they do and how they do it.[15]

As regards illicit substances, though there may be 'commercial' violence resulting from a desire to dominate drugs distribution or extort money from sellers, there is no evidence that the pharmacological effect of cannabis, hallucinogens, or opiates makes people violent: if anything, the reverse is true. There is a more plausible link between violence and amphetamines and solvents but, as with alcohol, demonstrating the causal link is confounded by the intervening personality variables.

Field suggests that the strong relationship between violent crime and per capita consumption reflects the fact that affluence leads people to go out more, increasing their risk of victimization, while a reduction in unemployment slightly counteracts what otherwise would be a stronger use in violence.[16]

We have learned a great deal in recent decades about patterns of violent behaviour and the factors that influence them, such as social class, ethnicity, and gender. The learning from role models on screen and in (ever more fractured) families and neighbourhoods about how to respond to tensions, plus differences in individual temperament and life circumstances, play a major part in accounting for variations in rates of violence. Retrospective accounts by killers and rapists help us to make sense of 'why it happened', why outside of learned and/or biological gender variations, people, even sometimes those from the same family and brought up apparently similarly, turn out to have different temperaments and cognitive sets remains mysterious. Becker, in an attempt to mitigate attacks on the idea that the labelling of people as 'criminals' intensified their involvement in crime, observed that he had not really meant to put forward a 'theory', merely a 'perspective' in which he would 'illuminate things formerly obscure'.[17]

Political Offences

Another way of looking at crime is with reference to its political and non-political overtones. Ordinarily crime against person and property or even organized crime may be confined to non-political considerations. However in the context of violence, one interpretation of political crime is that it is characterized by any 'subversive acts which threaten the safety and well-being of State and are intended to undermine or overthrow parliamentary democracy by political, industrial or violent means.'[18]

Political offences are legitimately divided into two categories: one is purely political offences, such as treason, sedition and espionage, and the other is relative by political offences in which a common crime is committed as a political offence. Most political offence issues naturally centre on what is the relative political offence and how it can be distinguished from common offences.

Various theories have been invented and carried out in many jurisdictions with regard to relative political offences. To summarize very briefly, there are three major theories and precedents:

- Political Incident Theory was developed by an English case. A three-fold standard is commonly applied in the theory to recognize political offence:
  i) There must be a political disturbance;
  ii) The act in issue must be incidental to the disturbance;
  iii) There must also be political motivation.
- Political Motivation Theory was developed in the Swiss courts in an attempt to modify the political incident theory. It provides the language of the Swiss extradition law. The standards for political offence in this theory seem to be:
  i) that the offence was committed for the purpose of helping or insuring the success of a purely political offence;
  ii) that there was a direct connection between the crime committed and the motive;
  iii) that the political element predominated over the ordinary criminal element;
  iv) The damage caused be proportionate to the result sought.

- The Injured Rights Theory originating in French law and developed in French tribunals, regards a political offence as an offence directed against the constitution of the government and against sovereignty, and judges the political character from the nature of the rights injured.

In very rough terms, both the Political Incident Theory and the Injured Rights Theory emphasize the objective elements of the act and, therefore, fall short of considering the subjective factors in total. On the other hand the Political Motivation Theory, though it seems to be more rational than the other two, is subjective to unpredictability because the judgement of the predominance of political nature would largely depend on the selection and weighing of the factors involved.[19]

Hijacking

The political offence issue becomes more acute when the offences are international or heinous crimes like assassination or injury of a state head or diplomats, hijacking, terrorism or war crime. The UN Model Treaty on extradition suggests including a clause, which would exempt any offence in respect of which the parties have assumed an obligation, pursuant to any multilateral convention, to take prosecutorial action where they do not extradite nor any other offence agreed by the parties not to be an offence of a political character. Adoption of such a treaty or national legislation in most member states will certainly preclude severe disputes over the issue, but with the non-existence of such favourable mechanisms, smooth extradition would be thwarted often. As one example, how to deal with the crime of hijacking, which has a high probability of occurrence in the future, is worth examining.

There were many cases in which defectors hijacked an aeroplane, in the 1950s. The first case was Kolcyznski, in which an English court denied extradition of a polish fisherman who had injured the captain and crew of a fishing trawler in order to escape from the State. Another was Kavic, in which a Swiss

Federal Tribunal rejected an extradition request from Yugoslavia on aeroplane crew members who had diverted a plane to Switzerland. The former was dealt with by the Political Incident Theory and the latter on the Political Motivation Theory.

The 1970 Hague Convention, in which more than 140 states have joined, obligates member states to extradite or prosecute hijackers, but the Convention could not reject the idea that some hijacking might be political offence, notwithstanding the vehement efforts by the United States and some other states. The position of the Convention and the above mentioned European cases seem to give hijackers special status, but many laws and treaties tend to exclude hijacking from the exception of political offence: Swiss law, Korean law, Australian law, the European Convention on Terrorism, the US-UK Extradition Treaty, and the US-Canadian Extradition Treaty.

In Japan in a 1989 hijacking case in which a Chinese national hijacked a China Airline in an attempt to reach Taiwan and eventually forced the plane to land at a Japanese airport on 16 December 1989, the Tokyo High Court had to decide on the issue of hijacking and political offence. The case was further complicated since the political motive of the hijacking was fiercely contested in the hearing, the offender claimed that he had been arrested, tortured and under watch by the Chinese security police for his participation in the Tiananman anti-government riot as a key member of the Chinese People Militants in June 1989, that he had unsuccessfully tried to escape from China several times, and that the hijacking was his last resort to escape possible persecution. The government (public prosecutor) contended that the offender had neither participated in the riot nor engaged in any serious anti-government activities in the past, that his arrest in October 1989 had been not for riot participation but for the embezzlement of public money, to which he had admitted guilt and been released on bail, and that he had desperately attempted to flee in order to get a job in Taiwan with his wife and son. The Tokyo High Court scrutinized the documents and witnesses on the factual issues but remained ambiguous, finding that the fugitive's claims could not be fully supported and his participation in the Tiananman riot, if found, might have been as an ordinary citizen. However the court decided that although some criminal acts in an attempt to flee from the Chinese political regime may be protected as a political offence, the hijacking of a civilian aircraft as a means of expatriation cannot be recognized as a political offence exception. The gist of the decision reads:

(a) Interpretations on the relative political offence differ from jurisdiction to jurisdiction, and the interpretation and its actual application to political offence issue are subject to changes reflecting society. Therefore, the court must examine the facts in any given contested case from all aspects, in order to find the magnitude of the political nature of the acts and make it clear whether the political nature of the acts, if any, is overwhelmingly predominant over the nature of the ordinary offence. The court then must make judgement in the case by means of common sense in terms of the interpretation of Article 2 of the Law. For the moment, the factors which seem to have relative significance in making the judgement, among others, are: whether the acts were done with genuine political motives; whether they can be objectively found to bear direct and material relevance in attaining political aims; whether the content, nature, gravity and other components of the acts are neither disproportionate to the intended objectives nor to be denied of deserving protection in the face of the commission of the crime.

(b) The most important factor, which should be taken into consideration in the present case is that the case relates to a crime in which a civilian aircraft was hijacked, endangering the safety of more than 220 passengers and crew members who had no relation with the intended political motives.

(c) In order to eradicate the crime of hijacking, in which the offender unjustifiably causes extreme terror to many passengers and crew who have nothing to do with the maintenance of a national regime or political order, it is useful and necessary for international society to make agreements to extradite such offender to the home country for the purpose of duly punishing the act of hijacking. Therefore, when a court is to find that the principle of non-extradition of a political offender should be applied to a particular case, the court must find that there is convincing reason why a number of civilian passengers should endure the disadvantages caused by the hijacking, i.e. that, in interpreting extradition law, there is a justifiable interest in the crime which is larger than and to be protected before the grave disadvantages imposed on the passengers.

(d) Examining all these points, even if the true motive, as the fugitive contends, were to escape from arrest and punishment by the Chinese authorities for the alleged participation in the demonstration activities in the Tiananman riot or other political activities, this court cannot find in the present crime of hijacking any justifiable interest which should be more fully protected than the actual suffering of the passengers and crew members in the case.

Conclusion

The analysis of violence with reference to individual incidents and various factors influencing its nature and magnitude in conjunction with political offences brings out a clear distinction between the two. Three objective elements make the political violence phenomenon distinct from ordinary violence, first violence is used, by stealth rather than in open combat. Explosive and incendiary devices are the archetypical weapons of terrorism, but there are others, including, kidnapping, etc. The second element is that the principal targets of violence are political, unlike in crime. Political targets include public meetings, religious or political figures, civil servants, military and police personnel, etc. The third distinctive element is that organized groups operating clandestinely to carry out these actions. The organization and not individual terrorists decide the targets as well as objective. The essence of terrorism is belief in the magic of violence and blood. The media, who are always inclined to give wide publicity to acts of violence, are the terrorists' natural allies. Conditions become conducive for political, religious, and ideological terrorism when there is a highly visible social group that sees itself as oppressed in political or economic terms. Deaths in ordinary crime and even street gang killings or organized crime mafia slayings do not affect the people much because the majority of citizens do not care about the victims. But in terrorist killings, a large group of people, emotionally attached to the victim, is aggrieved and motivated by revenge. Terrorism, thus, breeds terrorism.

NOTES

1. Gartner, R. (1990), 'The Victims of Homicide', *American Sociological Review*, 55, 1, pp. 92–107.
2. Braithwaite, J. (1989), *Crime, Shame, and Reintegration*, Cambridge, Cambridge University Press.
3. Burgess, R., and Draper, P. (1989), 'The Explanation of Family Violence: the Role of Biological, Behavioral and Cultural Selection', in L. Ohlin and M. Tonry, eds., *Family Violence*, Chicago, III, University of Chicago Press.
4. Wolfgang, M., and Ferracuti, F. (1967), *The Subculture of Violence*. London, Tavistock.
5. Davidoff, L., and Greenhorn, M. (1991), 'Violent Crime in England and Wales'. Paper presented at the British Criminology Conference, York.
6. Hanmer, J., Radford, J., and Stanko, E. (1989), *Women, Policing and Male Violence: An International Perspective*, London, Routledge. Also see Scully, D. (1990), *Understanding Sexual Violence*, London, Harper Collins; and Dobash, R. E., and Dobash, R. D. (1992), *Women, Violence, and Social Change*, London, Routledge.
7. Toch, H. (1969), *Violent Men*, Harmondsworth, Penguin.

8. Levi, M. (1997), 'Violent Crime', *The Oxford Handbook of Criminology*. Clarendon Press, Oxford, pp. 841–82.
9. Reiner, R. (1992), *The Politics of the Police*, 2nd edn., Hemel Hempstead: Wheatsheaf. Also see Skogan, W. (1990), *The Police and Public in England and Wales: A British Crime Survey Report*, London, HMSO; Which (1990), *The Police, Which?* May, pp. 258–61.
10. Bernard, T. (1990), 'Angry Aggression Among the Truly Disadvantaged', *Criminology*, 28, 1, pp. 73–93.
11. Wilson, J., and Herrnstein, R. (1985), *Crime and Human Nature*, New York, Simon and Schuster.
12. Farrington, D. (1989), 'Early Predictors of Adolescent Aggression and Adult Violence', *Violence and Victims*, 4, pp. 307–31.
13. Blumstein, A., Cohen, J., Roth, J. and Visher, C. (1986), *Criminal Careers and Career Criminals*, Washington DC, National Academy Press.
14. Farrington, D. (1991), 'Childhood Aggression and Adult Violence: Early Precursors and Later Life Outcomes', in D. Pepler and K. Rubin, eds., *The Development and Treatment of Childhood Aggression*, Hillsdale, NJ, Erlbaum.
15. Toch, H. (1969), *Violent Men*, Harmondsworth, Penguin.
16. Field, S. (1990), *Trends in Crime and Their Interpretation*, London, HMSO.
17. Becker, H. (1973), *Labelling Theory Reconsidered*, New York, Free Press.
18. Duncan, C. (1987), *Viewpoint—Reasonable Force*, 14 July, 10.30 p.m. London, ITV.
19. Horiuchi, K. (1995), 'Overview of Mutual Assistance and Extradition Issues', (The) Joint Seminar on Contemporary Issues Concerning Criminal Justice—A Comparative Perspective, 12–16 March, Rawalpindi.

5

HISTORICAL OVERVIEW OF LAW
AND ORDER IN PAKISTAN

This chapter contains a historical overview of law and order in
Pakistan with reference to the period of united Pakistan 1947–
71, further bifurcated into period of settling down (1947–58),
period of relative stability (1958–67) and interregnum (1968–
71) in juxtaposition with the post-1971 period further divided
into period of settling down (1972–1977), period of relative
stability (1977–88), period of political changes and uncertainties
(1989–June 1997) and difficult and challenging period (1998–
99). The classification of the periods, though arbitrary, is based
on variables like political stability or otherwise, levels and pace
of economic development and progress and geopolitical scenario
prevalent at that time. The idea is just to explain the changes in
the nature and pattern of crime over time and not to establish
linkages between various types of crime and their psychological
and sociological implications. This analysis of trends in crime
has, however, been used for determining the impact of
lawlessness on the economy as a whole.

Law and Order history of Pakistan may be categorized into
the following phases:

Period of United Pakistan 1947–71

Period of Settling Down (1947–58)

This period witnessed an upsurge under all major crime heads largely due to partitioning of the subcontinent and its aftermath. Every thing was in a flux. As is evident from crime figures, there was a phenomenal increase in both crimes against person as well as property. Increase in number of assaults on public servants and incidents of rioting were also reported. Similarly crime against property under all heads peaked. Due to a breakdown of moral social values and influx of a sizeable number of population from across the border, law-enforcing machinery found it difficult to tackle the situation on ground since it was neither trained nor properly equipped to deal with this type of a situation. During the early phase of this period, forcible occupation of property left by the Hindus was the order of the day. Mob violence also prospered. These two aspects of violence equated the concept of freedom and liberty with the negation of 'rule of law'. It also generated a sensibility, which accepted supremacy of material values over moral and religious values; hence the resultant 'Rehabilitation and Evacuee Property Grab Syndrome'. This syndrome has continued to affect the value system with attendant repercussions. Surprisingly, during this period, level of armament in terms of capture of illicit arms is relatively low as compared to preceding or succeeding years, both quality- and quantity-wise.

Period of Relative Stability (1958–67)

Political stability and economic growth characterize this period. Geopolitical scenario also favoured procurement of financial assistance from abroad till the early sixties. This period witnessed a downward drift in both crimes against person and property. The imposition of martial law and its continuation till 1962 may be an important factor in bringing about relative stability on the law and order front. This period also witnessed revamping of institutions and reinvigoration of the bureaucratic set-up. The process of industrialization unleashed new forces, which started affecting the character and sensibility of the rural population. Influx of rural population to cities started affecting both cities and rural areas as well as social and political ties. Anonymity of criminals started surfacing, the criminal now was part of the crowd. Another characteristic of this period is the increase in the number of weapons as evidenced in the figures of illicit arms recovered. Quantum and quality of arms used in crime/violence improved largely due to economic development. Since, during the early phase of this period, the process of economic development generated employment opportunities, the propensity to crime remained at a relatively lower level. The centralized writ also held in check the disturbing factors in the early phase. Machinery to deal with crime, too, was in better shape with low workload on the law and order front in the early phase.

The last phase of this period, however, is characterized by political and social turmoil largely attributable to social and economic inequities. The war of 1965 also took a heavy toll of the preceding economic development. Drift towards mob violence and the availability of better grade weapons started stretching the potential of law enforcing agencies to its farthest end. Unfavourable geopolitical scenario and perceived inequality in the distribution of income further precipitated the crisis resulting in the promulgation of the second martial law.

Interregnum (1968–71)

The aftermath of martial law witnessed cataclysmic changes on the political front with the deepening of the political divide between the East and West wing of the country. Since the entire nation was involved in the process of politicking and the subsequent electioneering over a prolonged period, criminal propensities generally remained in check due to the promise of a better future after elections. The crime figures of three years, however, are suggestive of increased criminal activity both against property and person. The number of arms recovered also indicated arming up of society. Political expression of social and economic discontentment under the framework of the martial law rule, however, kept the criminal propensities in check and underground. The war threat and the actual war in 1971 also minimized the role of such tendencies. This period witnessed the introduction of student and labour factors in politics. It also saw the politicization of campuses and introduction of weapons to students.

Post-1971 Period

Period of Settling Down (1972–77)

This interregnum between two martial laws witnessed a sharp rise in crime figures under all heads. If we inflate the figures by two to convert five-year figures to a decade, crime figures look horrifying. There was a sharp rise under all major heads of crime. Newly emergent crime pattern showed an increase in the incidents of armed robbery and various types of theft including those of automobiles and cattle heads. Juvenile delinquency and vandalism showed an upward trend. Food adulteration and misappropriation by government employees also increased. Political polarization gave birth to political offences. This period witnessed a mushroom growth of 'bara markets' signifying an increase in the volume of smuggled goods. Due to declining standards of discipline and social values in conjunction with the politics of divide between the rich and the poor, incidents of bribery in government offices and political matters, land disputes and attendant violent crime, abuse of women and prostitution, travelling without ticket in buses and trains, eve teasing, political murders and pornography showed a substantial increase. The demand for Pakistani labour in Dubai and the Middle East created what can be described as 'Dubai phenomenon' leading to illegal immigration and attendant incidents of cheating and fraud. Lax supervision of financial institutions resulted in the growth of fraudulent finance companies and emergence of white-collar crime. Phenomenon of child labour and 'begar camps' caused serious concern in the press. Display of fire arms and carrying of weapons became a fashion in many parts of the country. Due to insurgency in Balochistan, sophisticated weapons found their way to this part of the world. Mild wave of terrorism and subversion was witnessed particularly in the NWFP and Balochistan.

Period of Relative Stability (1977–88)

The imposition of the third martial law brought in check the rising graph of crime. The crime figures, under all major heads, registered a decrease. This may largely be attributed to the autocratic nature of the rule and discouragement of free registration. The fear of arbitrary punishments, delivered through the summary military courts also contributed to the relative stability of the period. Siphoning of western economic and military aid further contributed to the apparent calm on the surface. This period is, however, characterized by the fact that due to the heavy hand of martial law all criminal/political propensities of the society went underground. This period thus, for the first time in the history of Pakistan, witnessed active linkage between these propensities both on the domestic front as well as abroad. The crime pattern of these years is characterized by availability of sophisticated weapons. It was a natural outcome of the influx of three million Afghan refugees, break-up of national polity on ethnic *biradri* and sectarian affiliation and funding of disparate groups (ethnic/sectarian) by forces inimical to Pakistan largely due to Afghan war and the Saudi-Iran conflict. The Kashmir, Bangladesh and Afghanistan imbroglio and other related issues not only took us to war against the enemy but the enemy saturated us with bomb blasts, mines, subversion and terrorism using and encouraging the criminal elements within Pakistan also; this process gave an unprecedented boom and bonanza to organized and violent crime. The Afghan war, next door to Pakistan, brought in a devastating flood of the most lethal weapons into the hands of criminal elements in Pakistan. The moral and social breakdown, emergence of criminal mentality due to breakdown of constitutional norms, illegitimate governance and collapse of the system of justice followed by the availability of kalashnikovs, Uzis, mouzers and other such weapons gave the criminals tremendous confidence and courage against even the poorly equipped police. The result was that a peace-loving citizen remained under perpetual fear and suffered from a sense of insecurity.

Natural plant drugs like opium, cannabis and marijuana have been in vogue in our area since centuries. Their addiction was harmful, no doubt, but not cripplingly destructive to human soul and body. Free availability of new drugs like morphine, heroin and cannabis oil extracted through modern scientific methods and chemicals particularly during and after the Afghan war changed the scenario completely. The vicious circle of smuggling and use of drugs enhanced the commission of the worst type of crimes in Pakistan. The smuggling and trafficking in drugs along with the lethal weapons introduced organized crime, the drug mafia, a parallel illegal economy, money laundering and subversion of the entire criminal justice system through corrupt temptations. This period also witnessed the emergence of white-collar criminals as a strong lobby. It pressurized the government to revise its income tax proposals.

Uncensored and unscrupulous media, video and audio proliferation with unfettered objectionable and immoral material, easily available in every nook and corner, polluted and poisoned the young minds. Pleasure-seeking hedonism led to the growth of criminal conduct especially among the youth.

Over-emphasis on Islam led to the politics of religion. Caste and creed bigotry without enlightenment exhibited itself in crime. The result was that scoundrels took refuge in sectarian and ethnic causes. They involved themselves not only in sectarian killings and ethnic violence but also in bank dacoities and extortion of *'jagga tax.'*

This was a period where crime figures showed a decline but the lethality, mobility and resourcefulness of the criminal resulted in more deaths and damages both in terms of cost to the society, as well as the nation as a whole.

Period of Political Changes and Uncertainties (1989–June 1997)

This period was characterized by the fact that all forces, which were unleashed during the preceding periods, were operative in a democratic framework. Disruptive forces, generated during the last period, influenced the political process due to economic benefits accruing to them. Now crime and drug influence had a political cover and patronage, which resulted in increase in crime of all sorts and types. The will to bring criminals to book no longer existed due to political patronage. Public confidence in the rule of law was no longer there. Political influence was the law of the area. martial law and autocratic government characterized the rule of one man over the entire country. Different areas were being administered by the whims and idiosyncrasies of influentials of the area whose sole motive was to perpetuate themselves in offices of benefits.

Drug-related crime, sectarian killings and ethnic violence, gunrunning and *'qabza groups'* sponsored by political influentials flourished in a flawed democratic set-up. There was a mushroom growth of finance companies and co-operatives, which deprived a large number of people of their life-long savings. This was so because the crime received political patronage. In an environment of protection, incidents of kidnapping for ransom, bank dacoities/robberies and involvement of students in criminals activities showed an upward trend. Breakdown of social and moral values reached a point where power theft and non-payment of utility bills became a norm. Flawed democracy emanating from a desire to win elections at all costs led to the issuance of forged national identity cards on a massive scale.

Violence on a large scale in Karachi and virtual collapse of the administration in the city drove its younger, more political residence to exercise their frustrations in beating up people from other communities. Karachi, for most of the time, was a symbol of virtual anarchy and lawlessness.

Acts of terrorism and subversion increased in other areas of Pakistan as well; for example, bomb blasts. Only in the Punjab province, during the period from 1987–94, 207 persons were killed and 1472 injured in 114 incidents of bomb blasts. Bomb blast incidents from 1987 to 1991 and 1996 were quite frequent.[1] The situation was further aggravated by extra judicial killings by the police, especially in Karachi. This practice brutalized the criminals who would resort to violence whenever challenged by the police.

Period of Relative Stability (1997–98)

The sectarian violence and ethnic killings continued during this period because of the carry-over effects of the preceding seven years of virtual anarchy. However, in the aftermath of the 1997 elections, a beginning was made to deal with the law and order problem effectively. A number of known dangerous criminals were arrested, training of police officials was accorded due priority, a relatively better trained force designated as the Elite Police Force was raised to combat organized violent crime in the Punjab, anti-terrorist courts started functioning and ethnic and sectarian terrorist groups were exposed politically. The incidents of violence, kidnapping for ransom, sabotage and sectarian killings indicated a downward trend.

Difficult and Challenging Period (1998–99)

The fiscal year 1998–99 witnessed the full impact of testing a nuclear device by Pakistan on 28 May 1998. The freezing of foreign currency accounts, introduction of a dual exchange rate system on 22 July 1998, restriction on certain foreign payments and a continuous row between the government and the independent power producers resulted in an environment of uncertainty. Though violent crime and sectarian killings were on the decrease for a considerable time period yet white-collar, crime and dollar related lawlessness showed an upward trend. The pattern of crime included incidents of auto-theft, highway robbery, kidnapping for ransom, violence against women, suicides and power theft. However, during the first week of October 1999 a wave of sectarian killings in almost all provinces of the country sent shock waves and created a general sense of insecurity.

In December 1999 a letter by a psychopath, Javed Iqbal, a forty-two year old, twice divorced father of two, to police and a local newspaper in Lahore claiming that he had killed one hundred children, all boys, and erased their bodies in acid-filled containers jolted Pakistan. The murder spree began in June 1999 and sometimes the culprit killed two or three boys on the same day. This claim was substantiated when the police found bag of shoes and garments, as well as two skeletons floating in vats of sulphuric and hydrochloric acid. It was a commentary on child sexual abuse. The brutalization and dehumanization were part of the price Pakistan was paying as it stumbled towards modernity. The Afghanistan war left Pakistan awash with guns and heroin. The demographic pressures resulted in the breakdown of traditional safety nets. Inflation, unemployment, and poverty make the children of poor families fend for themselves.

Conclusion

The crime pattern in Pakistan, during the past fifty-three years, has undergone a sea change. Though this division into various phases is arbitrary yet all these phases are interactive, proactive and reactive. For example apparently one phase may appear very stable from law and order point of view due to different variables, but its cumulative impact on subsequent phases may be disastrous due to relative absence of stability factors of the preceding phase. Crucial operative variables during these phases generally were the existence or absence of political stability, levels and pace of economic development and progress and geopolitical scenario prevalent at that time. The interaction amongst the aforementioned factors also affected the changing patterns of crime with bearing on law and order. The crime pattern was affected by political, economic, social, administrative and cultural environment prevailing in the country during all these years.

NOTE

1. Special Branch, Punjab, Special Branch Report, 1994. Lahore.

6

PATTERNS OF LAWLESSNESS IN PAKISTAN

For a comprehensive analysis of the nature and magnitude of deviation from the rule of law, it is essential, in addition to a consideration of crime patterns, to examine the socio-economic patterns of lawlessness. This chapter discusses, in brief, socio-economic aspects of lawlessness with reference to corruption and white collar crime such as written-off loans and the co-operative scandal, smuggling and balance of favours mainly in the context of the 1990s. This is because this period witnessed large amounts of stuck-up advances and non-recovery thereof along with rampant corruption, breach of trust, violation of rules embezzlement of funds, wasteful expenditures, inefficiency and lack of accountability.

Corruption

Corruption, particularly at the top, is a complex socio-economic phenomenon. In terms of scope and level, corruption has no bounds and can take any shape. For example, it includes bribery, perversion of rules and procedures, nepotism, moral deterioration, maladministration, misuse of funds, abuse of powers, illegal appointments, hoarding, black-marketing, blackmailing, smuggling and scores of other corrupt practices. Some classify corruption into two types, direct and indirect. The former consists of bribes, commissions, kickbacks, embezzlements, etc.; and the latter refers to misuses of authority, patronage and organizational participation. However, monetary corruption is of the worst type.

Some argue that corruption is efficient; that it is simply the market asserting itself in the face of the government's inefficiency. To some extent this may be true. A businessman's consignment of raw materials may take a couple of months to clear from custom houses unless he pays a few thousand rupees as bribe. But, basically, corruption leads to malfunctioning of the system. It prevents the government from collecting taxes, allows people not to pay for public utilities, and enables inefficient persons to buy jobs which they do not deserve.

Normally, corruption is found at three levels of activity in the official sector; (i) policy planning, (ii) supervision and (iii) fieldwork. At the policy planning level, a decision may benefit an individual, firm or interest to the tune of millions of rupees. The decision at this level is usually too sophisticated or too high-footed for any anti-corruption agency to deal with. The supervisory level corruption means that senior officers overlook corrupt practices used by their field staff either because they get a part of the latter's illegal collections or because they are afraid of initiating action as they expect retaliation from corrupt subordinates. The field level corruption implies corruption by field officials who are the main instrument of collecting bribes and bypassing rules and regulations.

In the early years following independence, honesty and integrity marked our leadership. The Quaid-e-Azam never took a salary as the Governor General, and rather than taking from the national exchequer, gave out a lot for various worthy causes. Liaquat Ali Khan left no bank balance, at home or abroad, when he fell victim to an assassin's bullets in 1951. The same can be said of other early leaders of Pakistan.

In later decades, the rise of authoritarianism and the absence of accountability led to massive increase in corrupt practices, particularly at the top level. The situation by the year 1988 was that top rulers and officials had developed a lifestyle which, in a wider sense, bordered on corruption. For example, the Committee on the Study of Corruption, constituted by the Junejo

Government, taking notice of the top-level extravagant and corrupt lifestyles, recommended that the size, splendour and opulence of State banquets and receptions be drastically curtailed. To achieve this objective a precedent could be set at the top by ensuring that the President and the Prime Minister going abroad travel by normal commercial flights of Pakistan International Airlines, whenever convenient; when not, only the smaller jet planes (Boeing 737) were chartered. A low maximum ceiling should be laid down for the size of the President's/Prime Minister's entourage. The Committee further recommended the abolition of the practice of route lining by policemen for the President, Prime Minister, Governors and Chief Ministers travelling by road and discontinuation of reception lines at airports to receive or see off these dignitaries. Emphasizing the need for observation of traffic rules by every one the Committee suggested that there be no disruption of normal traffic for the quick passage of VIP cars. While recommending a low maximum ceiling for the size of the President's/Prime Minister's entourage, it also suggested that the various perks (facilities over and above salary, accommodation, car and telephone) authorized to public representatives holding office and senior government officials be critically reviewed and drastically curtailed. The Committee observed that 'the top leadership in the country must not be guilty of living off the State'. The other recommendations of the Committee included the curtailment of the size of government accommodation authorized for public representatives holding office and government servants to three thousands square feet area built on a plot not exceeding six hundred square feet and allotment, if at all necessary, of only one plot (six hundred square yards) at the reserved price in any urban residential area anywhere in Pakistan.[1]

There are interesting findings from two statistical surveys carried out by Gallup Institute of Pakistan on the question of corruption. 21,000 replies were received in response to Gallup's General Questionnaire. According to the replies, corruption was perceived to be in every section of the State apparatus and was felt to be up from an estimated 50 per cent ten years ago to a present 75 per cent. A vast majority of respondents to this questionnaire (70 per cent) felt that the common man could not secure his legitimate rights except through bribery or *sifarish*.[2] Gallup's second study, the National Statistical Survey, revealed that more than a third of the population attached no stigma to corrupt individuals. The majority of respondents felt that the government was not sincere in its public profession to wage a war against corruption, although over two-thirds felt that corruption could be controlled.[3] In other words, going by the survey, the popular view is that corruption can be controlled, but there is no will to control it.

The Committee on the Study of Corruption sent out 109 special questionnaires to selected citizens and organizations. Only fifty-five replies were received. Of thirty-nine federal ministers, ministers of state and advisers, only one responded. Eighty-eight Senators were asked for their views, only four responded. Similarly, nineteen Members of the National Assembly were sent questionnaires, and five responded.[4]

According to the first report, Transparency International, a global coalition against corruption in international business transactions, in a survey of forty-one countries finds Pakistan and India to be the most dishonest. Indonesia heads the list as the most corrupt country where commissions, kickbacks and influence peddling are a routine. New Zealand, Denmark, Singapore and Finland are among the least corrupt.[5]

Dirty and Poor, Clean and Rich

A recent index of polls ranking nations for corruption suggests that in general the less venal they are, the more their citizens earn.

FIGURE 6.1
Ranking of Nations for Corruption

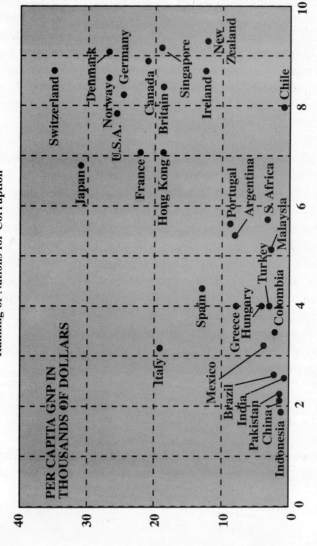

Source: Transparency International Index, World Bank.

The craze for quick money explains the strange success of rip-off investment companies in Pakistan. For three years, during 1985–87, companies offering investors 60 to 100 per cent a year mushroomed in Karachi. The companies could survive so long as new investments were higher than interest payments. By 1988, when about five billion rupees had been invested in about 300 companies, they began to go bust.[6] Some investors were uneducated workers, but the majority of them were retired army officers, bank employees and civil servants who must have known, had they thought about it, that the bust had to come. Yet the hope of quick profits overrode their common sense. The same story has been repeated in the case of co-operative credit institutions of the Punjab.

Press reports dating to autumn 1991 claimed that a total of 101 Finance Co-operatives stood registered in the Punjab at that time. Some were operational till the time of the crises, others were dummy corporations. Of these, fifty-one were registered with the Punjab Government's Central Registrar. As per balance sheet, at the time of the collapse, Rs 17 billion in depositors' funds stood locked up in these companies. An ex-registrar of co-operatives when interviewed, deposed that five of the 101 companies, i.e. National Industrial Credit Co-operative Finance Corporation, National Industrial Co-operative Finance Corporation, Pasban, Mercantile and Services Co-operative Credit Corporation held 91 per cent of the funds in the sector. However, according to the President of the Federation of Co-operatives, thirteen big co-operatives held about 90 per cent of deposits in the sector. The Judicial Commission appointed to look into the co-operatives affairs reported on eighty-seven co-operative companies. The Commission, on invitation from the public, received claims worth Rs 12.533 billion from a total of 217,945 claimants. The difference in 17 billion rupees and this figure is explained partly by some payments made till the initiation of the enquiry and partly for lack of claim forms a section of depositors who apprehended legal complications of various natures in the event of filing claims with the Commission.

The co-operatives had at the time of assessment by the Enquiry Commission invested a total of Rs 4.136 billion in assets such as lands, vehicles, etc. Rs 1.777 billion had been advanced as loans and as such the net position amounted to a liquidity of Rs 6.57 billion. Notwithstanding the highly irregular methods of investment in property and advancement of loans, the position of liquidity in hand cannot be defined as precarious, as per banking standards. This obviously has not been observed to understate the fact that the return of up to 37 per cent on fixed deposits being promised and paid by some of the companies was not sustainable over a long period and a crash was imminent later if not sooner.

The decline of the co-operatives began in July 1990, when the Habib Industrial Co-operative collapsed after it's management embezzled about 60 million rupees out of a total of Rs 300 million in deposits that it had. The second company to fall was the Services Co-operative Credit Corporation headed by the 'Islami Jamhuri Ittehad's' (Islamic Democratic Alliance) member of the Provincial Assembly, Zulfiqar Awan. Services Co-operative Credit Corporation was the second largest co-operative after National Industrial Co-operative Finance Corporation with deposits of over 2.5 billion rupees. After the fall of Habib Industrial Co-operative and Services Co-operative Credit Corporation, the remaining co-operatives fell like dominos.

Other sources of quick money in Pakistan have been employment in Gulf States, trade in heroin and market growth of smuggled goods. Indeed corruption has resulted in mafia type groups, particularly in large cities like Karachi. Land grabbers who chalk out plots and sell them to low-income and middle-income groups on the basis of affordable down payments illegally occupy State land. The land grabbers then collect the remaining portion of the price in instalment. Land development by co-operative housing societies has also become criminalized. Because no one holds legal title, the land grabber can only succeed in this business by the threat of force, which, again, is only possible with the connivance of corrupt officials of respective government agencies. These land grab operations have resulted in highhanded acts mafia style.

Financial Irregularities

The most common way for politicians to supplement incomes or do favours for friends has been through bank loans from nationalized banks, which guaranteed instant profit. Most of the projects sanctioned only ever appear on paper enabling investment figures to look better than they are. There are several popular scams. Up to 70 per cent of the value of the investment can be borrowed at a low rate. This can then be lent to someone else on higher interest, or the borrower's friend in high place declares it priority, he can then get a further 20 per cent in equity, and by over invoicing imported machinery, get the government to pay more than the total cost. So without putting up a single rupee of his own money a businessman can find himself in possession of sugar mills. Moreover there is a good chance he will not have to pay it back. In 1988, Rs 50 billion of loans from nationalized banks were declared non-performing.

The publication of lists of defaulters and beneficiaries of loans write-off and remission by the Pakistan Banking Council in August 1993 in pursuance of Banks (Nationalization) Act unravelled the 'loans scam of the century'. Spread over a period of eight years, it covers loans exceeding rupees one million. 261 top politicians and prominent business groups got loans amounting to about Rs 1.7 billion written off and 6670 of them defaulted on payment of their loans amounting to a total of over Rs 81 billion borrowed from major banks and financial institutions. Besides, a similar list of co-operative societies based on information provided by provincial government has also been issued by the Pakistan Banking Council, but is too lengthy and difficult to compute.

The details of loans exceeding one million rupees written-off during the period from 23 March 1985 to 30 June 1993 as published by the Pakistan Banking Council are tabulated below:

TABLE 6.1
Loans Written-off (Exceeding One Million Rupees)
23 March 1985 to 3 June 1993

Category of Receivers of Loan	Total Number	Amount Written-off (Rs in Millions)
Individuals	33	97.549
Partnerships	84	356.713
Corporate Sector	144	1162.092
Total	261	1616.354

Source: Pakistan Banking Council 1993.

The above chart shows that the main write-off pertains to the corporate sector, i.e. 69.73 per cent, whereas only 5.58 per cent relate to individuals. These figures also include foreign accounts (written off by foreign branches of Pakistani Banks) at Rs 53.277 million or 3.10 per cent. Again, loans written off by the ADBP (Agricultural Development Bank of Pakistan), obviously relating to agro-based industry or agriculture sector, Rs 3.368 million or 2.06 per cent of the total amount was also written-off during the period.

A similar exercise was carried out in respect of bank borrowers who defaulted on payment of loans. The same is tabulated hereunder:

TABLE 6.2
Defaulters on Payment of Loans

Category of Receivers of Loans	Total Number	Amount Outstanding (Rs in million)	Percentage with Total Outstanding Amount
Individuals	1232	6565	8.04 %
Partnerships	2931	23957	29.57%
Corporate	2446	44570	54.90%
Govt. Sector	61	6083	7.49%
Total	6670	81175	100%

Source: Pakistan Banking Council 1993.

The analysis of the above chart would reveal that corporate sector and partnerships were mainly involved in this scam.

Nationalization of commercial banks in 1974 showed record profits for a few years and phenomenal increase in bank deposits and advances. This became possible because of increased public confidence in banks due to government guarantee in addition to reflection in financial statements of profits concealed by the previous owners, unprecedented expansion of banks, elevation of bank executives in their position on merit before nationalization and excellent performance on their part. But this boom did not last long. There were successive changes in the political scenario. The country being ruled by military/civil bureaucracy and opportunist politicians to support and prolong dictatorial rule, political life having been mutilated like other institutions, banking and financial institutions were also corrupted. Stability of rule and popular support was ensured, besides other techniques, by misuse of financial institutions. Apart from recruitment of inefficient and unscrupulous officers and staff on politico-bureaucratic recommendations instead of merit, politicizing of top bank executives along with out of turn promotions and postings without merit contributed to the process of prostitution of financial institutions. Other factors responsible for this state of affairs were political loans under different schemes, agricultural loans under local political pressure, decentralization and delegation of powers to sanction loans to bank manager level. Furthermore, politicians used bank loans as a tool of horse trading to prevent floor crossing in Assemblies. Another technique of misusing bank loans consisted of *benami* and fictitious agricultural loans the real beneficiaries of which were big landlords who stood guarantee and subsequently got loans written off.

Credit facility was available in proportion to the size of the project—the bigger and foreign machinery-based the project, more was the loan, less equity ratio and more kickbacks. A new creed of politically influential but inexperienced industrialists entered the field. Average rate of floating new companies rose manifold. Since financial responsibility and accountability of directors/shareholders is limited, corporate sector proved to be a haven for financial burglers and white-collar criminals. There was visible discrimination in credit system being in favour of those with links to the banking world, political circles or government agencies. When projects were sanctioned on unreal feasibility reports over-projecting the project cost with the intention to set off loans against inflated price of machinery and to fleece funds even much more than the equity ratio in the form of kick-backs, installation of industry became a business in itself. Sale of a sanctioned project and handing over an industrial undertaking on 'turn key' basis was a new fashion in business.

This state of financial lawlessness gave birth to two types of adventurers on the industrial scene. The first category consisted of criminals indulging in corporate fraud after a process of assessing the rewards against the calculated risks. The second category included bonafide new entrants who were entrapped into financial stringency by entering in industrial sector with inadequate capital, poor entrepreneur-ship and mismanagement of the project, etc. In both cases, common practices were over-estimation of project cost through unreal feasibility reports and connivance with bank executives through financial malpractice or political influence/corruption. Banks, compromising adequate collateral, sanctioned loans. Since the project is initially over-burdened with loans (equity investment with profit having been drawn), expensive life style, Pajeros and big bungalows of the directors, the stage is setup for insufficient profits and consequent poor health of the industry. In such cases, professionals do not manage the projects and employee and agents are also prone to commit fraud against the corporation.

Genuine and experienced industrialists were also no exception to the phenomenon. They, too, would extract funds in similar way to set up more industries. They were also defaulters. They indulged in misrepresentation of industrial assets or net profits through accounting malpractice. All factors, international recession, bad crop, weak regulatory system to recover loans, etc., rendered textile units set-up in sixties, as 'sick' and government was pressurized to restructure/ reschedule loans and sanction fresh financial package through the recommendations of the Baig Committee to revive these units. It was due to defective planning, idiosyncrasies of the industrialists and procrastination on the part of decision-makers at policy-making level and more so lack of trust and understanding between the two. Nevertheless, a model was set that government comes in to relax the rules, inoculate fresh blood in financially sick units for whatever reason they become so, in the form of waiver, remission, write-off of loan or freezing of the interest payment. Such units in fact tend to be the liability of the financiers.

Pattern of Drifting Away from Self-reliance

In addition to financial irregularities the economic policies adopted by successive regimes contributed to the debt burden of the country and set up a course of dependence and living beyond means. For example, the comparative position of financial mismanagement with reference to 1988 and June 1999 and terms of public debt, stuck-up advances, 'qarz utaro mulk sanwaro scheme' (pay loans and build up the country), misutilization of foreign currency accounts and privatization proceeds tabulated below clearly reflects a pattern of financial indiscipline and drifting away from self-reliance.

TABLE 6.3
A Comparative Position of Public Debt, Stuck-up Advances,
Qarz Utaro Mulk Sanwaro **Scheme, Foreign Currency Accounts and**
Privatization Proceeds, 1988–June 1999

			(Rupees in billion)
Item	1988	June* 1999	Rise in 11 years
Public Debt	520	2800	2280
Stuck-up Advances	39	350**	311
Qarz Utaro Mulk Sanwaro Scheme	—	17	17

FCAs mis-utilized ($10 bn converted at prevailing rate)	—	510	510
Privatization Proceeds	—	59	59
Total	559	3736	3177

* Provisional position of June 1999.

** Includes advances re-scheduled/written-off in an unprofessional manner.

Source: Developed by the author on the basis of data collected from the Ministry of Finance, Government of Pakistan, Islamabad (December 1999), press reports and the annual reports of the State Bank of Pakistan for the relevant years.

Avoidance of Officialdom

The main reason the government has no money is tax collection. Out of the population of 110 million, only 1.1 million are registered and even fewer pay taxes.[7] Despite insistence by the World Bank, the agricultural sector, the country's biggest sector comprising 70 ¥ per cent of export earning and employing 55 per cent of the work force, had not been subjected to income tax till recently. This was an outcome of a landlord's dominated parliament.[8]

Many industrialists reacted to it by either not getting registered or by getting together with a landlord and declaring their earnings as agricultural income. Mostly transactions are not documented in an effort to evade income tax (for details of tax-culture see Appendix 3).

Smuggling

Pakistan's socio-economic structure has been seriously damaged by the widespread phenomenon of smuggling of foreign goods. In the beginning, smuggling in Pakistan was confined to a few items like gold, silver, narcotics and foreign currencies. With the passage of time, it gained momentum in terms of both quantity and variety of goods, mainly as a result of projectionist industrial policies followed during the period of second and third Five-Year Plans (1960–70) and subsequent ineffective checks in coastal areas and tribal territories bordering Afghanistan. Nowadays, smuggling is rampant all over the country in the shape of what are called *bara* markets (named after the town of Bara near Peshawar which is among the original centres of contraband trading).

A large variety of smuggled consumer durables and other goods of daily use manufactured in various countries of the world are available in the regular commercial areas of all the big cities like Karachi, Lahore, Quetta, Peshawar, Rawalpindi, and Abbotabad. Such goods mainly consist of gold, textiles, cosmetics, electric and electronic appliances, crockery, auto-parts, watches, cigarettes, liquor, cameras, *bidi* leaves, arms and ammunition. The goods, which are generally smuggled out of the country include food grains, narcotics, gold, silver and consumer manufactures like cooking oil.

No reliable study is available regarding the total value of smuggled goods. During 1989–90 contraband goods worth Rs 498 million (excluding narcotics) were seized by Pakistan Custom authorities.[9] This, however, represents only a fraction of the overall illegal business. During the same period 109 thousand kilograms of narcotics were also seized.[10] It thus appears that the actual value of total illegal import and export must run into billions of rupees. One seemingly outrageous estimate is Rs 150 billion ¥ which is equal to 16.6 per cent of our gross national product during 1989–90 (Rs 904 billion).[11] This estimate is staggering but so is the extent of smuggling as outlined above (also see Appendix 4 showing assets of some drug barons).

In 1999 it transpired that, apart from traditional items of smuggling, many life-saving and essential medicines were being smuggled to India and other countries where they fetched higher prices, causing shortages in local market. Dozens of widely prescribed medicines for heart, blood pressure, diabetes, thyroids, etc. were finding their way to India besides Sri Lanka, Thailand and Indonesia where these medicines commanded a higher profit margin as compared to Pakistan.[12]

Smuggling takes place on all borders of Pakistan, viz. borders touching Afghanistan, Iran and India. Coastal areas and ports of Sindh, Balochistan and International airports are also used to import and export banned items. Each border has its own special geographical, administrative and trade features but the most lucrative and large scale smuggling has been taking place along the Pakistan-Afghanistan border.

On the face of it, smuggling operations are conducted by shrewd tribal tradesmen who have their own business houses and have access to the most sophisticated trading and financial institutions all over the world, especially those in Dubai, Hong Kong, Singapore, Japan, New York, and London. There also exist loose-knit networks of thousands of exclusive wholesale and retail dealers of smuggled goods. The situation is further complicated by duty-free shops, which freely indulge in unauthorized sale of foreign goods. These shops are the outcome of current soft baggage rules. Other factors utilized by smugglers include sale proceeds of narcotics accumulated in foreign and private financial institutions, under invoicing of exports and over invoicing of imports and *hundi* transactions (non-banking transfer of remittances) of foreign exchange earned by overseas Pakistan workers. Furthermore, the smugglers take advantage of large scale smuggling of Pakistani currency to Gulf States and of illegal barter trade of such items as gold, gold jewellery, silver and watches between India and Gulf States through Pakistan. The sale proceeds of these items are used to smuggle more of these items or other articles in demand.

Conclusion

Successive regimes in Pakistan have had some common characteristics which highlight flaws in their *modus operandi* and point to their eventual failure. These include subordinating institutions to individuals, equating dissent with treason by failing to distinguish between the government (which is temporary) with the State (which is permanent), personalization of power with a 'man or woman of destiny' complex that equates the person with the nation, refusal to relinquish power voluntarily and gracefully, inability to build a viable system that is not sustained by force, proclivity to wreck a system when it does not quite serve personal interests, a practice of keeping a balance sheet of favours like getting for someone a prized posting thereby leaving him indebted all his life, inability to build and rely on a team of clean competent confidantes, inability to crack down on corruption, a culture of acceptance of the status of richness irrespective of the means of its acquisition, greater reliance on State apparatus than on the masses.

From the above fact sheet, it is obvious that the major cause of crime resulting in weapon and drug culture is the tendency to flout the law and the constitution. This tendency has led to what we may describe as a 'criminal mentality' which has given birth to the present situation of lawlessness symbolizing social breakdown resulting in a general sense of insecurity.

NOTES

1. Hussain, M., (1990), *Pakistan's Politics—The Zia Years*, Lahore, Progressive Publishers, Zaildar Park, Ichra.
2. Ibid.
3. Ibid.
4. Ibid.
5. *India Today* (1995), The Transparency International Survey is quoted in the 15 July issue of *India Today*.
6. Duncan, E., (1989), *Breaking the Curfew: A Political Journey through Pakistan*, London, Penguin Group.
7. Government of Pakistan (1995), Central Board of Revenue, Islamabad.
8. Ibid.
9. Government of Pakistan (1995), Central Board of Revenue, Islamabad.
10. Ibid.
11. Ibid.
12. Pharmaceutical Association of Pakistan (1999), Market Survey (unpublished), Lahore.

7

MAGNITUDE OF LAWLESSNESS

While attempting to determine the real magnitude of crimes in all the four provinces of Pakistan as well as in the overall context, special mention of Karachi is made because the crime situation in Karachi, by its nature, complexity and extent, has national and international ramifications.

The total cases registered in 1947 were 73,105, which doubled to 129,679 in 1971, during a period of twenty-six years. Rapid upsurge is observed since 1980. The total reported crime during the decade from 1980 to 1990 almost doubled from 152,782 to 403,078. Since 1951, the annual growth rate of crimes has generally been higher than that of population. This is despite the fact that almost 40 per cent of crimes remain unreported.

The population of Pakistan is growing at an alarming rate of over 3 per cent per annum. The total population at the time of partition was about 30 million, and now stands over 130.6 million (almost four times). Alongwith population growth, there has been corresponding increase in crimes. Table 7.4 depicts total population, total crimes, their growth rates and crimes committed in population of 100,000 of selected years from 1951 to 1998. Province-wise population/crimes ratio is indicated in Table 7.5.

Growth rate in population upto 1961 was 2.43 per cent and then increased to over 3 per cent per annum. A corresponding growth rate in crime is visible during all these years. Consistent increase in crime can be observed since 1951. The growth rate of crime was consistently higher than that of population during the period from 1961 to 1976. This was an era of agitation, political uncertainty, elections and war with India. During the period from 1981 to 1986, growth in crime rate had been over 4 per cent per annum which outstripped the population growth of 3 per cent. This was the era of martial law, Afghan war, flow of refugees in the country, narcotics trafficking, gun running, and kidnapping for ransom.

Population to crime ratios given in the same table reveal that in 1966 only 180 offences were reported in the population unit of 100,000. By the year 1991, crime increased to 257 in the same unit of population. This shows an increase of about 40 per cent. In 1992 almost one crime was being reported after every five minutes. The situation was further aggravated in 1998 when 325 offences were reported in the population unit of 100,000. This is an alarming growth in crime.

Pakistan's crime figures from year 1947 to 1999 are given in Table 7.1 showing separately crime statistics for the provinces of the Punjab, Sindh, NWFP, Balochistan, and the capital city of Islamabad. The real nature of overall crime scenario has been further clarified in Figure 7.1. Table 7.2 and Figure 7.2 indicate the growth of major categories of crime in 1981 to 1992. Table 7.3 and Figure 7.3 explain five years average in percentage terms of major crimes during the period from 1988 to 1992. Table 7.4 and Figure 7.4 make a comparison of population and crime growth rates for selected years from 1951 to 1998. Table 7.5 and Figure 7.5 represent province-wise population and crime growth with reference to years 1951, 1961, 1972, 1981, 1992, and 1998.

TABLE 7.1

Pakistan's Crime Figures for the Period 1947–1998

(Total Reported Crime)

S. No.	Year	Punjab	Sindh	NWFP	Balochistan	Islamabad	Total
1.	1947	47359	12144	12516	1086		73105
2.	1948	56429	13755	12914	1251		84349
3.	1949	52152	14816	11727	1241		79936
4.	1950	49549	16028	8970	1403		75950
5.	1951	50006	15518	9457	1538		76519
6.	1952	49409	17606	8474	1519		77008
7.	1953	47869	20355	10479	1204		79907

8.	1954	44538	19182	11128	569	75417
9.	1955	42854	18078	10179	831	71942
10.	1956	44136	22042	9760	1093	77031
11.	1957	43742	22437	10724	856	77759
12.	1958	42268	26503	11445	908	81124
13.	1959	37808	20972	10763	787	70330
14.	1960	42602	17704	13257	802	74365
15.	1961	46334	20997	11659	910	79900
16.	1962	44869	19471	10445	907	75692
17.	1963	49732	18981	11394	1060	81167
18.	1964	48487	18698	12421	1170	80776
19.	1965	48883	19424	12558	1154	82019
20.	1966	55280	20817	16406	1130	93633
21.	1967	60856	23936	17765	1337	103894
22.	1968	69258	29263	19064	1470	119055
23.	1969	68525	28005	19650	1515	117695
24.	1970	74284	27628	19386	1440	122738
25.	1971	77454	28932	21195	2098	129679
26.	1972	97503	33709	22736	2774	156722
27.	1973	98809	33646	22947	2767	158169
28.	1974	100206	32371	25237	2487	160301
29.	1975	104676	30217	27217	2309	164419
30.	1976	104509	29287	30720	2516	167032
31.	1977	84187	25049	29206	2883	141325
32.	1978	102720	28267	32308	2474	165769
33.	1979	84435	26121	30691	2659	143906
34.	1980	89475	27659	32815	2833	152782
35.	1981	99775	43159	35751	3281	1151	183117
36.	1982	97858	45422	38628	3447	971	186326
37.	1983	99300	41518	48774	3542	714	193848
38.	1984	111414	43987	51424	4124	854	211803
39.	1985	114486	48125	52217	4426	781	220035
40.	1986	138785	51267	47092	4308	913	242265
41.	1987	153042	49257	46774	4193	1240	254506
42.	1988	164649	48648	51765	4693	1248	271003
43.	1989	242813	58735	57827	5377	1400	366152
44.	1990	285891	53994	56696	4817	1680	403078
45.	1991	171805	41969	65407	4443	1803	285427
46.	1992	172865	40170	67409	4445	1494	286383
47.	1993	169680	49341	71740	4909	1337	297007*
48.	1994	197384	42264	74333	5307	1899	321187
49.	1995	201150	45132	80297	5635	1929	334143
50.	1996	191019	42476	81372	6096	2094	323057
51.	1997	235855	43099	80894	5901	2426	368175
52.	1998	286466	47703	85070	6606	2627	428472
53.	1999	263490	43808	91896	6942	2624	408760

Note: Excluding the crime falling in the jurisdiction of the Railways Police, Northern Areas and Tribal Territory.

Source: Central Police Offices of Lahore, Karachi, Peshawar, Quetta and Islamabad.

FIGURE 7.1
Crime Figures for the Period 1947–1998
(Total Reported Crime)

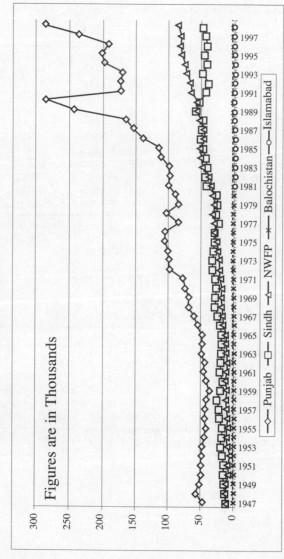

Source: Developed by the author with reference to the data in Table 7.1.

TABLE 7.2
Growth of Major Categories of Crime (1981–92)

Year	Murder	Crime against Person	Crime against property	Accidents	Local and Special law	Misc.
1981	4834	32135	32109	12258	59326	42455
1982	4811	31191	31781	12565	60632	45256
1983	4768	31132	31098	13447	65242	43024
1984	5222	32823	33323	11922	73693	54815
1985	5453	33645	33640	12073	80530	54694
1986	6209	35772	38163	12581	112290	37250
1987	6488	35788	34741	13330	127726	36433
1988	6928	36475	39942	14456	123474	49728
1989	7557	38670	46665	13897	211319	48044
1990	8226	36847	51593	12428	150563	43331
1991	7443	36246	45485	10656	129442	59443
1992	6943	39246	46826	11387	126171	593066

Source: Police Bureau of Research, Ministry of Interior, Government of Pakistan.

TABLE 7.3
Major Crimes
Average of 5 Years (1988 to 1992)

Murder	7441	2.5 %
Crime against Person	36115	12.2 %
Crime against Property	46102	15.6 %
Accidents	12565	4.2 %
Local and Special Law	148194	50.0 %
Miscellaneous	45970	15.5 %
	296387	100.0 %

Source: Police Bureau of Research, Ministry of Interior, Government of Pakistan.

FIGURE 7.2
Growth of Major Categories of Crimes (1981–92)

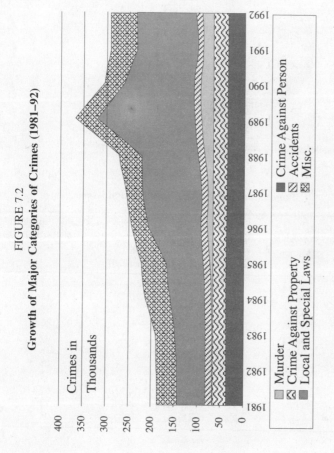

Source: Developed by the author with reference to the data in Table 7.2.

FIGURE 7.3
Major Crimes
Average of 5 Years (1988–1992)

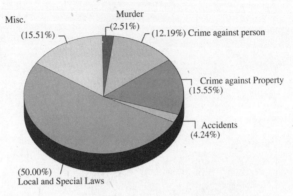

Source: Developed by the author with reference to the data in Table 7.3.

TABLE 7.4
Population and Crime Growth in Pakistan

Year	Total Population (Million)	Population growth rate (%) (annual)	Total Crime reported	Crime growth rate (%) (annual)	Crimes Population of 100,000
1951	33.82	–	76519	–	226
1958	38.12	2.43	81124	0.13	212
1961	42.97	2.43	79900	0.73	185
1966	51.98	3.08	93633	3.22	180
1971	62.88	3.08	129679	6.72	206
1976	73.20	3.09	167032	5.17	228
1981	84.9	3.0	183117	1.88	215
1986	97.5	2.7	242265	4.98	248
1991	110.8	2.5	285427	4.30	257
1992	113.6	2.5	286383	0.33	252
1998	130.6	2.4	428472	16.37	325

Sources:

1. Population Census, 1998 and Planning and Development Division, Islamabad.

2. Central Police Offices of Lahore, Karachi, Peshawar, Quetta, and Islamabad.

FIGURE 7.4

Population and Crime Growth in Pakistan

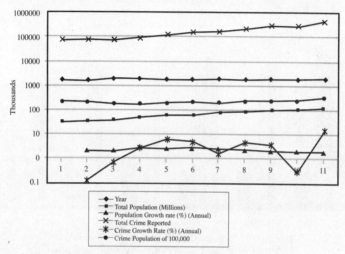

Source: Developed by the author with reference to the data in Table 7.4.

TABLE 7.5

Province-wise Population and Crime Growth

Total Crime Reported and Population/Crime Percentage of Selected Years

Year	Punjab		Sindh		NWFP		Balochistan	
	Popu-lation	Crimes	Popu-lation	Crimes	Popu-lation	Crimes	Popu-lation	Crimes
1951	20.55	50006	6.05	15518	4.58	9457	1.18	1538
	(60.8)	(65.36)	(17.9)	(20.28)	(13.6)	(12.36)	(3.5)	(2.0)
1961	25.50	46334	8.34	20997	5.75	11659	1.38	910
	(59.3)	(58.0)	(19.5)	(26.28)	(13.4)	(14.59)	(3.2)	(1.13)
1972	37.61	97503	14.15	33709	8.39	22736	2.43	2774
	(57.6)	(62.2)	(21.7)	(21.5)	(12.8)	(14.5)	(3.7)	(1.77)
1981	47.29	10096	19.03	43159	11.06	35751	4.33	3281
	(56.1)	(55.11)	(22.6)	(23.57)	(13.1)	(19.5)	(5.1)	(1.79)
1992	68.25	172865	20.73	40170	15.8	67409	6.16	4445
	(56.1)	(60.24)	(22.6)	(13.58)	(13.1)	(23.25)	(5.1)	(1.53)
1998	72.58	286466	29.99	47703	17.55	85070	6.51	6606
	(55.6)	(66.86)	(23.0)	(11.13)	(13.4)	(19.85)	(5.0)	(1.54)

Source: Central Police Offices of Lahore, Karachi, Peshawar, Quetta and Islamabad.
Notes:1. Population figures are in millions.
2. Figures for Islamabad and Federally Administered Tribal Area (FATA) are not included.

FIGURE 7.5
Province-wise Population and Crime Growth
Total Crime Reported and Population/Crime
Percentage of Selected Years

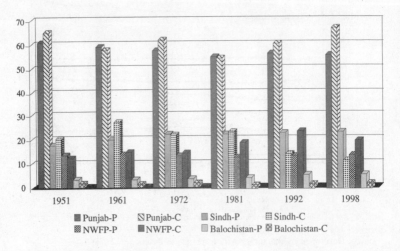

Key: P (Population), C (Crime).
Source: Developed by the author with reference to the data in Table 7.5.

Sectarian Situation

Sectarianism continues to exist in the Punjab, Sindh, NWFP, Balochistan and Northern Areas of Pakistan. The situation in the Punjab is particularly disturbing. It has brought the whole society to a point of virtual breakdown. The major threat to sectarian harmony comes from the Sipah-e-Sahaba Pakistan, its terrorist offshoot Lashkar-e-Jhangvi and their militant opponents, i.e. Sipah-e-Muhammad, and Tehrik-e-Nifaz-e-Fiqah Jafria (TNFJ). They stepped up violence as they attempted to implement their own vision of Islam. The terrorists from Lashkar-e-Jhangvi and Sipah-e-Muhammad resorted to mass indiscriminate murders motivated by religious imperatives. For them violence is a divine duty and morally justified. The intolerance and mutual hatred preached in their religious schools (madrassas) made them justify almost limitless violence against virtually any target, i.e. anyone who is not a member of their own religious sect. The confusion is worsened by their allied groups like Sawad-e-Azam Ahle Sunnat, Tehrik Haq Char Yar, and Immamia Student Organization whose religious fanatics continue to deliver objectionable speeches against each other. However, the Barelvi-Deobandi tussle is also being fuelled on the question of taking forcible possession of mosques of either sect by the other. A new organization the 'Sunni Tehrik' has been formed by one Saleem Qadri in Karachi. It has assumed the role of snatching 'sunni mosques' from the possession of Deobandis.

The recent years have witnessed growth of a large number of sectarian organizations wedded to their own narrow-minded goals. A list of such organizations is given in Appendix 5.

Province-wise Crimes Scenario

The total population of Pakistan, according to the 1998 Census, is estimated at 130.6 million. Out of this, the Punjab has 55.6 per cent (72.5 million), Sindh 23 per cent (29.9 million), NWFP 13.4 per cent (17.5 million), and Balochistan 5.0 per cent (6.5 million).

Punjab

The population proportion of the Punjab in relation to national population declined from 60.8 per cent in 1951 to 55.6 per cent in 1998. Correspondingly crimes reported in the Punjab were 65.36 per cent in 1951 and 66.86 per cent in 1998 of total crimes. Thus, more or less, the relative percentage share of crimes in the Punjab was according to population.

Table 7.6 gives an idea of law and order incidents of sectarian nature during the period 1995 to 7 June 1999.

TABLE 7.6

Punjab: Sectarian Incidents and persons killed

(1995 to 7 June 1999)

Period	Incidents	Persons Injured	Persons Killed
01-01-95 to 31-01-95	5	3 (3 Sunnis)	5 (Sunnis)
01-02-95 to 29-02-95	17	19 (17 Sunnis 2 Shias)	15 (11 Sunnis 4 Shias)
01-03-95 to 31-03-95	12	11 (10 Sunnis 1 Shia)	10 (6 Sunnis 4 Shias)
01-04-95 to 30-04-95	9	6 (6 Sunnis)	5 (1 Shia 4 Sunnis)
01-05-95 to 31-05-95	5	8 (4 Shias 4 Sunnis)	—
01-06-95 to 30-06-95	13	13 (8 Shias 5 Sunnis)	3 (3 Shias)
01-07-95 to 31-07-95	7	7 (7 Shias)	4 (2 Shias 2 Sunnis)
01-08-95 to 31-08-95	4	6 (6 Shias)	—
01-09-95 to 30-09-95	4	1 (1 Sunni)	4 (3 Sunnis 1 Shia)
01-10-95 to 31-10-95	5	1 (1 Shia)	8 (4 Sunnis 3 Shias 1 Qadiani)
01-11-95 to 30-11-95	5	12 (1 Qadiani 11 Sunnis)	4 (1 Qadiani 3 Shias)
1996	40	107 (61 Sunnis 46 Shias)	94 (36 Sunnis 58 Shias)
1997	92	146 (128 Sunnis 18 Shias)	195 (76 Sunnis 119 Shias)
1998	37	43 (43 Shias)	82 (3 Sunnis 79 Shias)
1999 (till 7 June)	9	9 (9 Shias)	38 (38 Shias)

Sources:
1. Khan, M. Abbas (1996), 'Problems of Law and Order and Police Reforms', IGP's Briefing to the Prime Minister of Pakistan, 7 February.
2. Crimes Investigation Department of the Punjab Police (1999) Official Record, Lahore.

FIGURE 7.6

Punjab: Law and Order Incidents Resulting from Sectarian Trouble

(1995 to 7 June 1999)

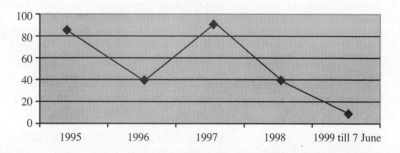

Source: Developed by the author with reference to the data in Table 7.6.

The following Figures (7.7 to 7.9) indicate the number of bomb blasts/sabotage activities including persons injured and killed (1990–1998), incidents of murder (1947–1998) and dacoity (1947–1998).

FIGURE 7.7
Punjab: Bomb Blasts
Incidents and Persons Injured and Killed

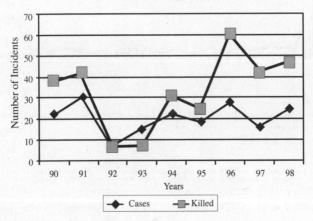

Source: Crimes Investigation Department of the Punjab Police, Lahore.

FIGURE 7.8
Punjab: Murders (1947–1998)

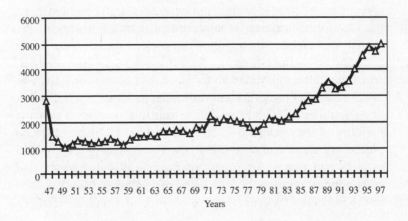

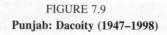

FIGURE 7.9
Punjab: Dacoity (1947–1998)

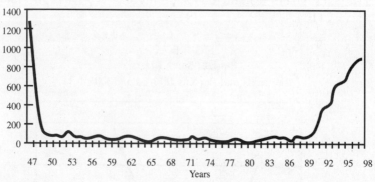

Sources:
1. Khan, M. Abbas (1996), 'Problems of Law and Order and Police Reforms', IGP's Briefing to the Prime Minister of Pakistan, 7 February.
2. Crime Branch of the Punjab Police (1999).

By the year 1990 the crime situation in the Punjab assumed alarming proportions. Sectarian violence, gunrunning, armed dacoities and police-public clashes, followed robberies and mysterious murders. For example, the Chiniot incident in which seven police officials, including a sub-Inspector, were killed in a citizen-police clash following a locals-dacoits encounter, which left two persons dead and six injured in the early hours on 24 January 1990. It occurred primarily because of growing resentment of people against police excesses.[1] The intensity of the Chiniot occurrence 'is unprecedented in the history of the Punjab in which ten including seven police officials were killed and more than forty injured.' A police party of Gujrat district, which was going to Mianwali to apprehend some criminals, was attacked due to mob fury and misunderstanding in Chiniot.[2] A news reporter of Lahore made the startling revelation that the majority of the '*thanedars*', i.e. Station House Officers (SHOs) posted in Lahore had been criminals. The crimes of these police officers had ranged from acts of professional dishonesty and corruption to murders.[3] In the wake of perceived injustice done to the police and a general sense of insecurity and interference in their duties, the Gujrat Police in 1990 went on strike. The policemen took out a procession that marched on the city roads, and was seen by the public and the media. The strike was discontinued on the intervention of a senior police officer who accepted their demands.

During the period ranging from March 1989 to 20 June 1991, mysterious murders resulted in incidents of violent protest and police-public clashes in Mughalpura (Lahore), Sheikhupura and Gujrat. Violence, breach of peace, kidnapping for ransom and dacoities resulted in a general sense of insecurity. The Punjab province became notorious for sectarian killings, proliferation of illicit arms and drugs and incidents of violent crime.

As regards the capital territory of Islamabad, the situation in 1990–1991 was hardly satisfactory. Some of the diplomats complained that law and order was deteriorating in the capital. Besides many break-in of homes belonging to the diplomatic community, they also alleged that cars carrying the diplomatic number plates were deliberately attacked.[4] From January 1997 to May 1999 five persons were killed in sectarian violence and one terrorist arrested in the Islamabad capital territory.[5]

The crime situation in the Punjab in 1994–95, too, was hardly satisfactory. Protests over the blasphemy case of Gujranwala and death of a young man by burning by a furious mob in the city of Gujranwala after snatching him from the custody of police caused embarrassment for Pakistan even at the international level. The beginning of 1996 witnessed a wave of lawlessness in and around Lahore. Unknown culprits gunned down important personalities like film star Sultan Rahi, well-known poet Mohsin Naqvi and Director Excise and Taxation Sajid Gillani, thereby causing a general sense of insecurity. The situation appeared to be completely out of control by the middle of the year when the Commissioner of Sargodha Division, Syed Tajammal Abbas and Deputy Commissioner Khanewal, Raza Ali were killed in quick succession by some unknown sectarian gunmen.

This trend of sectarian violence continued even in 1997, 1998, and early 1999. Muhammad Ashraf Marth was a brilliant police officer. While posted as the Senior Superintendent of Police in

Multan in early 1997, he unearthed a group of terrorists who had stormed the Iranian Cultural Centre and killed the inmates. He also located all their links, financial resources, hit lists and equipment to jam police wireless sets. They threatened to kill him if he did not give up his pursuit. Subsequently he was transferred to Gujranwala as the Senior Superintendent of Police. He continued his professional duty undeterred by threats. On 6 May 1997, he was gunned down by terrorists in front of his official residence.

The sectarian attack on a mosque in Muzaffargarh in 1999 established a strange pattern, making the month of January the favourite among a particular hardcore religious group to settle scores with its opponents. The killings of the people from a sect by a rival one in January seems to be a part of the 'routine' followed the second group. The latest attack suggested the particular group had not forgotten the loss of twenty-seven lives, including one of their leaders at the court bomb blast. This was apparent from the fact that the sessions court bomb blast took place on 13 January 1998, and the Karamdad-Muzaffargarh tragedy happened on 4 January 1999—the sessions court explosion killing twenty-seven people including Zia-ur-Rahman Farooqi which led to the twenty-five shia deaths in Mominpura and seventeen more Shias in Muzaffargarh. The retaliation in the Mominpura and Karamdad bloodcurdling drama provided another fundamentalist approach of ensuring death close to the sessions court blast. Apart from these incidents, January appeared to be the bloodiest month for the Punjabis as 101 lives had been lost with more than 200 injured over the last five years. These casualties were from eleven bomb explosions and seven sectarian attacks.[6]

As the government intensified efforts to bring terrorists to justice by prosecution and conviction before courts of law, the latter tried to intimidate the government by making an attempt on the life of the then Prime Minister of Pakistan. On 3 January 1999, a group of terrorists belonging to the Sipah-e-Sahaba Pakistan and the Lashkar-e-Jhangvi carried out an act of sabotage. A remote control device containing 180 kg of explosives was placed under the Bhobattian Bridge, Raiwind Road, Lahore, for assassinating the then Prime Minister of Pakistan, Muhammad Nawaz Sharif. The bomb went off at 9:55 am, shortly before Nawaz Sharif was due to travel along it. The explosion was so powerful that the concrete debris fell in houses as far as three kilometres away. An eight-kilogram slab landed on a shop in a market about 200 feet away and caused a one-foot wide hole in the roof. A welding plant, parked on the bridge before the blast, flew 400 feet right and landed twenty feet away from the place of the blast. The plant's wheels landed some 300 meters away. A tractor (OKA-312), parked beside the plant, was also damaged. The bicycle of one of the three dead persons flew fifty feet high and landed around 300 feet away from the place of explosion. One of the victims, later identified as Saleem of Mangamandi, flew several feet into the air and hit the iron fence along the bridge some twenty feet away from the site of explosion. Both his legs were severed. The other dead persons were identified as Ashraf Masih and Pitras Masih aged between 30–35 years. They were brothers and had four and five children respectively. It was a well-planned and thought out conspiracy hatched by the Sipah-e-Sahaba Pakistan and the Lashkar-e-Jhangvi. Although they failed in achieving their target because the device accidentally exploded before time, the blast resulted in death of three innocent persons besides extensive damage to the bridge itself.

NWFP

The trend of crime in NWFP shows that since 1961 the share of crimes compared to population has risen substantially. During the period form 1947 to 1998 the crime in NWFP rose by 629 per cent while the increase in population was 454 per cent.[7] The details are outlined in tables 7.7 and 7.8. However, in the years 1980 and 1992 while population proportion of the province remained almost constant (13.1 per cent), crimes increased from 19.5 to 23.5 per cent. This rise can be attributed to the influx of refugees from Afghanistan, abundance of weapons, narcotics trade and penetration of KHAD and RAW agents. NWFP remained in the front line during the Afghan war and still hosts over 1.5 million refugees. Recently violent incidents took place in Malakand division and certain tribal areas of the province.

TABLE 7.7

NWFP: Break-up of Heinous Crime and its Trend from 1970 to 1998

Year	All Reported	Against Persons	Kidnapping/ Abduction	Assault on Government Servants	Robbery/ Dacoity/Car Snatching	Burglary/ Theft
1970	25188	2714	285	55	66	1985
1980	33932	5970	559	106	33	1630
1990	56676	6915	498	159	156	1218
1991	65676	6616	414	165	216	1200
1992	67545	6454	405	200	239	1336
1993	71740	6612	427	182	242	1251
1994	74333	6990	462	108	308	1320
1995	80297	7421	464	98	283	1272
1996	81372	7783	463	110	895	1332
1997	80890	7771	503	93	393	1997
1998	85070	8562	557	143	418	2018
Percentage of Crime as compared with year 1970						
	338%	315%	195%	260%	633%	102%

Source: CPO Peshawar
1. Briefing in December, 1994.
2. Crime Branch Official Data, 1999

FIGURE 7.10

NWFP: Break-up of Heinous Crimes and its Trend from 1970 to 1998

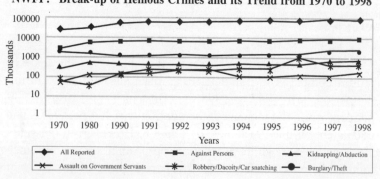

Source: Developed by the author with reference to the data in Table 7.7.

TABLE 7.8
NWFP: Comparison - Population, Crime, Proclaimed Offenders and Police Strength for Selected Years

Year	Population*	Crime	Proclaimed Offenders	Strength
1947	4,556,545	13516	2150	28945
1990	14,320,886	56676	12947	25903
1993	16,869,859	71740	11728	29663
1998	2,06,92,537	85070	8565	31310
Increase in percentage	**454%**	**629 %**	**398 %**	**108 %**

*Settled Area Population 20,692,537 and Tribal Area Population 3,137,863.

Source: CPO Peshawar;
1. Briefing in December, 1994.
2. Crime Branch official data, 1998.

Balochistan

Population of Balochistan is about 5 per cent of the national population but the crime share only 1.54 per cent. The recorded crimes relative to population reveal that the province of Balochistan witnessed less incidents of crimes than the other provinces. The crime situation in Balochistan has been fluctuating in the past few years, without assuming alarming proportions. In recent years, Balochistan has been plagued by theft of vehicles. 1990 was the worst year. Tribalism is peculiar to Balochistan.[8] Though better educational facilities and improved means of communication have made some dents in the system but it is so deep-rooted that its decline is woefully slow. A brief resume of the tribal feuds is given in Appendix 6. Since 1973, sensational tribal murders have been adversely affecting the law and order situation in Balochistan.[9] Added to this is the phenomenon of abduction of foreigners engaged in the exploration of oil and gas, arms proliferation, dealings in narcotics, activities of Afghan groups like the one headed by Mullah Rocketti who kidnapped a Deputy Commissioner, and a significant number of proclaimed offenders coming from the bordering areas of other provinces. A glance at Table 7.9 gives an idea of the recovery of arms and narcotics by the Balochistan Police during the years 1990–1998.

TABLE 7.9

Balochistan: Fire Arms, Hand Grenades, Rocket Launchers, Machine Guns, Bombs and Narcotics Recovered by the Police

Items	1990	1991	1992	1993	1994	1995	1996	1997	1998
All types Fire Arms	344	395	350	473	542	497	289	538	468
Hand Grenades	39	27	0	10	9	40	1	14	15
Rocket Launchers	6	0	0	225	537	3	3	0	4
Machine Guns	0	1	0	1	1	3	0	1	0
Bombs	3	2	1	7	47	2	0	1	0
Narcotics (Kilograms)	708.513	3259.605	804.711	603.857	884.4	1697.709	537.065	2014.358	1464.297

Source: Crime Branch, Quetta, 1999.

Sindh

In Sindh province, share of crimes was higher in 1951 (29.28 per cent and 26.28 per cent) against share of population. During 1972 and 1981, population and crimes have similar percentages. However, in the year 1992 and 1993 a substantial decrease in crime (13.85 per cent) was observed against population proportion of 22.6 per cent. This trend continued in 1998. With a population share of 23 per cent of the total population of Pakistan the crime in Sindh was only 11.13 per cent of the total crime of the country. This is an unnatural phenomenon, as Sindh had serious law and order problems during the last few years. Ethnic violence in major cities and dacoities and robberies in rural areas abounded. The province was virtually paralyzed by crime. It shows that crimes were not being reported or the police failed to register them. It also reflects a state of lack of mutual trust and confidence between the police and the public. Both considered each other as illegitimate. In fact, gangs of dacoits have been playing havoc in the rural areas of Sindh and appeared to be out of control for a considerable length of time. Kidnapping for ransom, highway robberies, armed encounters with the police and other law enforcing agencies became quite common particularly after the launching of the Movement for the Restoration of Democracy in 1983.

The law and order situation has remained equally disturbed in the urban areas as well since 1983. The following years witnessed an upward trend in crime. However, the situation took a different turn, when Altaf Hussain revived the Mohajir Quami Movement (MQM) in 1985–86. Taking the plea of injustices done to Mohajirs (Urdu speaking) an element of ethnicity was introduced in the politics of the country. After sweeping the local bodies' elections in 1986–87 the MQM became a force to be reckoned with. In the national elections of 1988 they won all the fourteen seats of the National Assembly from urban Sindh. The subsequent political developments made the MQM acquire arms. The intensity of the ethnic strife, which followed, can be gauged from the details of casualties given below:

TABLE 7.10
**Sindh: Killings in Karachi/Hyderabad/Sukkur Division
from 1986 to 1994**

Serial No.	Division	Punjabi	Pathan	Sindhi	Mohajir	Others	Total
1.	Karachi	330	299	88	696	404	1817
2.	Hyderabad	007	009	91	185	002	0294
3.	Sukkur/Larkana	003	-	11	038	003	0055
Grand Total		340	308	190	919	409	2166

Source: CPO Karachi, 1994.

FIGURE 7.11
Sindh: Killings in Karachi/Hyderabad/Sukkur Division
from 1986 to 1994

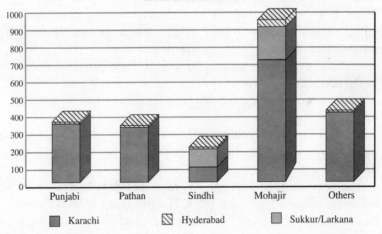

Source: Developed by the author with reference to the data in Table 7.10.

With the beginning of 1990s the law and order situation in the province of Sindh reached an extremely alarming state whereby the economic activity stagnated and peace-loving citizens in urban areas were demoralized. The common man in the rural area was desperate and fearful even during day time. A large number of gangs of dacoits were actively involved in criminal activities like kidnapping for ransom, murder, highway robbery, dacoity, firing on buses/trains/cars. The gangs of dacoits and urban guerrillas (terrorists) were roaming both in rural and urban areas and had spread a reign of terror.

Under such circumstances on 28 May 1992, proceeding under Article 147 of the Constitution of the Islamic Republic of Pakistan, the Federal Government entrusted to the army the functions of public security and maintenance of law and order. The army initiated a programme for elimination of gangs of dacoits and terrorists. It was named as Operation Clean-Up in Sindh. As discussed in Appendix 9, the operation resulted in many problems which adversely affected the citizens, the army itself and the government. There was no significant change in the worsening law and order situation. The degree of success of the army action can be determined with reference to tables 7.10 and 7.11.

TABLE 7.11

Sindh: Comparative Crime Statement for Year 1992–93

Serial No.	Heads	1992	1993	Difference
1	Murder	1566	1439	-127
2	Attempt to Murder	1756	1650	-106
3	Dacoity	339	289	-50
4	Robbery	246	295	+49
5	Vehicle Theft/Snatching	6208	6343	+135
6	Kidnapping/Abduction	1148	866	-282
7	Assault on Public Servants	792	706	-96

Source: CPO Karachi, 1994.

FIGURE 7.12

Sindh: Comparative Crime Statement for the Year 1992–93

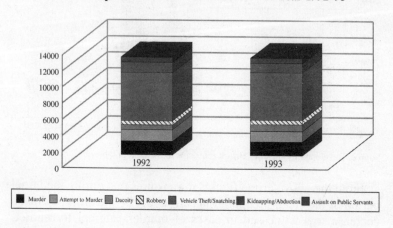

Source: Developed by the author with reference to the data in Table 7.11.

TABLE 7.12

Sindh: Comparative Crime Statement for Year 1993–94

Serial No.	Heads	Period 1 Jan 1993 to 15 Dec 1993	Period 1 Jan 1994 to 15 Dec 1994	Difference
1	Murder	1382	2024	+642
2	Attempt to Murder	1559	2214	+655
3	Dacoity	280	352	+72
4	Robbery	1067	1075	+8
5	Vehicle theft/Snatching	5868	6684	+816
6	Kidnapping/Abduction	839	854	+15
7	Assault on Public Servants	460	502	+42

Source: CPO Karachi, 1994.

FIGURE 7.13

Sindh: Comparative Crime Statement for Year 1993–94

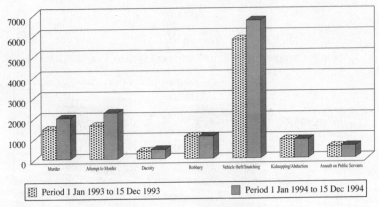

Source: Developed by the author with reference to the data in table 7.12.

From the above crime figures it transpires that during the initial period of the clean-up operation carried out by the army, a drastic decrease was witnessed in cases of murder, attempt to murder, dacoity, kidnapping, abduction and assault on public servants but incidents of robbery and car theft/snatching registered an increase. Another way to look at the situation in Sindh is to take into account police casualties.

TABLE 7.13
Sindh: Police Casualties

Year	Killed	Injured	Compensation in Rupees
1983	21	14	–
1984	56	58	1,000,000.00
1985	28	56	3.285,000.00
1986	95	176	5,400,000.00
1987	57	107	5,290,000.00
1988	40	99	3,300,000.00
1989	43	112	1,900,000.00
1990	95	183	7,120,000.00
1991	109	155	17,000,000.00
1992	98	123	11,240,000.00
1993	67	102	2,160,000.00
1994	73	26	22,308,000.00

Source: CPO Karachi, 1994.

FIGURE 7.14
Sindh: Police Casualties

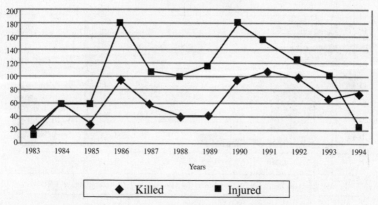

Source: Developed by the author with reference to the data in Table 7.13.

Sectarianism, too, continues to exist in Sindh and there are indications that it could lead to a major law and order problem anytime as is evident from the figures given in Table 7.14

TABLE 7.14

Sindh: Loss of life in Sectarian Violence in Sindh

Party	Killed	Injured
SSP	47	60
Sunni Tehrik	3	7
TNFJP (Shias)	35	72
Ahle-Hadis	0	0
Qadianis	0	6
Police	1	9
Others	5	26

Source : CPO, Karachi, 1994.

FIGURE 7.15

Sindh: Loss of Life in Sectarian Violence in Sindh

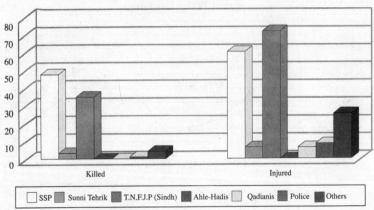

Source: Developed by the author with reference to the data in Table 7.14.

Lawlessness in Karachi

Extent of Lawlessness

After the initiation of the army action in Sindh, another faction of the MQM, known as MQM (Haqiqi or H) was created. The original MQM came to be known as MQM (Altaf or A). The killings in Karachi are attributed to factional fighting between MQM (A) and MQM (H). It is the fight to control the turf. The upsurge is also attributed to the attempts by both factions to strengthen their position on the bargaining table for negotiations with the government. Both groups of MQM have been fighting among themselves to settle scores arising out of issues such as collection of donations or distribution of money obtained through illegal means. The propaganda tactics adopted by the MQM's dissenting groups are to blame government for every thing. Following acts of violence and terrorism alleged to be committed by MQM (A) and MQM (H) depict the worsening law and order situation.

TABLE 7.15

Karachi: Losses in Terms of Killings, Injuries, Abduction and Damage to Property and Vehicles

(December 1993 to December 1994)

Month	Killings	Injuries	Abduction	Damage to Property	Damage to Vehicles
Dec.93	3	5	1	-	-
Jan. 94	3	13	1	8	3
Feb. 94	16	21	-	8	5
March 94	14	37	-	28	4
April 94	14	80	3	27	12
May 94	36	87	1	54	22
June 94	22	10	1	3	-
July 94	12	14	2	16	2
August 94	26	30	1	19	-
Sept. 94	24	36	-	9	-
Oct. 94	35	15	1	9	-
Nov. 94	64	106	2	20	8
Dec. 94	19	15	-	-	-

FIGURE 7.16
**Karachi: Losses in Terms of Killings, Injuries, Abduction and Damage
to Property and Vehicles**
(December 1993 to December 1994)

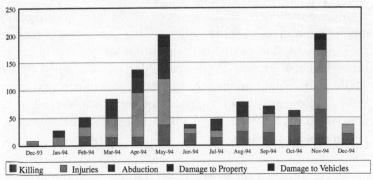

Source: Developed by the author with reference to the data in Table 7.15.

The break-up of aforementioned losses is indicated below in Table 7.16.

TABLE 7.16
Karachi: Break-up of Killings and Injuries
(December 1993 to December 1994)

PARTY	KILLINGS	INJURIES
MQM-A	108	73
MQM-H	79	40
PPP/PSF	6	7
POLICE	19	36
RANGERS	1	2
ARMY	1	7
OTHERS	1	29
TOTAL	**215**	**194**

Source: CPO Karachi, 1994.

From 1988 onwards industrialists began moving out of
Pakistan to Dubai, frightened off by the unstable political
situation, tension with India, and ethnic violence in Karachi, the
country's commercial centre where 47 per cent of industry and
all major headquarters are based. By the end of 1989 the

FIGURE 7.17
Karachi: Break-up of Killings and Injuries
(December 1993 to December 1994)

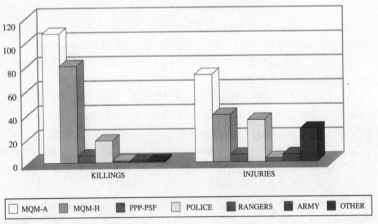

Source: Developed by the author with reference to the data in Table 7.16.

security situation was so bad in the southern part of city—that provides nearly three quarters of government revenues—that business was down to 50 per cent. Chamber of Commerce officials in Karachi said that Karachi was losing $42 million per day because curfew in most populated areas prevented workers from reaching factories.[10]

Leading business organizations brought in experts in dealing with kidnapping from the United States and Italy after more than eight businessmen had to pay ransom in six months. By August 1990, according to the Chairman of Adamjee Insurance, Mr.Chaudhry, the number of kidnappings had reached one a day and several hundred businessmen kidnap held insurance policies with Lloyds of London through the Company. Victims included the son of the State Bank Governor and the head of the stock exchange.[11] Bashir Ali Muhammad, Chairman of the All Pakistan Textile Mills Association, whose members had paid out more than 39 million rupees in six months, observed as under:

> Every day we hear of people we know personally being kidnapped or robbed. The highways are so unsafe that over a year we have not

been able to visit our factories. We cannot understand why the government is allowing business and industry to be driven out. Ultimately Sindh will lose.[12]

Similarly, Akhtar Hameed Khan, the Director of the Orangi Project, said, 'We are looking at the destruction of Karachi and that means the destruction of the Pakistan economy. Pakistan is trying to destroy itself.'[13]

The urban areas, specially Karachi, were in the grip of anarchy and chaos before the clean-up operation. The lives and property of the citizens were not safe. the city of Karachi was segregated into small pockets privately fortified by huge iron gates. Due to fear of terrorists, even access to common people into these areas was denied.

The activists of different organizations like MQM (A) and MQM (H) were employing tactics of blackmailing and coercion for collection of illegal donations to the tune of millions of rupees. In case of refusal to meet such demands for donations, innocent people were killed. This situation had created a sense of total insecurity amongst the people.

Following is a comparative crime position of the Karachi Division for the period from 1 December 1993 to 19 December 1993 and 1 December 1994 to 19 December 1994 after withdrawal of the army:

TABLE 7.17

Karachi: Comparative Crime Statement for 19 Days of Years 1993–94

Serial No.	Heads	Period 1 Dec 1993 to 19 Dec 1993	Period 1 Dec 1994 to 19 Dec 1994	Difference
1	Murder	19	98	+79
2	Attempt to Murder	30	78	+48
3	Dacoity	05	04	-01
4	Robbery	40	20	-20
5	Vehicle theft/Snatching	346	368	+22
6	Kidnapping/Abduction	21	07	-14
7	Assault on Public Servants	03	0	-03

Source: CPO Karachi, 1994.

FIGURE 7.18

Karachi: Comparative Crime Statement for 19 Days of Years 1993–94

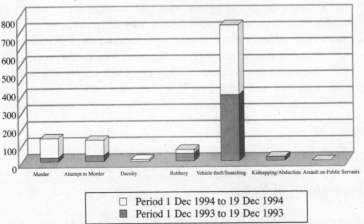

Period 1 Dec 1994 to 19 Dec 1994
Period 1 Dec 1993 to 19 Dec 1993

Source: Developed by the author with reference to the data in Table 7.17.

Examining the situation in Karachi, the participants of the 61st National Management course of the Pakistan Administrative Staff College, Lahore, observed as under:

Against the backdrop of massive killings of people in Karachi in the month of December 1994, a group of the Staff College visited the Sindh capital from the 26th to the 29th of December 1994 to study and prepare a report on the law and order situation of Sindh. The study group's visit coincided with the unscheduled visit of the Prime Minister of Pakistan to Karachi during the same time. The Prime Minister held a series of meetings with people from all walks of life including the state administrative machinery. By the time this group arrived in Karachi, more than 130 people had been killed and hundreds injured in the preceding twenty-five days. There was a total state of panic in the Karachi metropolis. Sniper firings and killings were the order of the day. There appeared to be total anarchy. The press every day had nothing but unwanted killings to report. Those who survived just kept on praying the whole time until the children were back home. Business came to a stand still. There were reports that essential supplies like 'atta', rice and other such articles were getting into short supply because the people had resorted to hoarding at individual house-hold level. All newspapers were reporting nothing but deaths—editors resorting to editorials nearly everyday, columnists crying for peace in their articles. There were a large number of people who were totally stunned by the day to day affairs—a leading editor being shot dead in the heart of city and in the midst of heavy traffic—the killers pumping bullets into him ensuring that he not only died but also bled in the process. The murder of Muhammad Salahuddin, in cold blood, was a defiance of forces of evil and darkness. This and other acts of terrorism are intended to terrorise the general public and to defeat their (public) will for dignity and freedom.[14]

Worsening Law and Order Situation in Karachi and Deployment of Rangers

After withdrawal of the army, in a meeting chaired by the Prime Minister of Pakistan, the Rangers were given police powers in Karachi. The meeting was informed that an agreement had been reached with a French company to monitor the crime in the city through latest technology. The estimated cost would be Rs 1 billion. The Prime Minister was informed that 132 condemned prisoners were languishing in different jails of the Sindh province out of which appeals of 123 were pending before the superior courts while nine had sent mercy petitions to the President.[15]

The month of March 1995 was marked by a state of violence and killing. Apart from other incidents, on 8 March 1995, a van carrying American staff of the US consulate was attacked by two terrorists in broad daylight at a busy intersection in Karachi. Two Americans were shot dead and a third was injured. All hell broke loose on 9 March 1995 when the *New York Times* reported that Pakistani gunmen had killed two Americans in Karachi. The report said, 'The two American who died, both with diplomatic status, joined more than 1100 people who have been killed in the past fifteen months, in a rampage of brutality driven by ethnic and religious hatred, as well as criminal gangs fighting for primacy in what has become Asia's prime narcotics-trafficking centre.'[16] Ms Bhutto condemned the attack and claimed that 'it was part of a well-planned campaign of terrorism.' This enabled the US Federal Bureau of Investigation (FBI) to invoke what is called 'its jurisdiction over terrorist attacks on Americans overseas', and to send a team of its agents to investigate the shooting incident. 'No self-respecting country would have permitted such intrusion into her internal administration', wrote Altaf Gauhar in an article in the daily *Nation*.[17] A formal appeal for American aid for fighting terrorism was made by the Prime Minister. She said, 'We, in Pakistan, do not have the resources on our own to carry out the entire cleaning operation.'[18]

The businessmen convention called by the apex body of trade and industry, i.e. the Federation of Chambers of Commerce and Industry on 15 March 1995 was represented by more than one hundred trade and industry groups and associations from all over Pakistan. The Convention held at the Pearl Continental Hotel lasted for well over four hours and a number of business leaders and trade organization representatives lashed out at the criminal and wilful negligence on the part of the Sindh Government to stop killings of innocent people in Karachi. During the last three years 7500 people were killed and over 34,000 vehicles were snatched at gunpoint, the speakers pointed out. The Convention was presided over by Mr S.M. Muneer, President of FPCCI (Federation of Pakistan Chambers of Commerce and Industry), and was addressed by the leaders of the business community including past president of the Federation Mr Tariq Sayeed and KCCI (Karachi Chamber of Commerce and Industry) President Mr Ahmad Sattar and other leaders from all over Pakistan.

Angry business leaders were unanimous in demanding 'No Peace No Taxes' and called upon all the leaders and representatives of the business community not to co-operate with the government, and not to participate in any government invitation for visits abroad. They also decided that from 1 April 1995, all advertisements on the government controlled television would be stopped by the private sector trade and industry. Those who violated this decision would face boycott of their products at the retailers level. The speakers warned the government that if 'the law and order situation is not improved, they would stop paying all taxes and duties to the government which has failed to protect the lives of the people in Karachi.' They also blamed the government and its various agencies for their criminal neglect to control the senseless killings of citizens.

The Businessmen Convention, emphasizing the failure of all other agencies in bringing sanity in the city, demanded that the army should be called in, with full powers under Article 245 of the Constitution, to control and maintain law and order in Karachi. It was also demanded that night curfew should be imposed in Karachi to save the lives of the people from becoming targets of 'unidentified' terrorists and killers. The Convention further decided that if 'the situation is not brought under control in due course of time, the businessmen would observe indefinite strike and will stop paying all taxes to the government, including utility bills'. It was also decided that an All Pakistan Businessmen Convention be held in Lahore, and if needed, at Quetta and Peshawar, to take stock of the situation and to exert pressure on the government to bring peace in Karachi and to check the eroding economy resulting from the breakdown of law and order situation, which, if goes unchecked, 'will soon engulf the entire country', the resolution said.

Though it was followed by the removal and subsequently reinstatement of the office-bearers of the FPCCI by the Government of Pakistan and the action initially contemplated by the businessmen did not materialize, yet a feeling of mutual distrust between the government and the trading community persisted for a considerable length of time.

In June 1995 Interior Minister Naseerullah Babar stated, 'the current situation in Karachi is similar to the state of affairs that prevailed before the dismemberment of Pakistan in 1971.'[19] Similarly in a workshop sponsored by the Pakistan Association of Mental Health, it was agreed that there had been a steep rise in all sorts of psychological, psychosomatic and physical ailments among Karachiites who, having utilized their defence mechanism in adapting to the deteriorating civil life, were helplessly waiting for the worse.[20] In June 1995 a three-day mourning was announced by the Mohajir Qaumi Movement against the alleged rape of one Farzana Sultan. Following the completion of the three-day mourning the MQM announced to launch a new series of anti-government protest on every Friday and Saturday till the acceptance of its demands presented to the government a few days earlier. More than two hundred persons were killed in June and July 1995.

According to the report of the Human Rights Commission of Pakistan (HRCP, 14 July 1995): 'The situation is even worse than its was in East Pakistan.' According to the report 'people are facing terrible difficulties because of the terrorism in the city which is not only committed by unidentified men but also by the law enforcing agencies. They take boys of age group 19–25 years to unknown places to investigate and as result all these boys are turned into terrorists because of torture.' The President of Pakistan observed that 'war is being waged against state authority in Karachi at present which calls for national consensus to solve this sensitive issue.'[21]

Murder of Hakim Saeed and Imposition of Governor's Rule

On 17 October 1998 a former Sindh governor, founder of the internationally known Hamdard Foundation, Chancellor Hamdard University and Chairman Hamdard Foundation, Hakim Muhammad Saeed was assassinated. This was in continuation of terrorist attacks in Karachi. In a meeting chaired by the then Prime Minister, Muhammad Nawaz Sharif, an overall view of the Karachi problem was taken and important decisions were taken with reference to upsurge in lawlessness. Governor's rule was imposed and concrete measures were initiated to curb violence and restore peace in the city. Though there is a relative improvement in the law and order situation, yet from 18 October 1998 to 30 June 1999 thirty-three incidents of terrorism were reported in Karachi.[22] From 1 January 1996 to 30 June 1999,

234 police officials were killed and 421 injured in pitched battles with desperate criminals in Sindh.[23] The ethnic and sectarian violence in Karachi continues as is discernible from the figures pertaining to District East Karachi in tables 7.18, 7.19 and 7.20.

TABLE 7.18
District East Karachi
Persons Killed and Injured in Group Violence (1996–30 June 1999)

Year	Party	Killed	Injured
1996	MQM-A	16	13
	MQM-H	5	5
1997	MQM-A	12	7
	MQM-H	15	4
	PML-N	2	0
1998	MQM-A	18	23
	MQM-H	23	23
	Shaheed Bhutto Group	1	3
	Muslim League	1	1
1999		-	-

Source: Crime Branch, Karachi (1999).

TABLE 7.19
District East Karachi
Persons Killed and Injured in Sectarian Violence (1996–30 June 1999)

Year	Party	Killed	Injured
1996		-	-
1997	Sipah-e-Sahaba Pakistan	3	2
1998	Shia	2	3
1999	Deobandi	1	1
	Sunni Tehrik	0	1

Source: Crime Branch, Karachi (1999).

TABLE 7.20
District East Karachi
Persons Killed in Ethnic Violence (1996–30 June 1999)

Year	Punjabi	Pathan	Sindhi	Mohajir	Others	Total
1996	9	5	2	34	20	70
1997	19	21	12	62	38	152
1998	24	15	17	87	36	179
1999	5	2	4	7	7	25

Source: Crime Branch, Karachi (1999).

Conclusion

The analysis of magnitude of lawlessness in Pakistan leads us
to the conclusion that the origin of the present challenge of
lawlessness dates back to the time when Pakistan surfaced on
the map of the world. The creation of Pakistan witnessed social,
political, and economic convulsions of great magnitude. The
turbulence and violence, unleashed at that time, caused a major
breakdown of the law and order machinery. Communal turmoil
and violence, interspersed with criminal looting, changed the
sociological landscape of the new country with attendant
challenges for the law enforcing agencies of British vintage.
The existing law was the first casualty of such an upheaval,
followed by the community. Harmony, peace, fixate of social
roles and homogeneity of social outlook characterized such a
community. Criminal Administration Justice system was wedded
to the community with identifiable deviants of law and social
norms. Reprimand of the community operated both through the
law enforcer as well as on the law enforcer in cases of deviation
from social and legal norms. Community consensus on positive
social values was the dynamic force, which kept the community
as well as the law enforcing agencies intact and vibrant. Both
were supplementing each other. This was how the British Crown
tried to salvage the subcontinent out of anarchy and chaos of
the last days of Mughal Empire when its writ never went beyond
Palam, the suburbs of Delhi.

British Government took pride in the fact that it gave administrative unity to the chaotic Indian subcontinent. The underlying theme of this arrangement was an integrated system of Criminal Justice Administration in which community outfits responsible for crime control like the police, magistracy and judiciary were working in functional harmony with each other. Community, with such mechanics as '*Chowkidara*' and '*Zaildar*' System, was helping the police and magistracy to control and prevent crime. Conversely, elements of Criminal Justice Administration were throwing their weight around community institutions aforementioned in order to keep peace and order. The linkage between the community and Criminal Justice Administration was not something alien to Indian polity since Mughals also based their system of governance on this principle of harmonious interaction and symbiotic relationship. What caused havoc in the last days of Mughal Empire was lack of central writ or authority, which, the British Crown restored.

Last four decades have witnessed a steady corrosion of the inherited Criminal Justice Administration system in terms of both its authority as well as prestige. Linkage with the community is no more there due to palign into background of institutions of '*Chowkidara*' and '*Zaildars*', etc.

During all this time of turmoil, rapid industrialization with class polarization, urbanization, martial laws, refugee influx, introduction of drug culture, terrorism, ethnic hatred, and student violence grew. While the nation sat on a heap of kalashnikovs and ammunition, the only thing that never held the attention of any of forces which matter was the concept of nation building.

The present crime challenge, which appears stupendous, thus may be attributed to four decades of neglect of the Criminal Justice Administration system in terms of value engineering, community support, and material resourcefulness.

NOTES

1. *The Nation*, Thursday, 25 January 1990, Lahore (daily).
2. The Chiniot incident, which created the law and order situation took a violent turn when the dacoits allegedly backed by the local councillors could not be apprehended in the two incidents of dacoity in Usmanabad two days earlier. The residents of Mohalla Usmanabad started guarding the street by deputing four persons in the street in which the houses of Ghulam Shabbir and Muhammad were looted. The Chiniot City Police, it was alleged, did not pay heed to their repeated requests for registration of cases against unknown culprits.

On the day of occurrence, at 3 a.m., six persons armed with weapons entered the street and after coming across guards started firing. A bullet hit one of the guards, Bashir in the chest. He died on the spot while three others were injured seriously. After hearing the noise of indiscriminate firing, some neighbours came out of their houses and two of them sustained bullet injuries. During the gun battle between the locals and dacoits, two dacoits were injured while four conveniently escaped. Another injured also disappeared.

When the whole drama was going on, some labourers engaged in loading and unloading of trucks on Sargodha Road, were stated to have claimed that there had been a police Hilux jeep and a Suzuki jeep parked on the main road just at the entrance of the street. Shabbir of the same locality, who was an eyewitness, rushed to the main road and found seven policemen in the vehicle while another man in plain clothes sitting in the Suzuki jeep. Shabbir identified him as one of the dacoits who had just attacked his mohallah.

Many people, hearing about the identification, gathered there and started beating the man. Meanwhile, Deputy Superintendent of Police, Chiniot, Khurshid, reached there. He got the man released from the mob and took him to the police station. The seven policemen standing there started negotiations with the people to remove the injured dacoit to the hospital despite the fact that policemen had come to know that six locals were also injured in the encounter.

Who was the man identified as dacoit and later rescued from the people by the DSP, Chiniot, and admitted to the hospital, were questions begging for answers. However, the locals claimed that both the men had their connections with the police. The mob got furious on the issue as to why the DSP rescued the man identified as dacoit and why the party of seven policemen was insisting that the injured dacoit be handed over to them.

The negotiations between the locals and the policemen continued for about an hour after the occurrence of the incident, but both the parties failed to convince each other. The resentment of the people against the police came to surface that very moment and the people made the policemen hostage and then confined them in a barber's shop till about 9.30 a.m. During this time, neither the police nor the district administration, came there for negotiations to get them released.

Workers, students and people from different walks of life gathered at the shop where the policemen had been confined. It was stated that the PSF and PPP activists, taking advantage of the situation, aggravated it by raising slogans, 'these policemen are the real culprits'. On this the mob turned towards the shop where these policemen had been confined and started breaking the doors and roof and later set it on fire. The confined policemen tried to run away from the scene firing in the air but they had not gone far when they exhausted their ammunition.

The angry mob started pelting stones at them and put them to death brutally. It was reported that the bodies of the cops remained on the ground for about two hours and the district administration and the police failed to save the cops from the clutches of the mob. After putting the policemen to death the furious mob went to the district courts and the police station and damaged the property and raised slogans against the high-handedness of the police and the district administration. A curfew was imposed in the city and roads connecting it with other cities were closed.

3. *The Muslim*, Tuesday, 23 January 1990, Islamabad (daily).
4. *The Nation*, Friday, 19 July 1991, Lahore (daily).
5. *The News*, Wednesday, 30 June 1999, (daily), 'Statement of Minister for Information, Mushahid Hussain Syed in the Senate'.
6. Crimes Investigation Department, Punjab Police (1999), Official Data.
7. Crime Branch of the NWFP Police (1999), Official Data.
8. Following is the demographic distribution of major tribes:
   a) Zhob-Quetta-Loralai: This area is inhabited by Kakars, Zarkuns, Mandokhels, Brahuis, Balochs, Sulemankhels and Manzais.
   b) Marri-Bugti Agency: These agencies are predominantly Baloch. They have the reputation of being good fighters. They consist of Marris, Bugtis, Domkis and Jamalis.
   c) Nasirabad Division: Predominantly Baloch area. Other tribes are Magsi, Domki, Urmani and Khosa.
   d) Kalat Division (Jhalawan/Sarawans): The main tribe of this area is Brahui with prominent sub-tribes of Mengals and Zehris.
   e) Nushki/Chagai: This area is inhabited by Brahuis, Kambranis, Mengal, Hussanis, Raisani, Rind, Rakshani, Baloch, Ghilzai, Kakar, Tareen, and Notezais.
   f) Kharan: Main tribe is Nausherwani. Rakshanis and some other such as Hassanis, Nakis and Loris also inhabit Kharan.

g) Lasbela: Principal tribes are Jamote, Sheikh, Engaria, and Burrah.

h) Mekran: Main tribes are the Rinds of Mand, the Bizenjos and Nosherwani.

9. Some of the sensational murders are discussed below:

a) 2 December 1973. Khan Abdul Samad Khan Achakzai, founder of the Pakhtoonkhwa Milli Awami Party (PMPA), was murdered in a bomb attack while asleep at home in Quetta. Mystery still unresolved.

b) 19 June 1983. Barat Khant Ashezai, father of former MPA Naseer Bacha and an accused in the murder of Khan Abdul Samad Khan, was ambushed on Quetta Chaman Highway.

c) 1984. Sardar Rasool Bakhsh Zarakzai was shot dead while attending a *jirga* at the residence of former Senator, Mir Nabi Bakhsh Zehri, in Quetta.

d) 26 May 1987. Nawab Ghous Bakhsh Raisani, a former Chief Minister and Governor of Balochistan, was killed in an ambush near Dhadar while proceeding to his native village Surni Shoran in Bolan district.

e) 19 June 1990. Haji Eid Muhammad Notezai, MPA from Chagai, was shot dead while coming out of a mosque in Satellite Town. Mystery is still unresolved.

f) 20 September 1990. Haji Muhammad Khan Ghaibzai, an elder of the Ghaibzai clan of Achakzai tribe and his two sons, were ambushed and killed near Said Hameed Bridge on Quetta Chaman Highway while returning to Gulistan from Quetta. This murder triggered off the Hameedzai and Ghaibzai blood feud in which about a hundred people have been killed so far.

g) 28 October 1990. Saeed Khan Achakzai, brother of Abdul Hameed Khan Achakzai and an elder of Hameedzai tribe, was kidnapped and killed.

h) 14 April 1992. Sardar Taj Muhammad Rind was ambushed and killed alongwith eight bodyguards while going from Dhadar to Sibi.

i) 1 May 1992. Sardar Arif Jan Muhammad Hasni was ambushed and murdered on his way to Khuzdar. Mystery still unresolved.

j) 7 May 1992. Mir Hamza Bugti was killed during a visit to a polling station near Sui in Dera Bugti district on the eve of local bodies elections. The murder turned the political contest between the Kalpar family and Nawab Akbar Bugti into a blood feud.

k) 2 June 1992. Nawabzada Salal Akbar Bugti, younger son of Nawab Akbar Bugti, was shot dead while driving on busy Jinnah Road in the heart of Quetta city in broad day light.

l) 10 February 1994. Additional Deputy Commissioner Pishin, Sardar Faqir Muhammad Tareen, was attacked near Ziarat and killed. Sardar Yaqub Khan Nazir, a PML-N Senator and a former federal minister, was among those named in the FIR of this murder.

m) 24 August 1994. Sherbaz Bangalzai, Assistant Director of Labour, was shot dead in his office.

n) 27 August 1994. Three grandsons of Nawab Akbar Bugti (Dinar Domki and Salar Domki, sons of Sardar Chakar Khan Domki and Shahar Yar son of Shahid Bugti) were killed in a tribal clash at Sariab Road.

o) 7 January 2000. Unknown assailants gunned down a senior Judge of the Balochistan High Court, Justice Muhammad Nawaz Marri, while proceeding to the High Court.

All these incidents can be seen in the intricate context of Balochistan's feud-ridden life where tribal titles are bequeathed to generations along with the duty to handle unsettled scores.

10. Lamb, C. (1991), *Waiting for Allah: Pakistan's Struggle for Democracy*, New Delhi, Penguin Books.
11. Ibid.
12. Ibid.
13. *Time Magazine* (1990), 12 March 1990, USA (weekly).
14. Pakistan Administrative Staff College (1994), *Law and Order Report of Group 'A' of the 61st National Management Course*, 1994, Lahore.
15. Government of Sindh (1995), *Minutes of the Meeting Chaired by the Prime Minister*, March 1995, Karachi, Home Department.
16. *The New York Times,* 9 March 1995, New York (daily).
17. Gauhar, A., (1995), Observations made in an article published in *The Nation*, Wednesday, 28 June 1995.
18. Ibid.
19. *The News*, Tuesday, 27 June 1995, Lahore (daily).
20. Ibid
21. *The News*, Thursday, 22 June 1995, Lahore (daily).
22. Crime Branch of Sindh Police (1999), *Official Data, received vide Memo No. CB-SO/99/1287-92/Karachi, dated 17 July 1999.*
23. Ibid.
24. Ibid.

8

IMPACT OF LAWLESSNESS ON THE ECONOMY AS A WHOLE

This chapter explains the impact of lawlessness on the economy as a whole. Starting with a discussion on high risk economies and Pakistan's status as a volatile country, this chapter ventures an analysis of the socio-economic cost of lawlessness in the context of Pakistan in a chronological order through the application of the principle of correspondence and coincident. It further examines the significance of law and order/political instability as a variable of economic development. The argument advanced is based on empirical analysis of the essential ingredients which consist of conditions of war, strikes, political developments, ethnic and sectarian conflicts and miscellaneous factors of law and order situation. Measurement constraints notwithstanding, the chapter makes a distinction between autonomous political developments and organic events and then elaborates with reference to value assigned to weights/intensities of major events and value given to weights/intensities of recurring events and the value of the composite index of law and order. Having given a resume of a series of indices of law and order conditions in Pakistan from 1964 to 1994 this chapter discusses the use of series of index of law and order in the context of Modified Structuralist CGE Model of Economic Development.[1] Based on the tools thus developed, it examines the composite index and capital flows.

High Risk Economies

Modern governments are expected to perform two kinds of roles, conventional and developmental. The first consists of control of internal crimes, and safety from external aggression; the second relates to the development of socio-economic infrastructure. With the increase in kidnappings, hold-ups, and riots, the task of creating confidence among investors and citizens has assumed foremost importance. While other roles continue to be equally vital, the provision of security to those engaged in nation-building economic activities has become the first priority of law enforcing authorities.

Pakistan's ambitious programmes for economic liberalization may not be able to achieve much because of the increasing incidents of abduction and robberies in areas having potential for industrial and mineral-based take-off. The basic thrust of the recent policies is to open the economy to private and domestic investors with a view to accelerating the pace of industrialization. The factors which determine where and when investors will feel comfortable are many but the foremost is the presence of a secure and crime-free environment.

Peace and security are also important for general economic development, particularly for encouraging mobility of factors of production essential for their efficient inter-sectional and inter-regional utilization. Our economy has suffered serious setbacks due to lawlessness on many occasions in the past. For example, the breakdown of law and order during late 1960s led to a fall of annual growth rate to 1.4 per cent from the average annual growth rate of 5.5. per cent during early 1960s. The more recent example is that of Sindh where process of development has slowed down because of ethnic riots and kidnappings.

A recent report, based on a survey on international security risks conducted in 1995, says that Pakistan is rated a high-risk country for business along with Algeria, Burma, Cambodia and of all countries, Burundi. The survey by Control Risks Groups (CRG), a British consultancy that advises business on how to assess and manage security in volatile countries, rates Pakistan as high risk because of danger of ethnic rioting and street violence. Burma, though rated as high risk, is said to have prospects for improvement after the release of Aung Sun Su Kyi. Risk in Britain is assessed as low because of the Northern Ireland peace process, but it was rated medium in 1994. CRG said that it rated countries as high risk if conditions verged on war or civil war, if law and order were in imminent danger of breaking down or if there was a sustained campaign specifically directed against the personnel and property of foreign business.[2]

Impact of Lawlessness on Major Economic Indicators

Two Early Decades

Earlier we have discussed the pattern of crime in Pakistan in chronological order. With a view to establishing linkages between law and order and economic indicators, it will be appropriate here to consider, in their historical perspective, the corresponding macro-economic trends as well.

Following independence the basic framework of economic development emerged as a consequence of the creation of an administrative setup and other related activities. As indicated in Table 8.1 this process continued during the decade of the sixties. The rate of investment (the ratio of gross domestic investment to GNP) increased from 14.4 per cent in 1959–60 to 24.5 per cent in 1964–65 but it declined somewhat during 1965–70 due to the reduction of foreign assistance. The resultant average growth in real GDP, manufacturing and agriculture was 6.8 per cent, 9.9 per cent, and 5.1 per cent per annum respectively during the sixties compared with labour force growing at a moderate rate of around 2.0 per cent per annum. Coupled with low inflation rate (3.8 per cent) and high growth rates in major labour absorbing sectors (agriculture and manufacturing) absorbing about 72.7 per cent labour force, on the one hand, and moderate growth of labour force on the other, the unemployment rate remained at a very low level (1.43 per cent) during the sixties. The political turmoil in the late sixties also slowed down the industrial activity which eventually contributed to the rise in unemployment, particularly the educated youth.

Decade of the Seventies

The hope raised by the impressive performance of the economy during the 1960s was frustrated by the experience of the early 1970s. The disturbed political situation leading to the separation of the eastern part of the country in 1971, caused a major set back to the economy. The reforms introduced by the government in 1972–77 added a major element of uncertainty in economic relations, which could not be removed by subsequent assurances. Nationalization of a significant segment of industry and of the entire financial system, shattered the investor's confidence. Furthermore, the adverse weather conditions affected agricultural output in the mid-1970s. External factors also played a major role in slowing down the economic activity in the first half of the 1970s. The five-fold rise in oil prices coupled with a 56.7 per cent devaluation of currency in May 1972 accelerated inflation in the country.

The combined effects of both the domestic and external factors were far reaching. The growth rates of agriculture and manufacturing sharply decelerated to 2.4 per cent and 5.5 per cent respectively during the 1970s. Real GDP grew at an average rate of 4.8 per cent per annum during the decade of the 1970s. The drastic slow down in economic activity, particularly in agriculture and manufacturing, would have severely worsened the unemployment situation. The emergence of the Middle East boom and sizeable migration, however, changed the picture dramatically in the late 1970s and early 1980s. During the period of 1975–82 the emigration of workers was approaching two million. In other words, roughly 25 per cent of the incremental labour force moved out of the country during the period 1975–82.[3] Despite slowing down of the economy, the unemployment problem remained manageable during the 1970s—the average unemployment rate remained 2.42 per cent.

1980–86

The performance of Pakistan's economy during the 1980s was generally impressive and broad-based even in the face of a number of adverse internal factors. The real GDP grew at an average rate of 6.4 per cent per annum, manufacturing and agriculture grew at the average rates of 8.2 per cent and 5.4 per cent respectively. As a result of high rate of economic growth, a large part of the addition to the labour force was absorbed. These positive developments were offset by a larger than expected growth rate of population (3.1 per cent against the plan assumption of 2.9 per cent). The average unemployment rate during the decade of 1980s was 3.51 per cent.

1986–89

Due to the influx of Afghan refugees, introduction of drug culture and illicit sophisticated arms, foreign-sponsored terrorism, sectarian strife, flow of black money, political turmoil resulting in uncertainty, violence and organized crime took the entire country in its grip. In the Punjab and NWFP, a number of bomb blasts resulting in the deaths of important political personalities and mysterious murders by so-called 'Hathora Group' caused an acute sense of insecurity. In Sindh the robber barons created havoc. In Karachi ethnic fighting went on through. 1987, with 243 people (officially) being killed in smaller bouts. By 1988, the violence had further encreased, in May in Orangi and North Karachi, people in cars and on motor bikes were shooting randomly at rickshaw drivers and queues outside cinemas showing Pashto movies.[4] In Northern Areas sectarian upheaval claimed a number of lives. The obvious outcome was a decline in the annual growth rate of the GDP from 6.3 per cent in 1985–86 to 5.81 per cent in 1986–87 and 4.81 per cent in 1988–89. The growth rate of the manufacturing sectors fell down to 3.96 per cent per annum in 1988–89 from that of 7.55 per cent in 1985–86.

The 1990s

The period from 1988–89 to 1993–94 witnessed a marked slow down in economic activity. The real GDP grew by an average rate of 4.8 per cent per annum while agriculture registered an average growth rate of 3.6 per cent per annum. A significant slow down was experienced in the manufacturing sector which registered an average growth rate of 5.8 per cent per annum compared with 8.2 per cent registered during the 1980s. Apart from adverse weather conditions, among others, the disturbed law and order situation in Sindh in particular and elsewhere in general and political uncertainty contributed to the lacklustre growth performance during the above mentioned period.

The slow down in economic activity during the period from 1988–89 to 1993–94 worsened the country's employment situation. Prior to 1990–91, about one million work force used to remain unemployed but in recent years this number has crossed the two million mark. As shown in Table 8.1 and Figure 8.1, approximately 2.35 million or 6.7 per cent of the labour force was unemployed in 1993–94.

TABLE 8.1

Pakistan: Growth Rates, Inflation, Unemployment, and Labour Force
(1960s to 1993–94)

Year	GDP	Manu-facturing	Agri-culture	Rate of Inflation	Unemploy-ment (in million)	Unemploy-ment Rate (percentage per annum)	Labour Force (million)
1960s	6.8	9.9	5.1	3.8	0.25	1.43	17.20
1970s	4.8	5.5	2.4	12.3	0.54	2.42	21.50
1980s	6.4	8.2	5.4	7.3	1.00	3.51	28.45
1980-81	6.4	10.6	3.7	13.9	0.95	3.70	25.65
1981-82	7.6	13.7	4.7	11.1	1.00	3.81	26.27
1982-83	6.8	7.0	4.4	4.7	1.06	3.91	26.91
1983-84	4.0	7.9	-4.8	7.3	1.05	3.82	27.45
1984-85	8.7	8.1	10.9	5.7	1.04	3.71	28.00
1985-86	6.4	7.5	6.0	4.4	1.02	3.64	28.05
1986-87	5.8	7.5	3.2	3.6	0.90	3.04	29.60
1987-88	6.4	10.0	2.7	6.3	0.94	3.14	29.93
1980/81-87/88	6.5	9.0	3.9	7.1	1.00	3.60	27.73
1988-89	4.8	4.0	6.9	10.4	0.97	3.14	30.87
1989-90	4.6	5.7	3.0	6.0	1.00	3.14	31.82
1990-91	5.6	6.2	5.0	12.7	2.00	6.28	31.83
1991-92	7.7	8.1	9.5	9.6	1.93	8.85	32.97
1992-93	2.3	5.4	-5.3	10.6	1.99	5.85	33.97
1993-94	4.0	5.6	2.6	11.2	2.05	5.85	34.98
1988/89-1993-94	4.8	5.8	3.6	10.1	1.66	5.02	32.74

Source: Pakistan Economic Surveys for relevant years.

FIGURE 8.1

Pakistan: Growth Rates, Inflation and Unemployment (1960s to 1993–94)

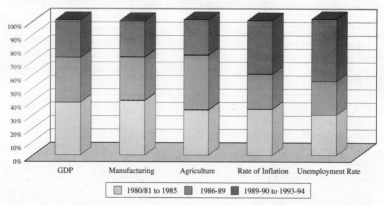

Source: Developed by the author with reference to the data in Table 8.1.

The impact of law and order situation on key economic indicators in macroeconomics framework, as analysed above, is summed up in Table 8.2

TABLE 8.2

Pakistan: Impact of Law and Order Situation on Economic Indicators

Economic Indicators	1960s (up to 1968)	1970s (up to 1977)	1980-86	1986-89	1989-94	1994-95	1996-97	1997-98	1998-99
	Political Stability	Disturbed Political Condition	Relative Politcial Stability	Disturbed Conditions especially due to Afghan War	Political Changes and Uncertainties			Relative Stability	Relative Uncertainty
GDP	6.8	4.8	6.4	4.8	4.8	4.7	1.3	4.3	3.1
Manufacturing	9.9	5.5	8.2	3.96	5.8	4.8	1.19	7.9	4.7
Agriculture	5.1	2.4	5.4	6.87	3.6	4.9	0.5	3.8	0.35
Inflation	3.8	12.3	7.3	5.8	10.1	8.0	11.8	8.2	6.1
Unemployment	1.43	2.42	3.51	3.14	5.02	5.37	6.10	6.10	6.10

Key: Unemployment, unemployment rate % per annum.
       Growth rates of GDP, manufacturing and agriculture are percentages of comparable years.
       Inflation figures are percentages.
Source: Developed by the author on the basis of data available in relevant Economic Surveys of Pakistan.

FIGURE 8.2

Average Growth Rate, Rate of Inflation and Unemployment Rate
(1960–68 and 1970–77)

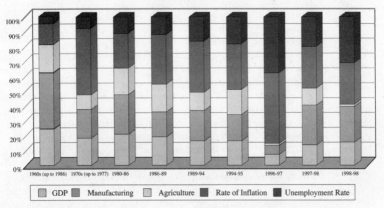

Source: Developed by the author with reference to the data in Table 8.2.

Notes: The corresponding law and order scenario for the above mentioned periods is as under:

1960–68   Period of consolidation, political stability and downward drift in crime against person and property.

1970–77   1969 to 1971 was a period of disturbed law and order and political situation resulting in the separation of the Eastern part of the country. Up to 1977, political polarization, land disputes and attendant crime, Dubai phenomenon and illegal immigration, insurgency in Balochistan and imposition of martial law in 1977 were significant features of the law and order situation in Pakistan and up to 1979, underground resistance movement had been launched in a high momentum.

1980–86   This period was characterized by a decrease in registered crime under all major heads due to fear of arbitrary punishments thereby forcing political/criminal propensities to go underground. The other features of this period include siphoning of Western economic and military aid, relative stability in the aftermath of 1985 partyless elections and the subsequent revival of political parties.

1986–89   Following are the main features of the law and order situation during this period:
-     Sectarian and ethnic violence
-     Bomb blasts and terrorism in 1987
-     Availability of sophisticated weapons due to the influx of Afghan refugees
-     Introduction of drug culture
-     Black Money/Crime Mafia like robber barons emerged
-     Fraudulent financial transactions

1989–94   These years was characterized by:
-     Virtual breakdown of law enforcement with resultant sense of insecurity

	Rising violent crime in Punjab, Sindh, NWFP, and Balochistan against person and property.
-	*Qabza* Group sponsored by politically influential persons
-	Gun-running
-	Drug related crime
-	Kidnapping for ransom
-	Terrorism and subversion

1994–96   The law and order situation during the year 1994–95 can be described as under:

State of anarchy and breakdown of law and order in Karachi resulting in at least 1300 deaths. Clashes and armed insurgency by TNSM (Tehrik Nifaz-e-Shariat-e-Muhammadi) in Malakand, trouble in Khyber Agency, kidnappings, hold-ups and dacoities in Sindh, Punjab, NWFP, and Balochistan. A deadly gang-up of drug barons, smugglers and 'mullahs' resulting in efforts on the part of warlords to establish their own turf

1997–98   A number of known dangerous criminals were arrested, anti-terrorist courts started functioning, police training was revamped, Elite Police Force was raised in the Punjab and top priority was assigned to law and order. Though incidents of violence, kidnapping for ransom, sabotage and sectarian killings continued as a spill-over effect of the past few years, yet a downward trend in overall heinous crime was visible.

1998–99   Incidents of sectarian and ethnic violence showed a downward trend. However, white-collar crime and US dollar-related lawlessness increased. There was uncertainty on account of freezing of foreign currency accounts, introduction of dual exchange rate system and the unresolved issue of the independent power producers. The pattern of crime included incidents of auto-theft, highway robbery, kidnapping for ransom, violence against women, suicides and power theft.

The above mentioned analysis indicates adverse effects of rise in crime and disorder on Pakistan's overall economic performance. During 1960s overall consolidation, political stability and downward drift in crime were matched by a growth rate of 6.8 per cent in GDP, 9.9 per cent in manufacturing, 5.1 per cent in agriculture with 3.8 per cent inflation, and 1.43 per cent unemployment. The disturbed law and order and political situation in the 1970s resulted in a decline in the growth rate of GDP (4.8 per cent), manufacturing (5.5 per cent) and agriculture (2.4 per cent). Rate of inflation rose up to 12.3 per cent and unemployment rate went upto 2.42 per cent. Relative stability of political and crime situation in the period from 1980–81 to 1985–86 also brought about an improvement in the growth rates of GDP (6.4 per cent) manufacturing (8.2 per cent) and agriculture

(5.4 per cent). Similarly, rate of inflation went down to 7.3 per cent though the unemployment rate increased due to other factors like increase in population and return of Pakistani immigrants from abroad. Sectarian violence and other features during the years 1986–89 resulted in a decline in the respective growth rates of GDP (4.8 per cent) and manufacturing (3.96 per cent). The rate of agricultural growth increased to 6.8 per cent due to better weather conditions and other economic factors. Unemployment remained a problem as it ever was. During 1989–90 to 1993–94 the complexity of crime problems indicated itself in declining growth rates of GDP (4.8 per cent), manufacturing (5.8 per cent) and agriculture (3.6 per cent). It was accompanied by rising inflation (10.1 per cent) and unemployment rate (5.02 per cent). The year 1994–95 was again affected by a state of anarchy and breakdown of law and order. This was obvious by a decline in the rates of growth of GDP (4.7 per cent), manufacturing (4.8 per cent), agriculture (4.9 against a target of 4.9 per cent). Rate of inflation and unemployment also presented a dismal picture.

If we take the average of loss owing to lawlessness and political instability, the fall in average rate of growth of GDP was 2 per cent in disturbed periods between 1960–95. The similar average loss in the rate of growth in manufacturing sectors comes to 4 per cent. The rate of inflation during the same period of disturbed law and order fluctuated on the average to the extent of 5.7 per cent.

Law and Order/Political Instability as a Determinant of Economic Development

The traditional models of economic development have been suffering from one of the singular inadequacy, namely, the neglect of law and order/political instability variable as a major determinant of economic development/employment, inflation, balance of payments performance, etc. An attempt has been made in this book (Appendix 1) to rectify this inadequacy of the traditional models of economic growth by developing a new

Computable General Equilibrium (CGE) model which specifically includes variable reflecting law and order/political instability conditions as an argument (or explanatory variable) of economic development.

Empirical Analysis—Essential Ingredients

From the theoretical structure, we have to move to the empirical analysis to discover some broad generalizations/approximations about the relationships between law and order conditions and economic development. In this regard, the composite or consolidated measure of law and order/political instability variable was identified as $Ø^c$ which is the weighted index of major (determinants) of law and order situation of a country consisting of conditions of war ($Ø^w$), strikes ($Ø^s$), political developments ($Ø^p$), ethnic and sectarian conflicts ($Ø^e$), and miscellaneous factors of law and order situation put under the symbol of $Ø^m$.

Measurement Constraints

In order to develop the composite index, it was also required to identify the values for intensities/weights of all the major (determinants) of Law and Order/Political Instability variable such as $α^1$ for conditions of war, $α^2$ for strikes, $α^3$ for reported crimes, $α^4$ for murders, and $α^5$ for miscellaneous factors.

The construction of the composite index of Law and Order situation, i.e. $Ø^c$ is a difficult and complex exercise as it incorporates both subjective (judgemental) values and objective (measurable) parameters. On the subjective side, we have the problem of assigning values to the weights or intensities ($α'Ø^s$) associated with the major constituents of the index such as war ($Ø^w$), internal political developments/upheavals($Ø^p$), strikes ($Ø^s$), ethnic and religious conflicts ($Ø^e$) and miscellaneous factors influencing Law and Order conditions ($Ø^m$). Considering these major constraints, a broader approach has been adopted with a view to arriving at the value of intensities (α's) through approximations as well as (value) judgements.

Besides the difficulties on account of estimating intensities (α's), there are equally binding complexities regarding the measurement of main components of the Law and Order index ($\emptyset^c$). For example, attempts to develop this index are seriously constrained by the absence of a uniform criteria or definition of ethnic and religious conflicts. How can we quantify these conflicts? Certainly, there are no easy methods for their calculation. Similarly, the question of how to estimate the miscellaneous factors ($\emptyset^m$) responsible for Law and Order situation would find diverse answers—depending upon the specific conditions of a particular country and its history of political evolution.

Autonomous Political Developments and Organic Events

Notwithstanding these difficulties, an entirely innovative approach has been adopted to develop the composite Index of Law and Order situation ($\emptyset^c$). According to this approach, all the determinants/factors of Law and Order/Political Instability situation are categorized into two distinct classes namely the 'autonomous' political developments and 'organic' events. In the first category, we include major macro level political events such as occurrence of war, or mass political unrest/movements, affecting directly or indirectly, a large segment of the population as well as the economy. These developments are generally of non-recurring nature and have their roots in 'exogenous' geo-political conditions. The second category of Law and Order situation includes the events which are micro-level developments and are of recurring nature. These refer to events like strikes, ethnic and sectarian conflicts/murders and other forms of crimes indicating the general state of lawlessness in a country.

Value Assigned to Weights/Intensities of Major Events

As part of the system of approximation for estimating the Composite Index, the major events of political upheavals/ changes including the phenomenon of war have been assigned differentiated weights/intensities ((α's) as detailed in Table 8.3. In other words, these weights are assigned considering the specific impact of these 'autonomous' developments (movements) on the political as well as the socio-economic patterns and conditions of the country. These weights/intensities are unique in the sense that the events are of non-recurring nature, and have lower frequency as pointed out above.

TABLE 8.3

Assigning Values to the Intensities/Weights to Autonomous Political Developments/ Upheavals

Year	Political Development/Event	Weights(α)	Index Points
1965	War with India	1.00	100
1968	Mass movement against Ayub Khan	0.25	25
1969	Martial Law	0.50	50
1970	Elections, Bangladesh movement	0.25	25
1971	War with India; separation of East Pakistan	1.00	100
1972	Urdu language movement in Sindh	0.15	15
1974	Anti-Qadiani movement	0.15	15
1977	Pakistan National Alliance launched a movement against Bhutto which culminated in the imposition of Martial Law	0.50	50
1979	Beginning of the Afghan problem	0.15	15
1983	Movement for the Restoration of Democracy launched; Anti-Qadiani movement in Punjab	0.15	15
1986	Sectarian conflicts	0.25	25
1988	Dissolution of Assembly; political crises; death of General Ziaul Haq and elections	0.25	25
1989	Confrontation between Federal and the Provincial Governments of Punjab and Balochistan	0.15	15
1990	Political unrest, elections and formation of the Nawaz Sharif government	0.25	25
1992	18 Nov. Long March/agitational politics against Nawaz Sharif government	0.25	25
1993	Nawaz Sharif government ended with the dissolution of National Assembly followed by elections	0.25	25

1994-96   Conflict with the MQM and trouble in Karachi;
            Dismissal of the Wattoo govt. in Punjab; Tehrik-i-
            Nijat movement against the Benazir govt; *dharna* by
            Jamaat-i-Islami; Dismissal of the Benazir government   0.35   35

Source: Developed by the author.

As may be seen from the table, the highest weight is assigned to the phenomenon of war, i.e. 1 which has been placed at 1.00 with the equivalent index value of 100. The phenomenon like abrupt change of the government such as imposition of martial law has been assigned a weight of 0.50 with the equivalent index value of 50. Similarly, the values of other weights follow depending upon the perceived impact of each event on the socio-economic system.

Value Assigned to Weights/Intensities of Recurring Events

The value assigned to weights/intensities defining the parameter of strikes is 0.50 taking into account the fact that strikes have a direct effect/bearing on the economic activity. The weight assigned to the total crime reported (other than murder) is equal to 0.25, for murders it is specified as 0.15 and for miscellaneous factors it 0.10. These weights/intensities are used to estimate the index of 'recurring events' determining the Law and Order situation.

It must be noted that for measuring ethnic and sectarian conflicts ($\emptyset^c$) as an argument for the composite index, the proxies used are those of total reported crime (other than murder) and the number of murders itself, with the weights of 0.25 and 0.15 respectively, as explained above. These proxies are useful and relevant as these fully encompass the ethnic and sectarian conflicts as well as the general conditions of lawlessness endemic to the society.

Values of the Composite Index of Law and Order

As a final step, the integration of the Law and Order indices of 'autonomous' political developments (Table 8.3) with the indices of 'organic' events (Table 8.4) gives the values of the Composite Index of Law and Order Political Instability condition which are provided in Table 8.5.

TABLE 8.4

Estimates of Indices of Law and Order/Political Instability Comprising Organic Conditions

Year	Number of Strikes	Total Crime Reported Except Murders	Murders (Ethnic Sectarian and Others)	Refugees	Weighted Index of Organic Law and Order Conditions
1964	330	52	68	0	188
1965	320	53	78	0	135
1966	264	61	79	0	150
1967	294	68	79	0	176
1968	222	78	77	0	143
1969	413	77	76	0	237
1970	440	80	85	0	253
1971	204	85	92	0	137
1972	1129	102	109	0	611
1973	777	103	107	0	430
1974	536	105	116	0	321
1975	377	108	107	0	231
1976	248	109	106	0	167
1977	117	92	101	0	97
1978	123	109	97	0	109
1979	94	94	87	4	
1980	100	100	100	100	100
1981	93	121	81	200	110
1982	38	122	112	250	92
1983	91	124	111	270	120
1984	117	139	121	280	139
1985	84	145	127	290	126
1986	38	159	244	300	111
1987	38	167	151	320	116
1988	26	178	161	330	115
1989	61	242	175	370	156
1990	143	199	191	370	192
1991	136	187	177	300	171
1992	58	188	161	250	125
1993	41	195	166	200	115
1994	36	216	193	150	116
1995	35	226	228	150	123

Source: This table has been developed by the author from the data collected from the Ministry of Labour, Government of Pakistan, Islamabad, Ministry of States and Frontier Regions, Government of Pakistan, Islamabad and Ministry of Interior, Bureau of Police Research.

TABLE 8.5
**Estimates of Composite Index of Law and
Order/Political Instability for Pakistan**

Year	Index of Organic Conditions of Law and Order	Autonomous Political Developments/Changes (Index value)	Composite Index of Law and Order/ Political Instability	Average Value of Composite Index	
1963-64	188	-	188		
1964-65	135	-	235		
1965-66	150	100	250		
1966-67	176	-	176		203.4
1967-68	143	25	168		
1968-69	237	50	287		
1969-70	253	25	278		
1970-71	137	-	237		
1971-72	611	100	716		
1972-73	430	15	445		
1973-74	321	15	336		316.0
1974-75	231	-	231		
1975-76	167	-	167		
1976-77	97	50	147		
1977-78	109	-	109		
1978-79	88	15	103		
1979-80	100	-	100		
1980-81	110	-	110		
1981-82	92	-	92		
1982-83	120	15	135		
1983-84	139	-	139	126.5	119.7
1984-85	126	-	126		
1985-86	111	25	136		
1986-87	116	-	116		
1987-88	115	25	140		
1988-89	156	15	171		
1989-90	192	25	217		
1990-91	171	-	171		
1991-92	125	25	150	158.8	157.8
1992-93	115	25	140		
1993-94	116	-	116		

Source: Developed by the author.

A Resume of a Series of Indices of Law and Order Conditions in Pakistan, 1964–94

Given the constraints mentioned in the preceding sections of this chapter, our innovative approach has helped in developing a series of indices of Law and Order conditions for Pakistan from 1964 to 1994.

The estimates of Law and Order/Political Instability Index for the period 1963–64 to 1993–94 were made taking into account the organic factors of Law and Order such as strikes, reported crimes, murders, and miscellaneous determinants (such as inflow of Afghan refugees) and the autonomous factors of political upheavals/change such as war, mass movements against particular leader, ruler or political set–up, sudden changes in the political framework say through a Martial Law or death of a ruler. These estimates in the form of values of composite index are given at Table 8.5.

The value of the composite index of Law and Order Situation/ Political Instability (which has been developed taking 1979–80 as the base), rises from 188 in 1963–64 to 235 in 1964–65 and 250 in 1965–66 (the year of war with India) but starts declining subsequently. However, from the year 1968–69 the index starts rising as the year depicts the mass movement against Ayub Khan culminating in the imposition of Martial Law in 1969. The value of the index for this year has been estimated at 287.

The traumic events and unprecedented political upheavals of seventies leading to war with India and secession of East Pakistan in December 1971 are duly reflected in the large magnitude (value) of the index of Law and Order situation. To track these events, the index for 1969–70 was estimated at 278, and for 1970–71 it comes to 237 rising steeply to 716 in 1971–72. The last year could be regarded as the worst year in the political history of Pakistan as it synchronized with the dismemberment of the country and the 'mass unrest' which was witnessed in the remaining (West) Pakistan.

The Law and Order Index remained quite high in 1972–73 and 1973–74 with the values estimated at 445 and 336 respectively, even though these values were lower than the 'peak' value of the index registered in 1971–72. In the following three (successive) years, the value of the index declined gradually to 231, 167 and 147, as the political scenario tended towards normalcy, notwithstanding a major change in the political set up in 1976–77 associated with the imposition of martial law by General Ziaul Haq.

The relative political stability and improvement in the law and order situation which prevailed during the military regime is fully reflected in the declining value of the Law and Order index with the values of 109 (for 1977–78), 103 (for 1978–79), 100 (for 1979–80 which is our base year), 110 (for 1980–81) and 92 (for 1981–82) — the year for which the index assumed the lowest value.

From the trough of 1981–82, the index shows an upward trend beginning with a higher value 135 for 1982–83 — the year when Movement for Restoration of Democracy was launched simultaneously with the anti–Qadiani movement (in Punjab).

The gradually rising index of Law and Order/Political Instability in the later part of eighties reaches a high level of 171 in 1988–89 — the year General Ziaul Haq died in the air crash leaving behind a trail of political uncertainty and an aura of agitation and confrontation. Due to these factors endemic to the fragile political system of the country as well as the pressures created by Afghanistan's internal turmoil for which Pakistan had to bear the burden of millions of Afghan refugees flowing in from across the border, the value of estimated index of Law and Order situation remained relatively high in the nineties, as may be seen from the table.

Use of the Series of Index of Law and Order in the Context of Modified CGE Model of Economic Development

Having developed the series of the index of Law and Order situation for Pakistan for the period 1964 to 1994, a period of thirty years, the question arises: what use of the series of index of Law and Order/Political Instability can be made in the context of the Modified CGE Model of Economic Development? The answer to the question is simple. The validation of the Modified CGE Model was contingent upon the availability of the value of the important variable of $\emptyset^c$—the composite index of Law and Order/Political Instability. The availability of estimates of the time series of $\emptyset^c$ ensures that the Modified CGE (The Computable General Equilibrium Model) is actually 'computable.' This series of the variable $\emptyset^c$ can be used for estimation, validation and simulation of the Modified Model for which $\emptyset^c$ is a basic input and thus critical.

The validation of the Modified CGE Model can be undertaken through the application of simultaneous-equations-regression techniques or the use of common statistical correlation methods. However, quite often, employment of simple principles of correspondence can help in obtaining results in analytical studies which are both robust and reliable. The same principles are therefore made use of in the process of validating the Modified CGE Model.

The Composite Index and the Real GDP Growth

As a first step towards that end, it to has to be recognized that, in all models of economic development, the variable of 'real GDP growth' holds the key position. This variable is of fundamental significance for the simple reason that all changes in different sectors of the economy such as agriculture, industry, mining or services, as these are affected by various economic and non-economic factors or determinants, are invariably reflected in changes in the real GDP growth. If these sector-wise changes are positive, these will be reflected in the real GDP growth rate in a positive way and vice versa. By focusing on the growth rate of real GDP, we can have the understanding about the most pivotal variable of any economy. Furthermore, by placing the variable of real growth rate in juxtaposition to any other variable, factor or determinant, an insight can be developed about their interrelationship or their cause-and-effect nexus.

This cause-and-effect connection is empirically established when the Composite Index ($\emptyset^c$) and fluctuations in the Index are studied in relation to the changes in real GDP growth of Pakistan for specified periods of time. The average value of the Composite Index of Law and Order/Political Instability situation ($\emptyset^c$) for the period 1969–70 to 1976–77 was estimated at 316.0 the highest value for other specified 'comparable' periods. The same period in the history of development of Pakistan is also identified as the period of lowest average real GDP growth of around 4.84 per cent. Thus by applying the simple principle of correspondence, it can be easily inferred that Law and Order/ Political Instability as reflected in a sizeable value of index, was a major factor in dampening the growth momentum of Pakistan in the seventies.

The average estimated value of 116.6 for the Composite Index ($\emptyset^c$) is lowest for the period 1977–78 to 1986–87, but at the same time this is a period of high average annual growth of real GDP equivalent to 6.51 per cent. This correspondence between relative political stability and higher growth rate of GDP again establishes that political stability is an important factor of economic growth of the country.

For the period 1987–88 to 1993–94 the average value of the Composite Index comes to 157.8 (the seven-year average) which obviously reflects repeated changes in governments, high intensity of sectarian and ethnic strife, political unrest and uncertainty, etc. This is also the period of an inconsistent performance of the economy in terms of lower average real growth of GDP equivalent to 4.16 per cent and thus provides evidence for the central hypothesis of this research that Law and Order/Political Instability conditions can undermine the process of economic development.

The average value of the Composite Index for the period 1963–64 to 1968–69 is placed at 203.4. This relatively large estimate of the Index (reflecting greater incidence of lawlessness) does not correspond with the high growth rates of GDP which characterized the economic performance of the sixties. This is primarily due to the fact that the Index has been prepared for the latter six years of the sixties during which a war was fought with India and, at the same time, the latter years of this specific period were marked with mass political unrest, upheavals, uncertainties leading to imposition of Martial Law in 1969. However, it can be safely concluded that if the Composite Index of Law and Order/Political Instability was calculated for the full ten-year period of the sixties, its value would be fairly reduced which would strictly correspond with the high growth of real GDP of the period.

The conclusion of the discussion is unequivocal that prevalence of general lawlessness and political instability is a basic factor which can undermine the growth efforts of any nation.

The Composite Index and Capital Flows

Another important barometer of economic performance of any country is the movement of private capital both inward and outward. In this context, flight of capital, is considered to be a phenomenon which is the direct response of and a reflection of political instability and lawlessness. The estimates of capital flight (gross) for Pakistan for the period 1971–72 to 1993–94, based on the World Bank definition, discussed in the next paragraph, indicate a close relationship between political instability and capital movement. The high degree of correlation between political instability and flight of capital reinforces our earlier conclusion that conditions of lawlessness and political instability weaken and corrode the economic structure of a country, creating serious constraints and blocks in its march towards growth and prosperity.

Flight of Capital

The above conclusion is reinforced by the state of capital flow into Pakistan, which is another important barometer of economic performance of any country. The movement of private capital both inward and outward is of crucial importance. In this context, the flight of capital is considered to be a phenomenon, which is the direct response to and a reflection on political instability and lawlessness. The estimates of capital flight (gross) from Pakistan during the period 1971–72 to 1993–94, based on the World Bank definition, are given in Table 8.6.[5]

TABLE 8.6

Flight of Capital From Pakistan

Year	($ in million) Amount
1972-3	88
1973-4	248
1974-5	-215
1975-6	-202
1976-7	244
1977-8	321
1978-9	19
1979-80	-154
1980-81	-158
1981-2	-22
1982-3	547
1983-4	-465
1984-5	-120
1985-6	441
1986-7	791
1987-8	1272
1988-9	-1245
1989-90	334
1990-91	1258
1991-2	1407
1992-3	-774
1993-4	-1036

Source: Mahmood, Z., and Nazli, H. (1996) 'Estimates of Unrecorded Accumulation of Private Foreign Assets' (unpublished), PIDE, Islamabad.

The table shows that during the seven-year period of 1972–73 to 1978–79, five years were characterized by capital outflow of various magnitudes, while only two years were marked with capital inflows. The flight of capital was only $88 million in 1972–73 which rose to $248 million in 1973–74. While the trend of capital flight was reversed in 1974–75 and 1975–76 (a period when political normality started to show some signs), the phenomenon of flight regained its momentum in 1976–77 and continued up to 1978–79 (a period of political change and upheaval).

During the eighties, the phenomenon of capital flight was transformed into a state of capital inflow equivalent to $154 million, $158 million, and $22 million, respectively, for the three years starting in 1979–80. With the exception of the year 1982–83, when the outflow of capital was to the tune of $547 million, capital inflows were resumed in 1983–84 (equivalent to $465 million) and 1984–85 (equivalent to $120 million).

The large quantum of capital outflow in 1985–86 to 1987–88 fully reflects the condition of internal political conflicts and the atmosphere of uncertainty prevailing in the country. Even though capital inflows of substantive proportions materialized during the years 1988–89, which were estimated at $1245 million, there occurred large capital outflows during the years 1987–90 to 1991–92, again showing a clear response to the climate of high political unrest and uncertainty.

During the first five months of the fiscal year 1999–2000 total foreign private investment was just $222.4 million. This included $250.7 million as foreign direct investment (FDI). However, portfolio investment registered an outflow of $28.3 million. The month of November 1999 was the most alarming with a net FDI flow of just $34.9 million.[6]

The average flow of foreign private investment in Pakistan was $1.2 billion during the period of 1994–98.[7] The nuclear tests of May 1998, problems with foreign investors mainly the independent power producers and mismanagement of the past several governments had damaged the investment climate of the country. In 1998–99, Pakistan received about $500 million in foreign private investment due to ongoing projects in the energy sector.[8] By January 2000 this phenomenon appeared to be over and flow of FDI seemed to be gradually evaporating. Sponsors of various foreign funded projects felt that Pakistan had lost its edge of free market, cheap labour and open investment policies due to its inefficient and corrupt governments. Inconsistent policies and law and order situation had further eroded the confidence level.[9]

Conclusion

The quantitative relationship between conditions of law and order and economic indicators has been analysed with reference to various periods of Pakistan's history keeping in view the state of political stability or absence thereof, level and pace of economic development, and geopolitical scenario prevalent at that time. Through application of the principle of correspondence and the use of Modified Structuralist CGE Model of Economic Development, it has been shown that law and order and economic performance are interdependent and mutually supportive.

NOTES

1. For details see Appendix 1.
2. CRG, (1995), Survey Report by Control Risks Groups, British Consultancy.
3. Kemal, A. R. (1987), 'Pakistan's Experience in Employment and Manpower Planning', in R. Amjad (ed.), *Human Resource Planning: The Asian Experience*, New Delhi, ARTEP.
4. Duncan, E. (1989), *Breaking the Curfew: A Political Journey through Pakistan*, London, Penguin Group.
5. Mahmood, Z., and Nazli, H. (1996), 'Estimates of Unrecorded Accumulation of Private Foreign Assets' (unpublished), PIDE, Islamabad.
6. Nadeem, M. (2000), 'Foreign Investment Nosedives', *The News*, Friday, 14 January 2000, Lahore (daily).
7. Ibid.
8. Ibid.
9. Ibid.

9

IMPACT OF LAWLESSNESS ON SELECTED MICRO-ECONOMIC SECTORS

With a view to determining the impact of lawlessness on selected micro-economic sectors, this chapter deals mainly with violence in Karachi and its impact on the economy during the 1990s. However, certain selected micro-economic sectors like the size of black economy, budget deficit, non-recovery of stuck-up loans, national savings and import-export gap have been discussed in a wider context of law and order situation in the country as a whole.

The Karachi situation, being a very obvious indicator of the impact of lawlessness on economic performance, is being discussed below with reference to general impact and the impact on Karachi Stock Exchange.

General Impact

From 1988 onwards, industrialists began moving out of Pakistan to Dubai, frightened off by the unstable political situations, tensions with India and ethnic violence in Karachi; the country's commercial centre where 47 per cent of industry and all major headquarters are based.[1] By the end of 1989 the security situation was so bad in the southern part of the city, that provides nearly three quarters of government revenues, that business was down to 50 per cent. Chamber of Commerce officials in Karachi said

Karachi was losing $48 million per day because curfew in the most populated areas prevented workers from reaching their factories.[2]

The Karachi Chamber of Commerce and Industry carried out a study on the production losses suffered by the city owing to disturbances during the first six months of 1995.[3] According to the study the losses were estimated at Rs 2.817 billion per day. It includes Rs 602 million in export, Rs 958 million in import, Rs 192 million in the manufacturing sector, Rs 638 million in other non-agricultural sectors and Rs 427 million in tax revenues. It further revealed that Karachi's contribution towards the country's manufacturing sector fell from 60 per cent to 40 per cent during the second half of the fiscal year 1994–95. Karachi's share in the growth of gross domestic product which was 2 per cent a couple of years ago had come to nought and the value-added production had been reduced to half.

On the basis of this report, it can be worked out that the three-day mourning observed in the last week of June 1995, during which all economic activities were completely suspended, caused a loss of Rs 8.5 billion to the national economy. But this was not the end. According to a subsequent announcement a two-day weekly protest on Fridays and Saturdays was to continue to be observed until the demands of the MQM were met. An appeal was also made to close shops, trade centres and offices and keep public transport off the road. The appeal was well-responded and the city gave a deserted look on the weekend. Besides, all economic activities remained suspended.[4]

'This means that if the MQM decides to carry on with the protest to press for the acceptance of its demands until end July this year (1995) the accumulative losses to the national economy will be as high as Rs 65 billion.'[5] This is more than double the amount of Rs 14 billion we are getting from the IMF for which we have sacrificed our economic sovereignty. Further, this is equivalent to nearly one-third of our defence expenditure, 18 per cent of our annual export earnings and 10 per cent of the total outlay of our federal budget.

In terms of human suffering, too, the scenario is equally depressing. Half of the twelve million population of Karachi, being daily wage earners, are deprived of a significant portion of their monthly income and denied a chance to lead a normal life.[6]

It will be appropriate to consider press report highlighting the impact of the strike in June 1995.

During the strike from 22 June to 27 June 1995 yet another trade fair, the 2nd International Jewellery Exhibition, fell victim to the persistent law and order problem in Karachi causing a loss of around Rs 0.5 million to the Export Promotion Bureau that was spent for publicity purpose. The chances of the two-day exhibition scheduled to be held on 26–27 June 1995 were very dim. From upcountry the jewellers were reluctant to bring in their ornaments fearing security risks involved in the troubled Karachi city.

Similarly, local jewellers were also apprehensive that the exhibition could prove a fiasco in terms of business on account of the prevailing law and order situation which would shy off many potential foreign buyers.[7]

A survey conducted by a reporter of the daily News published on 2 July 1995 indicated that business activities throughout the city remained suspended on Saturday, the second day of the two days protest call, given by the MQM. Production work in all the five industrial areas in the city stopped. The workers could not turn up because of non-availability of public transport. Similar was the case at both the ports where the activity remained low. Bazaars, cloth markets and main shopping centres at Saddar, Tariq Road, Hyderi, Sarafa Bazar and the electronic market at Abdullah Haroon Road gave a deserted look. Reports prepared by various trade bodies put the losses suffered by the city in recent strikes to more than Rs 6 billion while a report of the Industry mentioned a 50 per cent reduction in import and export through Karachi in the recent past.

Survey conducted by journalists showed that Karachi was coming close to severe food shortage due to frequent protests and strikes. This situation had paralyzed the normal life in the city. Meanwhile the import and export activities were also affected both at Karachi Port Trust and Port Qasim. Cargo handling at the KPT was thin. Low attendance of labour and other staff including the custom personnel were the chief reasons for slow activity.

The city was, in July 1995, at the threshold of a big vegetable and food crunch as wholesale dealers stopped supplying consignments to the only port city of the country due to fear of loss of goods. Tomatoes, which were just selling between Rs 12 to 16 per kilogram during the last week of June 1995 had skyrocketed to Rs 30 per kilogram in July 1995. The famous brands were fast running out of stock in many general stores. Meanwhile, fruit and vegetable dealers in the *sabzi mandi* reported very slow inflow of perishable goods mainly vegetables.[8]

The MQM's mourning day also badly affected the import and export activities at both the ports of the city—Karachi Port and Port Qasim. A KPT employee said cargo handling was also affected as drivers were not ready to take consignments for upcountry fearing burning of their vehicles. However, on some berths, transport was available but cargo handling was affected because labour and technical staffers were not present. Similar situation prevailed at the Karachi fish harbour, which presented a deserted look. All the floors of the Customs House were empty as 90 per cent staff of Custom House preferred not to show up due to impending violence in the city. Working at the income tax building was also severely hit on the mourning day as almost all the staff of IT zones and circles was absent. A number of assessees could not respond to the notices whose deadline was Sunday, issued by the Income Tax department. Officials said that the Department would reconsider all those cases of appeal and would issue fresh dates for the hearing of such cases. Business centers like electronic market, Jodia Bazar, timber market, paper market, chemical and dyes market also remained closed throughout the day which resulted in suspension of wholesale commodities trade to the upcountry. All banks, shopping centres, business houses, I.I. Chundrigar Road,

Jewellers markets at Saddar and Bohri Bazaar were also completely shut.[9]

The city with five huge industrial estates is home to 80,000 commercial entities that collectively provide around 60 per cent of the government's overall revenue stream. An estimated 30 per cent of all these tremendously important facilities have now been shut down.[10] The city provides direct employment to three million workers who feed nine million of their dependants and all that in return provides all life line to the rest of the country's industrial base. The country's premier stock exchange has been the source of a Rs 150 billion loss over the past year (1994) alone.[11] The government's economic policy has, as a result, been badly shaken. Export growth is a full billion dollar short of target. Total revenue collection target in 1994–95 was roughly 75 per cent fulfilled causing a loss of more than Rs 50 billion to the exchequer. The current account deficit that, according to IMF target, was not to exceed 3.5 per cent of GDP may have actually ended up at a colossal 5 per cent. GDP growth itself was below 5 per cent as opposed to targeted rate of 7 per cent. The worst performance so far has been on the inflation front where prices continue to increase at an officially admitted rate of more than 14 per cent as opposed to a target of 7 per cent.[12]

According to city industrialists, government suffers approximately Rs 800 million per day on account of central excise duty (CED), sales tax, professional and other taxes due to the closure of business and industrial activities in the city. The government loses another Rs 300 to 400 million per day in the shape of customs duties, withholding tax, container charges, income tax, and other surcharges.[13] According to the industrialists they are doomed to lose an amount of Rs 750 million as production losses and in the shape of enhanced expenditure, banks mark-up, cancellation of orders and delayed shipments. Similarly the importers face losses in the form of demurrage container charges, port and shipping levies, perishing and theft of cargo, and fluctuation of prices.[14]

One day's closure of trade activities results in four days disturbance of trade transactions affecting huge financial losses of the importers, said Chairman, Karachi Keryana Merchants Group (KKMG) Rais Ashraf Taj Muhammad.[15] The account holders of foreign banks were perturbed as none of their branches in the city were opened during the last three days.[16] Karachi Stock Exchange remained closed for the second consecutive day on Monday following a call given by Altaf group for three days mourning.[17]

Impact on Karachi Stock Exchange

Another way to look at the relationship between law and order situation and economic performance will be to have an overview of the disturbed law and order situation and the trends in the Karachi Stock Exchange market. For this purpose different time series marked by lawlessness may be examined with reference to the trends in the stock exchange market. This will include, in particular, certain months during the period from 1990 to June–July 1995.

The strength and survival of the country depend on the strength and survival of democracy in the country. There is no better guarantee of democracy than a strong and vigorous capital market and widespread dispersal of ownership of economic assets. In Pakistan neither the prescription for self-reliance nor the transfer of economic responsibility from the State to the private sector will succeed without a well-functioning capital market.

The stock market in our country is passing through a developmental stage as Pakistan makes a shift from an agricultural to industrial economy. In the development process financial institutions, commercial banks and leasing companies play an important role. The promotion of capital and stock markets is also linked with financial institutions such as leasing and *mudarabah* companies and investment and private commercial banks.

Within a short span of two years, i.e. from 1989 to 1991, the number of shareholders increased fourfold to one million, and aggregate market capitalization tripled to Rs 182 billion. This included about $200 million worth of foreign investment. In 1991 a record of 15.2 billion shares were traded on Karachi and Lahore stock exchanges which saw 61 new companies listed as against 41 in 1990.[18] Table 9.1 gives a bird's eye view of this state of affairs. It may be added that 1990 was a year of relative political instability, religious, ethnic and drug related terrorism whereas the situation was being brought under control during the last months of 1991.

These developments are remarkable by any financial yardstick. However, the big question is whether they can be taken as a barometer of sustainable tendencies reflection in the nation's inherent economic health. Already there were signs of ups and downs. General price index of share prices fell from 193.92 in January 1992 to 159.47 in November 1992 (Table 9.2) when Long March and political turmoil had started surfacing. It started rising once again though at a slower pace. Stock markets are notorious for their volatility, reflecting the impact of global, regional and domestic socio-economic conditions. By its free market policies and expanding links with international courses, Pakistan has linked itself to international funds transfer system.

TABLE 9.1

Pakistan's Stock Market Sector: A bird's eye view 1992

Shareholders	1 m (Oct 1992)	0.25 m (March 1991)
Market capitalization of Shares	Rs 200 b (Oct 1992)	Rs 67 b (March 1991)
Foreign investment	US$ 200 m (Oct 1992)	
Share transacted in Lahore and	15.2 b (1991)	
Karachi new listed companies	61 (1991)	41 (1990)
Highest transaction of shares recorded on single day	9.164 m (9 Sep 1991)	
Turnover of shares	9.164 m	255.39 m (1990)

Source: State Bank of Pakistan (1992) Bulletin, February and December, Karachi.

Stability Criteria

Stable stock markets are those that grow steadily in volume and value with minimum of ups and downs. It is growth and not merely size that attracts investors. A large market that is declining drives investors away. A small market that is growing and shows potential for growth attracts investors provided it is located within a deregulated and stable socio-economic environment. But too rapid a growth, which promotes bullish tendencies invariably, leads to adjustment processes, which are often painful to new investors and harmful to further growth.

TABLE 9.2

Pakistan's Stock Markets September 1991–November 1992

Sectors	Issued Capital	Market capitalization shares				SBP general indices of shares price			
		Sep 91	Jan 92	Sep 92	Nov 92	Sep 91	Jan 92	Sep 92	Nov 92
Banks and Other Financial Institutions	11,693	10,580	39,373	29,396	27,959	148.25	181.62	131.20	126.62
Banks and Investment Cos	5,469	3,061	18,514	16,334	14,397	170.62	276.13	158.53	140.69
Mudarabah	4,428	2,966	11,457	5,811	5,496	129.31	145.72	82.24	70.77
Leasing Companies	1,168	1,112	4,017	3,156	3,811	129.47	161.09	136.87	139.38
Insurance	628	3,441	5,385	4,095	4,255	163.61	143.52	147.17	155.65
Cotton and Other Textile	15,854	17,579	42,482	58,159	39,966	141.24	191.94	144.18	141.13
Textile Spinning	8,059	10,317	18,829	15,200	14,349	147.43	193.95	133.14	124.55
Textile Weaving and Composite	4,573	5,715	11,576	11,318	11,204	145.20	204.47	150.82	143.55
Other Textile	3,222	1,547	12,077	11,641	14,413	131.10	177.39	148.57	155.28
Pharmaceuticals	5,237	13,279	19,983	35,250	26,321	143.36	199.67	196.26	209.50
Chemical and Engineering	808	1,324	1,725	1,481	1,523	134.18	171.22	140.23	127.38
Auto and Allied	1,992	3,409	4,722	7,334	7,602	134.84	170.16	153.34	157.04
Cables and Electrical Goods	571	1,660	2,438	2,860	3,427	134.61	166	178.86	206.72
Sugar and Allied	2,834	4,974	7,002	7,647	7,962	111.08	140.68	125.70	130.30
Paper and Board	766	1,966	3,282	3,358	3,890	114.96	158.52	124.13	133.77
Cement	2,705	2,697	4,218	8,669	10,007	145.46	217.81	270.86	333.46
Fuel and Energy	4,474	17,747	32,605	32,922	29,395	149.77	232.96	196.47	190.63
Transportation and Communication	4,1213,4	9,841	8,070	7,161	115.66	233.53	224.29	198.26	77
Miscellaneous	4,220	11,974	17,418	19,525	20,615	130.21	155.06	137.86	137.96
Jute	443	777	981	891	832	141.57	164.77	118.91	111.17
Food and Allied	1,122	6,177	10,356	11,890	12,867	135.97	175.52	171.72	171.48
Glass and Ceramics	515	531	730	803	785	122.21	156.77	135.44	129.29
Vanaspati and Allied	267	555	694	492	502	128.37	118.71	103.93	102.36
Others	1,873	3,934	4,657	5,450	5,629	122.93	160.05	159.28	175.49
Aggregate Market Capitalization	55,275	90,666	185,089	194,671	185,828	136.91	161.15	159.47	

(Aggregate Market Capitalization: General index)

Source: State Bank of Pakistan (1992) Bulletin, February and December, Karachi.

New issues over 1991–92 were more than 100 (Table 9.1). Daily turnover in stock exchanges of Karachi and Lahore averaged 3 million shares as against a little over one million in 1990. Market capitalization increased from Rs 61.75 million to over Rs 182 billion.

Causes of Jerks in 1992–93

The fall in share prices in 1992–93 can be attributed to both global and domestic factors. Uncertainties on the international scene were caused by succession of events including non crystallization of political developments after the break-up of Soviet Russia, prolonged USA-ECM trade negotiations, doubtful future of Mastricht scheme of single European currency, continuous economic recession in the United States, and Germany's economic crisis after unification. These developments did cast a shadow on trade and investment markets of Pakistan. As for domestic factors, the following have been relatively more important:

i.   Large supply of securities during twenty months preceding June 1993;

ii. Sudden increase in the supply of *Mudarabah* shares which led to a fall in their prices;

iii. Impact of fall in *Mudaraba* shares on banks and leasing companies;

iv. Diversion of funds towards privatization at the cost of stock market;

v.   Global recession in the textile market which is Pakistan's largest stock exchange sector. A year ago when the textile sector joined stock market run up, its bullish flames engulfed the entire share market;

vi. Improper interpretation of State Bank's Prudential Regulations by some banks in respect of advances against the shares of listed companies (a manifestation of the culture of lawlessness);

vii. Shock of the 1992 widespread floods causing great damage to standing crops and communication infrastructure; and

viii.Non-emergence of wider political consensus on crucial economic issues (a symbol of political instability, unrest and out-break of terrorism resulting in violence and killings).

The fall in share prices was triggered by so called panic selling by investors who had borrowed excessively and beyond their means. Since investors were paying high financial cost to banks, they had no alternative but to sell their stocks to meet commitments.

The Year 1994

The year 1994 proved to be the bloodiest for the Karachiites. With high mortality—shooting upto 400 per cent—violence continued unabated costing 561 lives and wounding 601 in almost 879 incidents of widespread violence.[19] A series of investigations showed that police officers and one captain of the Rangers were also included among those killed in Karachi in 1994 in regular rounds of violence. Up to ten people were being killed daily in political or criminal shoot outs. According to statistics, a total of 795 people had been killed and another 1421 injured in the 1999 violent incidents between June 1992 to October 1994. Of 795, almost 121 lost their lives in the seven months of 1992—from June to December—and another 113 in 1993. But this number increased abruptly to 561 in 1994, thus showing a relative rise of 400 per cent in death toll. Most of the police stations in District East and Central came under attack and firing on police vehicles became a routine.[20]

Despite the fact that Karachi is not a metropolis but a megalopolis and has a population far in excess of many small countries of the world, the impact of strikes, strife, riots and breakdown of law and order had made itself visible in trends of general index for share prices and aggregate market capitalization in the Karachi Stock Exchange market. During the financial year 1992–93 (from July 1992 to June 1993) the general index for share prices came down from 88.5 in 1991–92 to -14.2. Aggregate market capitalization declined from 219.1 in 1991–92 to -1.8 in 1992–93.[21]

The Karachi Stock Exchange Index, by taking Thirty Day Moving Average represents the impact of the prevailing environment of lawlessness. From 11 November 1993 to December 1993 the Karachi Stock Exchange was at its lowest ebb and recovery took the shares to the peak 2650 (indicating 100 per cent recovery) during a period of relative calm ending on 22 March 1994. In the last week of March, trouble started in a big way following an unsuccessful raid by law enforcement agencies for the arrest of an alleged terrorist. As stated already, violence, killings, attacks on police officials and buildings resulted in the erosion of confidence and despite the speculative nature of the stock exchange business, there had been almost a consistent downward trend in the movement of the share market till 16 November 1994.

Even on 26 November 1994 the woes of the share market were multiplying in geometric progression. Ten days earlier it was completely thrown in doldrums due to fresh eruption of violence. Many of the investors had beaten a hasty retreat, off loading their holdings to book the available margin. Not only were the foreign country funds conspicuous by their absence, local investors, bargain hunters, and speculators avoided making any fresh commitments. Even the institutional buyers could not retrieve the situation despite their best efforts.[22] Analysts said that at a time when everybody was worried about their family security, who would care to invest in shares.[23] On 23 November 1994 the business community held a peace rally under the aegis of the FPCCI to express its anguish and dismay over the fast deteriorating law and order situation. 'Peace or no tax' shouted the processionists.[24]

As a result of sell off, only by 16 November 1994, Rs 14 billion were eroded from the aggregate market capitalization. The figure tumbled from Rs 370 billion to Rs 356 billion on 26

November 1994.[25] More disturbing was the fact that price index breached the resistance level of 2100 points and hit 2088 in the wake of selling pressure. If the process continued and the index breached 2000 barrier, that would have signified a crash. Progressively the aggregate market capitalization had declined from Rs 420 billion to Rs 348 billion and a recovery of about Rs 70 billion was not an easy task.[26]

Index and Lawlessness from August 1994 to March 1995

A glance at the Stock Exchange Index in Figure 9.1 with reference to important events from August 1994 to March 1995 makes the adverse impact of lawlessness and violence on the Stock Exchange Index quite obvious. Events like placing of the Capital Bank's Chief Executive's name on the exit control list, strike call on 11 October 1994, probe of the Highnoon Scam, shooting down of the editor of the *Takbeer*, Salauddin, killing of twenty persons, murder of two US citizens with diplomatic status on 8 March 1995, and prediction of death of 250,000 persons by the MQM leader Altaf Hussain indicate a direct and proportionate relationship between lawlessness and depressant trends in the Stock Exchange Index. The extent and magnitude of violence in December 1994 and March 1995 has already been highlighted in Chapter 7.

April – July 1995

On 6 April 1995 KSE's price index declined by 19.66 points at 1711.71 as against 1731.37 a day earlier, reflecting the weakness of base shares.[27] Of the 311 active issues, 109 posted gains while 131 showed losses and 71 remained unchanged.[28] Turnover on Thursday (6 April 1995) totalled 17,304,800 shares as compared to 37,470,140 shares a day ago.[29]

Most analysts said that there was no hope of a sustainable rally because of many destabilizing factors. The law and order situation was still far from satisfactory and cases of murder, robbery and sniper firing were still being reported daily. The political and economic scenario, already grim, was punctuated by soaring inflation, stagnant exports, and widening budgetary gap. With further enhancement of utility charges and additional taxation in the offing, the industrial circles were worried about the shape of things to come. They were fast losing their competitive edge in foreign markets due to erosion of the value of the rupee and subsequent rise in import cost of basic raw materials.

In the aftermath of the protest convention of businessmen and industrialists on 15 March 1995, the war of nerves between the business community and the government was still continuing and the former's convention had been banned. The businessmen had challenged the removal of the top office bearers of the FPCCI. Thus the atmosphere was hardly congenial for investment. The government, which was faced with a serious financial crunch, needed businessmen's co-operation rather than confrontation.

KSE's price index recorded a nominal decline of 2.14 points at 1709.57 as against 1711.71 reflecting relative weakness of base shares. Of 330 active issues, 75 posted gains while 199 showed losses and 56 remained unchanged. Turnover on Sunday (9 April 1995) stood at 18,103,700 shares as compared to 17,304,800 shares at the last weekend.[30] The share market sank into deeper depression on Sunday (9 April 1995) in the wake of fresh eruption of violence in the city which claimed eight lives on Saturday (8 April 1995). Bomb scare in New York resulting in the cancellation of a shopping plan by the prime minister and continued protest against human rights violations in Karachi by MQM activists made the investors jittery. There was heavy selling pressure on many counters which led to widespread erosion of values.[31]

The overall outlook was gloomy despite the reported signing of MoUs worth six billion dollars by US investors in energy

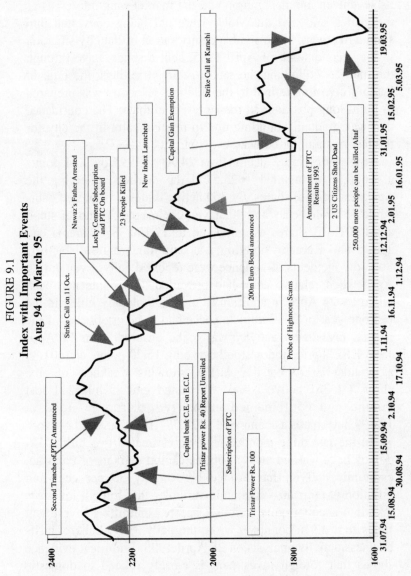

FIGURE 9.1
Index with Important Events
Aug 94 to March 95

Source: Developed by the author.

and other sectors. It went to the credit of the then government that MoUs worth twenty billion dollars had been signed during its seventeen months tenure. Yet, the market sank into crisis as the critics said that the MoUs were not being converted into solid agreement.[32] The sudden deterioration of the city situation in the second week of April 1995, sent a shock wave through the market. Following the report of fresh killings, the bulk of leading investors retired to the sidelines. Nobody was prepared to build long positions in their present climate. The confidence that was gradually building due to relative calm in the city for the last two and half weeks was sharply eroded.[33]

KSE's price index declined on 24 April 1995 by 2.64 points at 1620.93 as against 1623.57 a day earlier, reflecting the weakness of base shares. Of 360 active issues, 114 posted gains while 156 ruled easy and 90 stayed unchanged. Turnover stood at 11,501,673 shares as compared to 17,150,385 shares a day ago.[34] The Karachi situation was still far from satisfactory. Sporadic incidents of violence were reported daily. Even during April when relative calm had prevailed, 69 people had been killed by 24 April in addition to the 1500 already killed in the last one year or so. Complete peace had to be established if the normal investment activity was to be ensured.[35] On 19 April 1995 KSE's price index stood down by 15.20 points at 1601.83 as against 1617.03 a day earlier, showing weakness of blue chips. Of 361 active issues, 85 posted gains while 211 lost ground and 65 remained unchanged. Turnover stood at 12,299,810 shares as compared to 20,587,100 shares a day ago.[36]

'In the last three months or so an estimated two billion US dollars have washed away from the capital markets of Pakistan, economic activity has eroded by roughly 30 per cent and inflation is rampant—economic variables that foreign investors take into account quite seriously before committing investment funds to a given country', wrote the daily *Jang*, Lahore, in its business activity analysis on 25 April 1995. Empirical evidence shows that foreign investment is closely related to domestic investment. This makes sense because it is difficult to rationalize as to why a foreigner should like to invest in a country where domestic investors are not. The country has experienced a deterioration of law and order and sectarian violence for long, particularly Karachi. However, the Government sponsored hostility towards the business community is independent of these factors and has greatly diminished the prospects of any fresh domestic investment in the country.[37]

No economy, more so one which purports to have embraced *laissez-faire*, should expect to receive foreign investment without the support of the country's entrepreneurs. Unfortunately, not only has the government created an ever widening gulf between the business community and itself, it never seemed to be cognizant of the enormous scope that loomed large on the international financial horizon, and therefore, a whole array of opportunities may have been missed for sometime to come.[38]

On 27 June 1995 KSE 100 index declined by 13.69 points at 1597.36 as against 1611.05 a day earlier reflecting the weakness of base shares. Of 296 active shares, only 88 posted gains while 151 showed losses and 57 remained unchanged. Turnover on Tuesday (27 June 1995) stood at 8,659,966 shares as compared to 9,518,011 shares a day ago.[39] The near term outlook of the share market appeared to be quite gloomy. The most disturbing factor was the law and order situation, which was quite alarming. The city was in the grip of an insurgency, which posed grave threat to the integrity of the country.

The market circles said that only a miracle could save the market from imminent disaster. All the odds were in favour of the bears who had been holding sway for the last six months. The bulls, who made a feeble attempt to stage a comeback after the budget, drawing strength from the technical factors, had beaten a hasty retreat and there was little hope that they would gather courage to assert themselves in the present adverse circumstances.

The MQM had disrupted life completely and even trading on the stock exchange was suspended for two days. Since the MQM had decided to observe strike every two days in a week until the acceptance of its six demands, the danger of fresh eruption of violence continued to loom large on the horizon. Thus, the majority of the investors preferred to sit with their fingers crossed. They said it was better to adopt a wait and see policy until the city returned to normal which appeared to be a remote possibility.

Even base shares came under selling pressure, losing heavily. Selling originated from all quarters which clearly demonstrated the bearish mood of the market. Small business volume was largely attributed to the dearth of demand. Even blue chips like Dewan Salman, Lucky Cement, and Dhan Fibres were neglected by the investors. The 1600 point was again breached by the KSE price index which tumbled to 1597 reflecting the weakness of base shares. Market circles apprehended that if selling pressure continued unabated, the index might fall below the 1500 point barrier soon.[40]

The last week of June 1995 was conspicuous by unprecedented violence and killing resorted to in the wake of MQM's protest and strike call on the issue of the alleged rape of one Farzana Sultan. The KSE 100 Index at one stage was down more than fifteen points but some 'forces' seemed to have entered in the rings in an effort to keep the Index above 1600 points level. *The News*-MCB Composite shed 1.25 points, seemingly under pressure due to the financial sectors as whole, as usual. Tuesday (27 June 1995) was declared the last day of the clearing week whose clearing was on 3 July. The financial sector lost 1.48 points with all the sub-sectors losing in terms of points. The leasing companies suffered the greatest fall. To a lesser extent, fall was also registered in insurance, mutual funds and brokerage firms. The banks and investment companies stabilized but there were very strong chances that this sub-sector would come back after suffering major setbacks in the past two or three trading sessions. This particular sub-sector, it seemed, was the one under severe pressure from short selling measures resorted to by all the major speculators in the market. Short selling creates artificial supply which puts downward pressure on prices and the resulting inertia is used by the speculators to make money. Incidentally, short selling is prohibited in the law books but every one expected the government knew that it was rife in all the country's capital market dealings. In the Industry, nineteen out of thirty sub-sectors posted decline in prices from start of trading till the end while only ten could post gains. The losers were led by apparels, cement, energy and food and confectioneries sub-sectors. The gainers had the sub-sectors of vanaspati, toiletries, transport and communications, and textile weaving in the lead. In the industrial sector, cement sub-sector had become the worst sufferer at the hands of bears. The sluggishness in the market was the result of oversupply of cement in the country as well as pessimistic opinions regarding the Federal budget on this sub-sector. Coming to the twenty most active scripts of Tuesday, fifteen declined in ending values while only four went up. PTC came below Rs 34 mark and going by its record in the previous several trading days, it was becoming less risky. Hubco came down to Rs 18.8 after going well over Rs 19 in the last three trading sessions. Alico seemed to be caught in the bears and lost further to finish at Rs 22.75. Dhan Fibres became valued at Rs 9.30 and in a couple of trading days, it was expected to become an attractive short-term buy. Asian Stock Fund was the fourth most active script with 578,000 shares changing hands—with surprisingly only one transaction. MCB, whose 3000 shares switched ownership was supposed to start the day at Rs 38.98 after becoming ex-rights but there seemed to be some adjustment in its ex-rights date because of call coming at Rs 46, instead of Rs 38.98.[41]

According to Network Securities and Services, the market was expected to stay under pressure during the next clearing because of the political situation in Karachi.[42] KSE 100 index declined by 10.94 points at 1586.72 as against 1597.66 a day earlier reflecting the weakness of base shares. Of 329 active issues 77 posted gains while 185 showed losses and 67 remained unchanged,[43] Turnover on Wednesday (28 June 1995) totalled 7,317,714 shares as compared to 8,569,966 shares a day earlier.[44] It was agreed by all concerned that the ongoing mayhem had caused a colossal loss of industrial production and government revenue, which would eventually tell badly on the health of national economy and industrial profitability.[45]

Institutional support was also grievously lacking which aggravated the situation. The analysts were unanimous that unless the financial institutions lent aggressive support to the sagging market it could not be pulled out of the present morass. Besides individual investors, speculators and bargain hunters were also sitting on the fence waiting for some positive development on the law and order and political front. There were no encouraging reports from the corporate sector either.

Observers apprehended further deterioration of the law and order situation in the wake of the MQM chief's alleged demand for a separate province for Mohajirs. This had already evoked sharp reaction as it was allegedly aimed at the division of Sindh which was unacceptable to other sections of society. Worse still it had been alleged that Altaf Hussain had said that this demand could go even further meaning disintegration of the country. The comments in the press highlighted the adverse effects of the law and order situation in their articles, editorials, and business reviews. For example:

> Already the violence in Karachi has acquired ethnic dimension as Sindhis, Balochis and Pathans have been targeted by the killers. The solution lies in the acceptance of recommendations of Human Rights Commission. Meanwhile the confidence of the investors has been sharply eroded and they are reluctant to take new positions. The market has been left completely at the mercy of jobbers and day traders.[46]

MQM-Government Talks and the Karachi Stock Exchange

On 16 July 1995 KSE 100 index lost 32.06 points at 1632.81 as against 1664.87 a day earlier reflecting the weakness of base shares. Of 335 active issues, 74 posted gains, 182 showed losses and 79 remained unchanged. Total turnover on Sunday (16 July 1995) stood at 9,756,135 shares as compared to 12,388,665 shares a day ago.[47] Among the most active issues were PTC, down by 90 paisa at Rs 34.25 on 3,151,800 shares; Faisal Bank, down by Rs 1.80 at

Rs 29.00 on 1,728,100 shares; Hub Power, down by 40 paisa at Rs 18.30 on 973,500 shares; Pel Appliances stood at Rs 50.00 on 704,000 shares; and Dewan Salman, down by Rs 4.25 at 108.25 on 569,500 shares.[48] Major gainers included Pel Appliances, up by Rs 3.00; Millat Tractors, better by Rs 2.00; Emco Industries, higher by Rs 1.75; and BP Board, dearer by Rs 1.50.[49]

In the minus column, Nestle Milkpak eased by Rs 10.00, Orix Leasing lost Rs 9.00, Dewan Salman fell by Rs 4.25, and MCB declined by Rs 3.00.[50] In the third week of July 1995 the dwindling hope of the success of the PPP-MQM talks threw the share market into a tailspin contrasting the buoyancy of the last week which was generated by the report that the talks had started on a positive note. The optimism proved short-lived as reports poured in that the talks were heading towards a collapse. The growing tension in the city created by on-going operation by Rangers and rumours that the parleys were going to end in a fiasco soon made the investors jittery forcing them to unload their holdings in haste. Their optimism evaporated in thin air with the fading away of the hope that at least this time a sincere effort would be made by both the sides to resolve the crisis and restore to normalcy this strife-torn city which had hit hard the economy. It had put foreign as well as local investment in grave jeopardy while the stock exchange was in the grip of protracted bearish spell chipping away at the value of shares.

Jobbers and sundry day traders resorted to panic selling while bargain-hunters and speculators beat a hasty retreat to the sidelines. Investors and brokerage houses were also buying very discreetly, picking up only risk free issues. There was preponderance of losers due to heavy selling pressure. It was feared in July 1995 that unless some miracle saved the talks from collapse the index might soon go down the 1600 resistance level.[51] What intrigued the investors was the continuing operation by Rangers, which was hardly conducive to peace talks. The twenty-one demands put forth by the government had also vitiated the climate for talks, therefore, most of the investors were highly sceptical about their success. Fortunately the two sides decided to continue the dialogue and to continue their effort to find a solution to the festering problem.

The reports in the international media about possible change of government also made the investors chary. Analysts said that unless there was political stability and law and order situation was satisfactory, both local and foreign investors would back out of their commitment to invest in Pakistan in view of the Karachi situation. 'The already ailing industrial sector is likely to suffer further setback if peace is not restored to Karachi soon. Thus the enthusiasm generated in the wake of a record export of worth 8.4 billion dollars in the outgoing fiscal year (1994–95) is fading away.'[52]

Analysts were unsure about the direction of the market in view of discouraging reports about the talks. Particularly, interviews of the leader of the MQM team had taken the wind out of the sails of the investors who were thinking of ways and means to wriggle out of their commitments. Analysts feared that as a selling frenzy had presently gripped the market, even sound technical position reflected in highly oversold position could not avert a possible crash. Only some positive developments in the talks could turn the table and the market again witness a buying euphoria. Thus, much depended on the news from the political front. Only stabilization of the present democratic process and amicable settlement of the Karachi tangle could have a salutary effect on the market. However, 'there may be a partial recovery if heavy short covering surfaces on technical grounds', said the analysts.[53]

The responsiveness of the trends in the Karachi Stock Exchange can be further illustrated with reference to comments and analysis in the press. The following are some of the excerpts:

Karachi: As the law and order situation worsens further, in the wake of MQM Chief Altaf Hussain's announcement for a five day mourning—three day for Farzana case and two day for S.M Tariq murder—the chances for trading look bleak. Not to talk about the market performance.[54]

'Karachi: the market may not remain as buoyant as in the last week, yet keeping in view the past three days the behaviour of the trading it looks like that everything at Karachi Stock Exchange is hinged upon the Government-MQM talks.[55]

A positive result will swing the KSE 100 index upward and a negative outcome will simply wipe out all the gains of the last three days.

'Although fundamentals are weak yet any positive outcome of Government-MQM talks will put the market back on the tracks', said Nadim Ahmad Siddiq, and Khadim Ali Shah Bukhari, dealers in Stock Exchange.[56]

Analysts expect that trading in the coming week will remain more subdued in comparison to the last week. However, local institutions activity will probably continue in selective scripts. The blank-sellers are also likely to take full advantage of this development with the vengeance to repay the bulls back with interest.[57]

The situation is so sensitive that the slightest depression will discourage weak investors and set-off panic selling, said Imran Arif Motiwalla at Ali Hussain Rajabali.

Foreign institutions are indeed picking up scripts, but on the other hand they are still in the process of unloading scripts that are not as feasible as they were at the time of purchase. Over the past one month, we have witnessed various dips, where the political instability and disorder in the city has weakened the market and substantial decline. At many a time the market-men had come to believe that a revival was in process, but later on the market presented a different picture.[58]

On 17 July 1995, KSE 100 index declined by 15.95 points at 1603.21 as against 1619.16 a day earlier reflecting the weakness of base shares.[59] Of 337 active issues, 96 posted gains while 155 showed losses and 86 remained unchanged. Turnover was placed at 7,919,352 shares as compared to 7,595,361 shares a day ago.

In the light of foregoing analysis it is obvious that the most destabilizing factor is the volatile law and order situation. Even the visit of the President of Pakistan to the city to review the situation and help restore peace here failed to yield any palpable result. There was no hope of early return of normality to this tormented city because of the rigid stance of both the government and MQM. It is further clear that unless the Karachi crisis is resolved, there is little hope that local and foreign investment will gain any momentum. It is agreed on all hands that Karachi is the hub of the national economy which contributes 60 to 65 per cent of total national revenues, houses most of the industries and business houses, the entire export and import trade of the country is routed through its two ports and hence it cannot be left at the mercy of terrorists and murderers.

The alarming slide in the Karachi Stock Exchange, which reflects the sad state of other exchanges as well, has continued for too long a time now with only minor interruptions. The KSE index came down from its peak of 2661 points in July 1994 to 1546 on Tuesday (18 July 1995) when it registered an increase of thirty-two points. When the index crashed through 1500 last month, i.e. June 1995, and a broker of KSE won a bet of Rs 10 million on that basis, the fear was that the slide might continue and the index return to the low 1200 mark of February 1993. However the index bounded back soon to above 1500. But the aggregated market still continued to lose. Capitalization had been around Rs 150 billion.[60]

September 1995

The State Bank General Index of share prices showed a grim situation of the capital market in the first week of September. The General Index (1990–91) depicted a downturn of 4.20 points and stood at 204.82 on 7 September as compared with 209.02 on 31 August. The index touched the highest level at 206.25 on 5 September and the lowest at 204.82 on 7 September. During the week ending on 7 September, the total volume of business decreased from 42.753 million shares to 23.827, giving average business per day as 8.550 million shares and 7.942 million shares respectively.[61]

The foregoing analysis provides sufficient evidence that the movements in the capital market are interwoven with the law and order situation and a culture of observance of laws. For the crash of the stock exchange market the causes are political, economic, fiscal, and external:

- There is a lack of confidence among the investors in the political system and its readiness and competence to cure the economic ills of the country. Investors complain that in its anxiety to woo foreign investment the government is neglecting local investors although if the local investors are reluctant to invest in Pakistan the foreign investors will not be over excited about making investment except in the very lucrative power production sectors.

- Likewise, investors in KSE who were sensitive to political trends were upset by the lasting confrontation between the government and opposition and then appalled by the confrontation between the government and business which now appears to be coming to an end and the prolonged and escalating Karachi killings which result in frequent closure of industries or financial institutions in the city or partial attendance of the staff on other days.

- High taxation, which sought to collect an incredible 40 per cent more revenues in 1995 than last year (1994) and the large volume of smuggling it spawned especially through the Afghan transit trade, high prices of power, gas and water and the endemic load-shedding hit the industries and lowered their profits.

- Finally came removal of the cap on maximum rate of interest which sent interest rate soaring and increased the financial charges of companies. Simultaneously, the government offered higher rate for money it needed and investors preferred buying bonds or making long-term deposits with their cash while the shares were giving poor dividends.

- The foreigners who earlier pushed up prices of some of the good shares soon capitalized on them, made large profits and left the country. The result was that the prices came tumbling down. As a result PTC shares which they had bought abroad at Rs 55 crashed and had been selling close to Rs 30 discouraging foreign portfolio investment to a large externt. If some foreign buying is taking place now it is because the prices are very low and those with ample surplus cash can afford to take the risk.

- High cost of production, heavy taxes, and high cost of credit and the utilities will erode the profits of companies, stunt their growth and encourage smuggling.

These observations are supported by the findings of the Prime Minister's Special Committee on Stock Market's Decline. According to the Committee, liquidity constraints, Mexican peso crisis, law and order situation in Karachi, and PTC shares behaviour were the chief factors responsible for the market's fall (PM's Special Committee's Report on Stock Market's Decline, 1995). KSE's half-yearly report has also suggested these factors responsible for the decline of the capital market.[62]

1996–99

For the past few years the stock market in Pakistan has been witnessing declining business trends which continued in 1998–99 also, due to some unfavourable domestic, regional and international factors. The declining trend continued during the first six months of 1998–99. The Karachi Stock Exchange (KSE) 100 index, which was at 1746 points at the beginning of 1998, touched its lowest ebb at 766 in July 1998. A number of factors were responsible for this decline which included: contagion effects of South East Asian financial debacle, global recession, crash of stock markets of some leading economies, imposition of economic sanctions on account of nuclear tests in May 1998, and local factors, such as, law and order situation, freezing of foreign currency accounts, and unresolved dispute with the Independent Power Producers. During July–March 1998–99, general index of share prices increased by 4.3 per cent as compared to a decline of 11.5 per cent in the comparable period last year. Out of twelve major trading groups, indices of the six groups recorded positive growth. These included auto and allied (0.5 per cent), fuel and energy (15.8 per cent), transport and communication (16.7 per cent), banks and other financial institutions (3.6 per cent), and miscellaneous (0.4 per cent).[63]

During May 1999, investor's confidence was at the lowest ebb as it oscillated in a narrow band within the last category very low.[64] As measured through the VIS, Stock Market Confidence Barometer, the confidence level ranged between 18 per cent to 24 per cent and in the process recording the lowest level, 18 per cent, in the third week. However, at the end of April 1999, the confidence level stood at a comparatively higher mark of 45 per cent. On an aggregate basis, confidence level was registered at 20 per cent entering the verily low category as compared to 46 per cent in April 1999.[65]

The month (May 1999) started with a bullish trend in the stock market. Abnormal gains were achieved in anticipation of a tax-free Federal Budget. But, traders and investors restricted themselves to blue chips and multinationals and staying away from other than safe haven stocks. Then came the selling pressure as the Indo-Pak tension rose high at the Line of Control. The retailers could not hold their positions, which resulted in drastic loss of values across the board with favourites taking heavy beating from the institutions and individuals.[66]

Share of Karachi's Industrial Units in Value Added

According to the FPCCI, the share of Karachi's industrial units in the overall value added of the manufacturing sector of Pakistan fell down from 45 per cent in 1985–86 to 20 per cent in 1993–94. The average annual rate of growth of GDP came down from 6.4 per cent in 1985–86 to 4.0 per cent in 1993–94. The average annual rate of growth from 1988–89 to 1993–94 did not go beyond 4.8 per cent. Thus it may safely be presumed that there was no shifting of investment funds from Karachi to any other part of the country. Most probably the process resulted in the flight of capital out of the country.

There are, however, some cases of shifting of capital to other parts of the country which have been highlighted by the press. Shifting of capital and business from Karachi to Punjab had been expedited in the last week of June 1995 when, at least, seven industrialists and a family of stock broker shifted to Lahore. It also transpired that many industrialists and businessmen who arrived in Punjab set up their respective business in Bhai Phero, Chunian, and Lahore. Those who had shifted their business to Lahore were of the view that if the situation in Karachi continued to prevail as it was then hundreds of businessmen would shift to Punjab. In addition, they added, Punjab would become the future market for traders and foreign investors would invest in the provinces of Punjab, NWFP, and Balochistan instead of Karachi.

In the wake of growing lawlessness in Karachi, foreign investment had nearly become stagnant in the city besides many industries had also been shifted to other parts of the country. In the same vein the volume of business in the Karachi stock exchange was on the decline with each passing day whereas business in Lahore and Islamabad stock exchanges increasing. It was also feared that income tax, sales tax and excise duty targets for Karachi would not be met. Shifting of industries from Karachi further aggravated the already existing unemployment problem in the city.[67]

Following the industrialists, federal employees were reluctant to serve in Karachi and were trying to get themselves transferred in other parts of the country. It was believed that more than one thousand business houses had become dormant to date.[68]

Impact on Government Revenue

Revenue Zones

Lawlessness affects not only the revenue collection activity of the government but also hampers attempts at broadening the tax base and diversifying the sources of funds. For instance, in case of revenue collection target in Pakistan for the year 1994–95 the Central Board of Revenue revised downward the annual tax collection target for the second time within a week to Rs 230 billion. The original target of Rs 259 billion was revised to Rs 240 billion in the second week of April 1995, which was revised, down to Rs 230 billion in the third week. The first revision was announced at a press conference by Vice Chairman Central Board of Revenue Alvi Abdur Rahim. He, however, had not stipulated the causes of the revision.[69]

The collection of direct taxes in the southern region of the Income Tax Department further deteriorated with the shortfall climbing to Rs 4.2 billion by 31 March, despite Rs 1.5 billion cut in the revenue collection target.[70] The southern region with a revised collection target of Rs 38.5 billion for the financial year (1994–5) had netted Rs 24.6 billion up to the first week of April.[71] However the revenue collection target set for the third quarter ending on 31 March, was Rs 28.87 billion.[72] By collecting Rs 24.6 billion by 31 March, the southern region had itself widened the gap between target and collection as now it had to net Rs 13.9 billion in the last quarter. It implied that in the remaining three months the southern region had to collect more than Rs 4.63 billion per month to cover the short fall. However, the department collected Rs 2.4 billion during the month of February 1995, nearly Rs 300 million less than the previous years corresponding month when the department had collected Rs 2.7 billion and in March indicated that ambitious target of direct tax collection would be hard to achieve. During the year 1994–95, the monthly collection target was Rs 3.20 billion which was 38 per cent more than that of last year's.[73]

The bad patch in revenue collection started in February (1995) when the law and order situation in the city hit revenue collection drive, said a senior official at the Income Tax Department. But in March (1995), the Southern Region has collected 24 per cent more revenue as compared to the corresponding period last year. Until 31 March 1995 the collection of direct tax stood at Rs 24.6 billion which is approximately Rs 5 billion more as compared to Rs 19.8 billion during the same period last year. During the month of March the Southern Region has collected Rs 3.8 billion which is a sign of relief for the Department if the collection is compared with that of February. During the current financial year the collection has increased by 154 per cent as compared to that last year's. Furthermore, out of total collection during the last quarter, approximately 85 per cent, has been collected through the efforts of the Department. The final quarter of financial year is always lucrative in terms of revenue collection. The past experience of the revenue collection indicated that approximately 20 per cent of direct tax collection has been made in last month alone, the official maintained.[74]

In this connection, the target for the Southern Region income tax fell from Rs 40,000 million to 38,000 million primarily due to the deteriorating law and order situation in the city while, on the other hand, the target for Central Region and Northern Islamabad/Rawalpindi were raised from Rs 11,019 million to 11,250 million and Rs 90,000 million to 95,000 million respectively. The Southern Region of income consisting of twelve zones had collected Rs 17,638.8 million out of the downward target of Rs 38,000 million.[75]

Likewise the Northern Region of income tax consisting of eight territorial zones collected Rs 6640.5 million out of upward revised target of Rs 95,000 million. Further break-up of the collections tells that the two company zones of the Central Region had netted income tax dues of Rs 5534.8 million up to April 1995 as against Rs 3828.1 million during the corresponding period of previous year which gave a percentage increase of 44.6 per cent which was Rs 1706.7 million more than the previous year. Similarly, three territorial zones of the same region collected Rs 931.2 million against 528.7 million of the previous year giving percentage increase of 76.1 per cent which was Rs 402.5 million more than the previous corresponding period.

In the Southern Region, from four companies, the income tax authorities collected up to April 1995 Rs 16,193.9 million as against Rs 12,646.2 million of the previous year showing a percentage increase of 28.1 per cent which was Rs 3547.7

million more than the same corresponding period last year. Likewise, six territorial zones without companies of the paid Region, collected Rs 9195.2 million as against 7462.4 million of previous year giving a percentage increase of 23.2 per cent which was Rs 1732.6 million more than the previous year. However the two territorial zones with companies of the Karachi region collected Rs 1444.9 million as against Rs 865.3 million showing an increase of 67 per cent which is Rs 579.6 million more than the previous year.

TABLE 9.3

Collection from Different Revenue Zones (1994–95)

Zone	Collected	As against the previous year
I Lahore	2132.5	1767.5
II Lahore	3402.3	2060.6
I Karachi	10967.3	8380.7
II Karachi	3000	3088.2
III Karachi	1656.4	1147.6
IV Karachi	570.2	29.7
A Lahore	97.2	82.6
B Lahore	712.8	382.2
C Lahore	121.2	63.9
A Karachi	102.1	160.7
B Karachi	76.1	
D Karachi	37.4	1016.6
E Karachi	52.3	0.6
F Karachi	8777.8	6069.1
A Peshawar	761.9	604
B Peshawar	554.6	156
Hyderabad	822.7	779.5
Sukkur	822.7	85.8
Faisalabad	899.1	611.1
Sargodha	324.4	189.3
Gujranwala	316.4	188.1
Sialkot	394.6	296
Multan	603.2	489.4
Sahiwal	133.8	73.2
Bahawalpur	220.4	125.3
Rawalpindi	1578.2	1703
Islamabad	1811.3	1158

Source: Central Board of Revenue, 1995.

The Northern Region consisting of eight territorial zones, with companies netted Rs 6640.5 million as against Rs 4906 million collected in the corresponding period of the previous year which was Rs 1734.5 million more than the previous corresponding period.[76]

It is worth mentioning that the collection in the Company Zone II Karachi, Hyderabad Zone, Rawalpindi Zone, and Zone D Karachi had gone down from previous year (1994). The fall in the collection in Karachi and Hyderabad was the natural outcome of the deteriorating law and order situation in these parts of the country.

According to the latest figures revealed by the Central Board of Revenue, on 30 June 1995, a sum of Rs 226.38 billion was collected in all categories of taxes in the year 1993–94 which exceeded the target of Rs 225 billion by Rs 1.38 billion (Rs 225 was the latest revised target scaled down from an earlier target of Rs 240 billion, which in itself had been reduced from the original budgetary figure of Rs 259 billion). This was Rs 54 billion or 31.2 per cent more than the collection in the previous year. Seen in the context of claims for refund, these figures were not likely to stand the test of a minute scrutiny. It appeared that even unjustifiable taxes were collected, later on to be returned by way of meeting claims for refund, simply to show improved performance on the part of tax collecting authorities.

Corporations

Major public and private sector corporations that fell under the direct tax net during the financial year 1994–95 for the first time are listed in table 9.4. The amount of tax levied relates to one year and the Income Tax Department had levied the tax. The short fall in the amount recovered can be attributed to a fall in production owing to distrubed law and order conditions.

TABLE 9.4

Public and Private Sector Corporations Falling under the Direct Tax Net (1994–95)

Organization	Revenue levied million (rupees)	Amount recovered million (rupees)
Lahore Stock Exchange	43.5	6.4
Shezan International Ltd.	20	20
Sui Nothern Gas	206	20
Sufi Soap	2.6	2.6
Pak Fruit Juice	3.7	1
Toyota Garden Motors	8.7	Nil
Karachi Port Trust	1582	3
Pakistan Refinery	280	Nil
KESC	140	Nil
State Cement	250	250
KDA	32	6
Port Qasim Authority	47	21
Defence Housing Authority	30	30
NDFC	215.0	215
ADBP	69.5	69.5

Source: Central Board of Revenue, 1995.

FIGURE 9.2

Public and Private Sector Corporations Falling under the Direct Tax Net (1994–95)

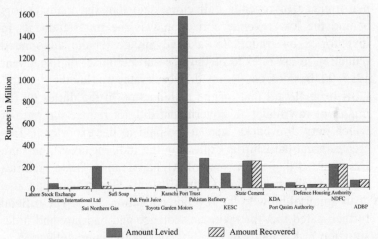

Source: Developed by the author with reference to the data in Table 9.4.

The indirect tax collection slipped further down in the third quarter of fiscal year 1994–95 as the overall shortfall climbed to Rs 11.25 billion at the end of this quarter sending shock waves to the government quarters seeking to bolster the revenue position from all avenues available. By the end of the third quarter, the Customs department had netted Rs 57 billion against the revised revenue collection target of Rs 91 billion. The revenue collection target set for the customs for each quarter was Rs 22.75 billion which the department failed to meet in any of the three quarters gone by.

The performance of Customs during the third quarter showed signs of slight improvement as the department collected Rs 21.8 billion between 1 January to 31 March 1995. In this quarter the month-wise collection average stood at Rs 7.2 billion. Before the take over of the 1995 hierarchy at the Central Board of Revenue, the indirect tax collection in the first two quarters stood at Rs 35.1 billion. The Customs authorities collected Rs 16 billion in the first quarter and approximately Rs 19.1 billion in the second. If the annual revenue collection target of Rs 91 billion was to be achieved the Customs authorities would have to collect Rs 12.3 billion which would remain an elusive pursuit.

A senior official at the CBR, while commenting on the poor performance of revenue collectors, said that the main factors behind the low revenue collection was the mis-statements in inventories by traders to take advantage of the announced reduction in tax rates to be enforced at the outset of fiscal year 1995–96. Besides, cut in duty drawback rates was another factor.[77] CBR official said that inspite of reduction in the duties on the import of raw material, government did not reduce the ratio at which duty drawbacks were to be paid to the exporters. 'This creates great hardship in collecting the indirect taxes', he said. He admitted that the misuse of Afghan Transit Trade facilities as well as the corruption in the Customs Department had also dealt a mortal blow to the revenue collection drive. The official further stated that the sporadic violence and bad law and order situation in Karachi had also affected the revenue collection as the traders were very reluctant to venture in exports or imports.

He, however, claimed that, against all odds, Customs would not only achieve its 1995–96 budgetary target but also make rich amends for the last year's shortfall. 'We are quite satisfied with our performance during the third quarter as the collection is the highest if compared with the previous quarters', an official added.

The Pakistan Telecommunication Corporation

The Pakistan Telecommunication Corporation, Karachi Region, had missed its revenue target by a staggering amount of Rs 800 million for the year 1994–95 although the Corporation's countrywide bill collection showed a rise of Rs 400 million. The PTC Karachi Region collected a revenue of Rs 5400 million during 1993–94 against the Rs 6200 million target. The other PTC regions efforts in revenue collection enabled the corporation to exceed its 1994–95 fiscal year target by more than Rs 400 million. The total PTC revenue collection stood at Rs 28.4 billion against the goal set for Rs 28 billion.[78]

One of the major factors in the shortfall in Karachi Region's revenue collection was a decline in the billing amount which remained far below expectations and constituted almost 50 per cent of the total shortfall. Against the set target of Rs 6200 million, PTC Karachi region's billing did not exceed Rs 5800 million—thus showing a wide gap of Rs 400 million. Karachiites made less calls in 1994–95 than expected mainly due to the fact that trade and business activities dropped due to worsening law and order of the city. The PTC Karachi region's shortfall in revenue target was not much if we keep in view the troubled days that country's commercial capital witnessed during the year 1994–95. The remaining Rs 400 million gap in PTC Karachi region's revenue collection was because of the 'age old' problem of the non-payments of bills.[79]

The Sindh and the Federal governments collectively owed PTC a massive Rs 269 million amount. Out of this total, Rs 220 million were outstanding against the Sindh Government, while Rs 49 million against various federal government departments.

The rest of the money was outstanding against the private subscribers. The PTC Karachi Region's revenue collection for the year 1995–96 had also made a bad start because of the continuing killings and violence in Karachi. Against the set target of revenue collection of at least Rs 600 million per month, the PTC Karachi had collected only Rs 99.376 million in the first eleven days of July 1995. The chances that the monthly target would be met during July 1995 seemed remote as the on-going violence had again resulted in the non-distribution of bills and decline in trade and business activity.[80]

TABLE 9.5

Sources and Amounts of Financing the Consolidated Budget Deficit of Federal and Provincial Governments

	Consolidated budget deficit	Deficit as % of GDP	Banking System amount	%	Non amount %	Banking amount	External (Net) %
1980-81	14.6	5.3	2.4	16.1	4.5	30.9	7.7	52.9
1981-2	17.2	5.3	5.5	32.1	6.3	36.8	5.3	31.1
1982-3	25.7	7.1	6.1	23.9	14.4	56.0	5.2	20.1
1983-4	25.1	6.3	7.9	31.3	12.3	48.8	5.0	19.9
1984-5	36.8	7.7	18.7	50.9	12.9	35.0	5.2	14.1
1985-6	41.6	8.1	6.1	14.6	27.0	64.7	8.6	18.0
1986-7	46.7	8.2	10.9	23.4	27.4	58.6	8.4	18.0
1987-8	57.6	8.5	13.9	24.2	30.9	53.7	12.7	22.0
1988-9	56.9	7.4	0.8	1.4	37.9	66.6	18.2	32.0
1989-90	56.1	6.5	3.5	6.3	29.6	52.8	22.9	40.9
1990-91	89.2	8.7	43.5	48.6	23.7	26.6	22.1	24.8
1991-2	90.0	5.8	12.9	14.2	55.0	60.0	22.8	25.1
1992-3	107.7	8.0	62.6	58.1	19.7	18.3	25.4	23.6
1993-4(PA)*	90.7	5.8	12.9	14.2	55.0	60.0	22.8	25.1
1994-5(BE)**	71.9	4.0	15.0	20.9	26.3	36.6	30.6	42.6

*   Provisional Actual
**   Budget Estimates
Source: State Bank of Pakistan.

Budget Deficit

Table 9.5 explains the sources and amounts of financing the consolidated budget deficit of federal and provincial governments from the year 1980–81 to 1994–95. Net budget deficit was 20.6 per cent, 20 per cent, 32 per cent, 40.9 per cent, 25.1 per cent, 25.1 per cent, and 42.6 per cent in the financial years 1985–86, 1987–88, 1988–89, 1989–90, 1991–92, 1993–94 and 1994–95 respectively. These years were marked by violence, sectarian conflicts, political divide, arms proliferation, ethnic trouble, emergence of organized, white-collar and drug-related crime, growing incidents of kidnapping for ransom, and erosion of financial and commercial discipline.

FIGURE 9.3

Budget Deficit and Law and Order Situation

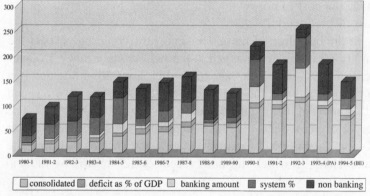

Source: Developed by the author with reference to the data in Table 9.5.

Thus the relationship between net budget deficit and law and order situation has been positive. Keeping in view the law and order situation in Karachi and elsewhere, various targets set in the budget 1995–96 looked ambitious particularly in view of our past performance. Overall economic growth rate had been fixed for 1995–96 at 6.5 per cent against 4.7 per cent achieved in 1994–95. In industry the target was 7.5 per cent while achievement remained at 5 per cent. In the investment areas it was fixed at 17.5 per cent as against achievement of 15.5 per cent. National savings were 15.6 per cent of the GDP in 1994–95. Budget deficit was aimed to be brought down to 5 per cent while it could be materialized in the 1995–96 to only 5.7 per cent and finally inflation, which was targeted at 7 per cent in 1994–95 but rose to 13.7 per cent. However, in the year 1995–96, again the target was fixed at 9.5 per cent.

Apart from the targets which appeared to be on the higher side, we were repeating the same mistakes which led to the failure in the realization of desired results during the year 1994–95. Hardly had the fiscal year 1995–96 started that the gas tariff was revised. Prices of petrol and petroleum products were enhanced by 5 per cent in the budget. Above all, the government gave a free hand to State-owned corporations to revise the power and telephone tariffs at will. It may be mentioned here that the State Bank of Pakistan lifted the cap on lending rates which made the cost of borrowing dearer, leading to an increase in the cost of production.

In the backdrop of these decisions how could one expect the inflation rate to be contained at 9.5 per cent as against 13.7 per cent in 1994–95? With the expected high inflation rate and low economic activity due to increase in the cost of borrowing and other adverse factors, the situation of stagflation continued. The target of net federal revenue receipts for 1995–96 was fixed at Rs 249.24 billion as against the revenue collected during the year 1994–95 which did not exceed Rs 220 billion by the end of the fiscal year.

Non-recovery of Stuck-up Loans

How is one to bring off recovery of stuck-up loans amounting to Rs 8.20 billion against 6799 defaulters? Whether yet another publication of defaulters list in newspapers shames them into paying their outstanding debts to lending banks and development financial institutions or it will prove to suggest that what the government could do is over.

Prior to 1970 the banking sector in Pakistan was as much efficient as it should be anywhere in the world. Capital base of banks was substantial. Their employees were efficient. Loans recovery was sound. Bankers were quick to ascertain safety, liquidity and profitability of funds lent to borrowers. The repayment of loans was guaranteed. Securities pledged against loans by borrowers were sufficient enough to recover outstanding loans. Irrespective of inadequate credit flow to needy sectors of the economy, the banking system had been performing well. It was nationalization of banks that changed the whole banking system in Pakistan. The capital base was eroded. Bank employee became inefficient. Rate of stuck-up loans increased. Merit in appointment and promotion of top bank officials as well as other employees was neglected. Attributes of 'safety, liquidity and profitability' changed to 'preference, public retaliating and monetary benefits' to bank officials.

The World Bank, in its report on Pakistan's financial sector in 1987, had raised the alarm situation on stuck-up loans. The report suggested public disclosure of defaulters as a last resort which became a reality in 1993 when a former Vice-President, Moeen Qureshi, a Pakistan national, was brought in Pakistan as chief executive of the country. The interim government, headed by Mr Qureshi, planned to put the whole economy, in general, and financial sector, in particular, on sound footing within weeks. It published loan defaulters list of banks and development financial institutions in newspapers on 28 August 1993 which showed stuck-up loans of greater than Rs 1 million to the tune of Rs 64 billion up to end 1991. The list was updated, revised and made public on 9 September 1993. The new list including stuck-up loans of greater than Rs 1 million till June 93 was to the tune of Rs 82.20 billion.[81]

FIGURE 9.4
Stuck-up Loans and Their Recovery up to End June 1995

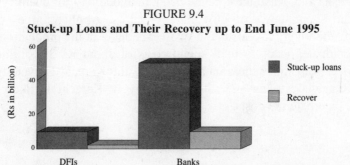

Source: Developed by the author on the basis of the data obtained from the National Banking Council of Pakistan.

The Government of Pakistan, given the typical political and social culture in the country, has striven for the recovery of stuck-up loans but proportion of recovery to outstanding debt remains grim. Position of outstanding loans and their recovery as on end of June 1995, showed that recovery rate was a mere 16.59 per cent. Out of total outstanding debts of Rs 71,430.1 million, only Rs 11,850.00 million had been recovered. Recovery rate by banks was mere 18.38 per cent and stood at 9.29 per cent in case of development financial institutions.[82]

The number of sick units increased from 2500 to 5000. Industrialists were actually thriving on the sickness of these units. Writing off a specific percentage of stuck-up loans and their restructuring and rescheduling cannot improve recovery rate since most defaulters obtained these loans as gifts to their influential status in Pakistan.

When the government in the 1970s changed objective of banks from 'private' to 'public' the whole scenario changed within weeks. Recently privatized Muslim Commercial Bank recovered stuck-up loans of Rs 1160.0 million out of the total outstanding debt of Rs 4670 million which shows recovery rate of 24.84 per cent whereas Habib Bank's loans recovery rate was mere 11.13 per cent as on end June 1995.[83]

Social Cost of Closure of Karachi University

Pasha and Wasti have developed a methodology for quantifying the social costs of university closures. Application of this methodology reveals that a two-years delay in the production of graduates leads to total social costs of about Rs 332 million, over four times the annual budget of the Karachi University.[84] Repeated strikes and virtual anarchy in Karachi is likely to exacerbate the costs.

Sick Units

In 1995, according to the Pakistan Banking Council standards, there were 3296 sick industrial units in the country.[85] During January 1994 to March 1995 banks and development financial institutions rescheduled and restructured loans of over 250 sick units.[86] It was expected that the reactivation of these units would help the country's economy. At that time the following twenty-nine units were expected to be privatized:[87]

Sindh Engineering; Republic Motors; Trailer Development Corp; General Refractories, Thatta Cement Associates; Cement Ravi Engg; Ittehad Chem; Textile Machinery; Pak Engg Co., Pakistan Factor; Hazara Phosphate Fert.; Lyallpur Chem. and Fert., National Fert. Marketing; Pak Arab Fert.; Pak Saudi Fert.; National Petrocarbon; Nat. Refinery; Pak Hi Oils; Nowshera Chem.; Shikarpur Rice Mills; Cotton Ginning Factory; Swat Ceramics; Progressive Papers; National Press Trust Newspapers and Malam Jabba (Tourist Ski Resort).

The development financial institutions had sanctioned 300 projects involving a sum of Rs 9398.272 million during January 1994 to February 1995.[88]

Size of Black Economy

It is difficult to measure the exact size of black economy. However, the fact remains that black money is not only eroding Pakistan's corporate sector but also fragmenting the country's economy by choking the artery of industrialization and leading to undocumented transactions where people either put their money in the bearer certificates or even under the pillow. Over the years Pakistan had witnessed little or no growth in terms of real income and savings though simultaneously there could be seen 2000cc cars racing down the streets, signifying a prosperous nation. The presence of a select elite in juxtaposition with the culture of indulging in fraudulent tactics has been instrumental in distorting smooth distribution of income, restricting savings, choking investments, and artificially restricting consumption.

According to an estimate the magnitude of black money in 1995 stood to around Rs 120 billion against the money supply of around Rs 350 billion.[89] Measured with reference to GDP the black money in 1995 was around 19 per cent of the GDP.[90] Under the exchange controls, if the rupee is overvalued, we can see black money through dollars. Similarly, if the interest rates are controlled, we see parallel market of credits. Not only is the tax evasion a vibrant portion of the country's economy but also the non-tax-paying sector, called the informal sector, is playing a major role in the development of the country.

Tax evasion in Pakistan has been generally caused by high tax rates, provision for tax exemptions to certain industries on account of their location resulting in unfair competition and price war, the deteriorating law and order situation, crumbling utility services, and preferential tax treatment towards certain segments of society, like the agricultural sector.

We can supplement the above mentioned observations with the obvious statement that black money created through smuggling, drug-related trade, tax evasion, and other corrupt practices is utilized for consumption and partly hoarding or investment. The black money not consumed is utilized in one or more of the following ways:

a) Utilized in business not recorded in books.
   It may be in the form of:
   i   Undeclared stocks;
   ii   Undeclared capital investment;
   iii   Unrecorded trade receivable;
   iv   Fictitious loans/payable.
b) Kept in cash in home safes or banks safe deposit vaults.
c) Converted into gold, diamonds or other valuables.
d) Deposited in Banks in the form of Fixed Deposit Receipts in fictitious names.
e) Converted into Bearer Bonds, Prize Bonds, Saving Certificates, Foreign Exchange Bearer Bonds, etc.

f) Invested in stock /shares.
g) Invested in real estate.
h) Used for private lending.
i) Used in furnishing bungalows, acquiring cars and other luxuries.

The ill effects of black money on the economy and the society are too well-known to warrant detailed discussion. In case of Pakistan these may be identified as:

a) Being a major cause of inflation.
b) Promoting wasteful consumption.
c) Generating further black wealth.
d) Creating currency-in-circulation problems.
e) Leading to the creation of black market for precious metals and stones thereby promoting their smuggling.
f) Instrumental in raising the prices of building materials.
g) Promoting holding of speculative stocks of commodities thereby causing their shortages.
h) Corrupting the banking system by encouraging deposits in fictitious names.
i) Making corruption a way of life in Pakistan.

National Savings

One can visualize the scope of national savings, which were targeted at 15.6 per cent in 1995–96 as against 14.8 per cent achieved in 1994–95. When the rate of inflation was running at 13.7 per cent officially and 18 to 20 per cent by independent source who would like to save for meagre 5 to 8 per cent in profit and loss account and even for 12 per cent in National Saving Schemes. The 12 per cent return means a negative yield in the wake of higher rate of inflation than return. In fact only those people are investing in the government saving schemes who have no other option. Bulk of the investment in national saving schemes comes from employees' provident funds, etc. where managers are least bothered about the rate of return.

There is a clear link between law and order situation and national savings. If the law and order situation is not satisfactory there may arise negative expectations that the future situation is going to be worse than the present one. In such a case people are likely to save more to meet the future contingencies expected from the overall situation. However, the channels of such savings, in view of low return offered by government-sponsored saving schemes, will be extra legal. This is exactly what happened in Pakistan. Lack of national saving schemes, which can offer at least 5 per cent over and above the rate of inflation, led to the emergence of fraudulent investment companies and co-operatives created only to swindle the people.

Apart from the above phenomenon, adverse law and order situation may slow down economic activity which results in lower growth in income thereby leading to lower savings. Thus a vicious circle is built up. For example, in the large scale manufacturing sector, growth rate was recorded at 2.7 per cent in 1994–95 as against the target of 4.5 per cent. It is surprising to note that the policy makers had set the target for the year 1995–96 at 6 per cent. Was there any logic to expect such a high growth rate when over 3000 industrial units had fallen sick and many more were to follow suit?

The gap between the national savings and investment is rising over time in Pakistan. National savings financed almost 79 per cent of total investment in 1980s. This figure declined to 74 per cent in the first eight years of the 1990s.[91] The saving-investment gap is currently financed through foreign savings thereby accumulating foreign debt. The high levels of external debt (48 per cent of GDP) and heavy debt servicing burden (62 per cent) of export earnings make continued reliance on foreign savings which is unsustainable over the medium term.[92] There is, therefore, a need for raising the savings rate in Pakistan. The public savings, initially financing growth, would stimulate economic activity in Pakistan, leading to increase in income, which would, in turn, increase household savings. For increasing public savings, a series of actions in the areas of tax policy, expenditure management, law and order and public sector enterprise reform would be needed.

Imports-Exports Gap

The state of trade and current accounts for the years 1990 to 1995 with the forecast for 1996 and current account deficit have been explained below with reference to Figures 9.5 and 9.6 respectively.

FIGURE 9.5
Trade and Current Accounts

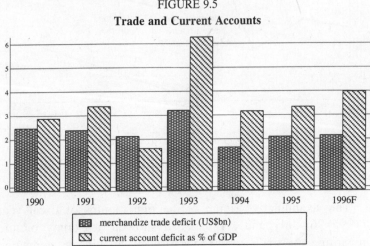

Source: IIF, Baring Securities.

The Balance of payments, during the month of August 1995, was not in Pakistan's favour as the exports came down and imports went up as compared with the corresponding period last year (1994–95). Similar was the case during the first two months of the fiscal year (1995–96) showing a trade gap of 608.355 million between exports and imports. According to the provisional figures, compiled by the Federal Bureau of Statistics for 1995–96, Pakistan's total export reduced by $9.637 million as compared with the corresponding month in 1994–95: from $561.708 in August 1996. On the other hand imports went up by $112.914 million: from $750.735 million of 1994–95 to $863.659 million in August 1996.[93]

FIGURE 9.6

Balance of Payments

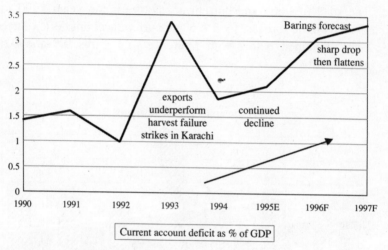

Current account deficit as % of GDP

Source: IIF, Baring Securities.

The accumulative figure of the first months of fiscal year (1995–96) July and August also showed a gloomy picture regarding the trade gap. The gap was widening as compared with the corresponding period 1994–95. In 1995–96 total exports of two months were of $1.070 billion while in 1994–95 Pakistan had exported goods worth $1.116 billion: showing a decrease of 146.169 million. Total imports during July and August 1995 were $1.678 billion as compared with $1.424 billion of 1994–95: showing an increase of $254.574 million. Out of twenty-two major items of export, rice, cotton fabric, guar and guar products, knitwear and towels showed an improvement while raw cotton, cotton yarn, fish and fish preparations, leather, raw wool, carpets, bed-wear, sports goods, ready-made garments, tarpaulin and canvas goods, other textile made-ups, synthetic textile fabrics, fruits, vegetables, leather and surgical goods depicted a downward trend. Main items of exports during August 1995 were cotton yarn ($94.772 million); cotton fabrics ($63.889 million); knitwear ($48.218 million); ready-made garments ($40.647 million); synthetic textile fabrics ($29.309 million); bed-wear ($26.666 million); rice ($24.093 million); leather manufactures ($17.355 million); fish and fish preparations ($14.359 million); towels ($14.359 million); other textile made-ups ($12.71 million); raw cotton ($5.214 million); sports goods ($5.102 million); and surgical instruments (4.784 million).[94]

The main items of imports during August 1995 were machinery, excluding transport equipment ($203.089 million); chemicals ($153.237 million); edible oil ($83.065 million); petroleum products ($75.603 million); petroleum crude ($42.954 million); iron and steel ($40.724 million); road motor vehicles ($30.461 million); synthetic fibre ($14.223 million); tea ($13.184 million); and paper and paper board ($9.988 million).[95]

The main causes for the decline in export were increase in raw cotton prices and input costs. These had a negative impact on the viability of mills, and resulted in a drop of approximately 100 million kgs of yarn production in 1994–95. This led to a state of financial squeeze on the textile industry. By June 1995, 114 units out of 493 units were closed. According to a survey, the main reasons for the closure were market recession, over-capitalization, unfeasible performance, uncertain viability, financial constraints, lack of modernization, inefficient management, labour problems, law and order situation and power failures.[96]

Thus it is obvious that socio-economic lawlessness alongwith unsatisfactory law and order situation contributed in the imports-exports gap. This observation gets further support by the result of a study conducted by the daily *News*.[97] Statistics from police and hospitals said that up to 602 people were killed during June and July 1995. Of the total number, 394 did not have any political affiliations. The rest — 206 victims of violence — included 71 from the law enforcement agencies, 42 from the

Mohajir Qaumi Movement (MQM), 17 from the MQM Haqiqi, 11 from the Pakistan People's Party (PPP), one each from the PPP Shaheed Bhutto Group and Islami Jamiat Talaba, and 65 from other smaller groups and organizations. Most of the innocent citizens were killed in cross firing in districts Central, East and West which are the most violence plagued areas of Karachi. Obviously, business and export activities suffered during this period.

Karachi Port Trust

Following is the description of the social and economic cost in terms of the activities of the Karachi Port Trust with reference to strike in June 1995. City disturbances left both the importers and exporters worried as the former had to pay huge demurrage on piling up of goods at the port and the latter lost millions thanks to the cancellation of export orders, trade sources said.[98] According to port sources the offices of pre-shipment inspection (PSI) companies remained closed during city strife resulting in delay in issuance of clean report of finding, by eight days of strike in June 1995. Adding further the sources said normally the PSI companies take three days to issue the CRF (Clean Report of Findings) but with the delay the importers had to pay a demurrage for eight days. Citing an example the sources stated that the CRF was to be issued to an importer on 3 July 1995 but owing to closure of the PSI offices it was issued on 10 July 1995, as result the importers had to pay a demurrage for eight days.

Secondly the disturbances also affected the working at the Customs office as it had thin attendance during the period. No processing of the consignments was done, the source added. According to Collectorate of Customs Appraisement the revenue collection under customs duty in the first ten days of the month, i.e. July 1995 showed a drastic reduction of 50 per cent as the Collectorate, which normally collects the revenue at an average of Rs 150 million per day, had lost more than Rs 500 million in the 10 days.[99] The Karachi Port Trust, on the other hand, was not going to waive off the demurrage incurred during the period of disturbance which would inflict a blow to the importer who in turn would pass it on to the consumer.

According to KPT sources the port ran normally during the strike days. The only work affected was the lifting of cargo by the importers that was not the fault of port. They said that the wharfage section remained open during that period and work was done despite the fact that there was thin attendance of the clerical staff.

The importers, however alleged that the cash department of the wharfage section was closed and was opened the next day for only three hours which, caused inconvenience to importers. Regarding export, the sources claimed that many orders amounting to millions of rupees had to be cancelled as no transportation was available. How can you risk your goods with such a dangerous situation where trucks were torched if found on road, said an exporter.

Due to the uncertain situation, many exporters cancelled the shipment and the orders.

Loss in Insurance Premium

The Insurance companies of Pakistan had witnessed a significant decrease of more than Rs 160 million in gross direct premium during the period 1994–95. This was announced by Munirul Haq, Chairman Insurance Association of Pakistan, while presenting a report in the 34th Annual General Meeting of the Insurance Association of Pakistan.

According to the report the total gross premium was Rs 5.29 billion in 1994 against Rs 5.46 billion in 1993. According to the break-up, from fire insurance it was about Rs 1.7 billion, from motor and working compensation about Rs 1.55 billion, from marine Rs 996 million, from tariff business Rs 4.3 billion and from non-tariff business Rs 982 million.

The decrease in gross premium which was 3 per cent less in 1994 as compared with 1993 was due to economic depression and particularly due to the law and order situation in Karachi.[100]

Conslusion

The forgoing discussion clearly indicates that the impact of lawlessness on the economic performance of Pakistan has been very significant both at the macro and micro levels. The economy of Pakistan is facing great challenges with limited options. The GDP growth rate was on a steady decline during 1988–96 and further declined to 3.5 per cent over the period between 1997 and 1999. The capital market, revenue collection, national savings, exports and other micro-economic indicators received big jerks from the year 1969 onwards. Particularly during the period from 1989 to 1996, on account of virtual anarchy, unbridled occurrence of terrorist attacks, violent acts and rising crime in Karachi and general socio-economic and political lawlessness in the country as whole, the losses suffered by selected micro-economic sectors were significant.

NOTES

1. Lamb, C. (1991), *Waiting for Allah: Pakistan's Struggle for Democracy*, New Delhi, Penguin Books.
2. Ibid.
3. KCCI (1995), *A Study on Production Losses During the Past Six Months*, Karachi Chamber of Commerce and Industry, Economic Wing, 1 July.
4. Ibid.
5. Ibid.
6. Ibid.
7. *The News*, Thursday, 22 June 1995, Lahore.
8. *The News*, Thursday, 2 July 1995, Lahore.
9. Ibid.
10. *Pakistan and Gulf Economist* (1995), Report on Karachi, March.
11. Ibid.
12. Ibid.

13. Ibid.
14. Ibid.
15. *The News*, Tuesday, 27 June 1995, Lahore.
16. Ibid.
17. Ibid.
18. State Bank of Pakistan (1992), Bulletin Karachi, February and December 1992.
19. Central Police Office, Karachi (1994), *Official Data*.
20. Ibid.
21. Ali, Amir (1994), *The Bloodiest Year for Karachiites*, Lahore, *The News*, 26 November.
22. FPCCI (1994), *Analysis of Stocks*. Report, Federation of Pakistan Chambers of Commerce and Industry, November.
23. Ibid.
24. Ibid.
25. KSE (1994), *Daily Situation Report*, Karachi Stock Exchange, 26 November.
26. Ibid.
27. KSE (1995), *Daily Situation Report*, Karachi Stock Exchange, 7 April 1995.
28. Ibid.
29. Ibid.
30. KSE (1995), *Daily Situation Report*, Karachi Stock Exchange, 9 April 1995.
31. Ibid.
32. Ibid.
33. Ibid.
34. KSE (1995), *Daily Situation Report*, Karachi Stock Exchange, 24 April 1995.
35. Ibid.
36. *The News*, Thursday, 20 April 1995. Lahore.
37. *Jang*, Tuesday, 25 April 1995, Lahore.
38. *The News*, Thursday, 20 April 1995 Lahore.
39. KSE (1995), *Daily Situation Report*, Karachi Stock Exchange, 27 June 1995.
40. *The News*, Wednesday, 28 June 1995, Lahore.
41. Ibid.
42. Ibid.
43. KSE (1995), *Daily Situation Report*, Karachi Stock Exchange, 28 June 1995.
44. Ibid.
45. KCCI (1995), *Survey Report, 1995*, The Research Cell, Karachi Chamber of Commerce and Industry.
46. *The News*, Thursday, 29 June 1995, Lahore.

47. KSE (1995), *Daily Situation Report*, Karachi Stock Exchange, 16 July 1995.
48. Ibid.
49. Ibid.
50. Ibid.
51. *Recorder*, 18 July 1995.
52. *The News*, Monday, 17 July 1995, Lahore.
53. Ibid.
54. Ibid.
55. Ibid.
56. KSE (1995), *Interview with Nadim Ahmad Siddiq and Khadim Ali Shah Bukhari*.
57. Ibid.
58. Ibid.
59. KSE (1995), *Daily Situation Report*, Karachi Stock Exchange, 17 July 1995.
60. State Bank of Pakistan (1995), *Bulletin*, Karachi, June, July and August 1995.
61. State Bank of Pakistan (1995), *Bulletin*, Karachi, September 1995.
62. KSE (1995), *Bulletin*, Karachi Stock Exchange, July 1995.
63. Government of Pakistan (1998–9), *Economic Survey*, 1998–99, Finance Division, Economic Adviser's Wing, Islamabad.
64. Statistical Scale for News-Orix Confidence Barometer very high 80% or more high to very high 70% to 79% moderate to high 60% to 69% low to moderate 50% to 59% very low to low, 30% to 49% very low less than 30%
65. The News Journal (1999), *The News Investor's Business and Financial Journal*, June, 1999, p. 2
66. Ibid.
67. *The Nation*, Wednesday, 28 June 1995, Lahore.
68. Government of Pakistan (1995), *Establishment Division*, Islamabad.
69. Government of Pakistan (1995), *Central Board of Revenue*, Islamabad.
70. Ibid.
71. Ibid.
72. Ibid.
73. Ibid.
74. *The News*, Thursday, 13 April 1995, Lahore.
75. Government of Pakistan (1995), Central Board of Revenue, Islamabad.
76. Ibid.
77. *The News*, Sunday, 16 April 1995, Lahore.
78. PTC (1995), Briefing, The Pakistan Telecommunication Corporation, Karachi.
79. Ibid.
80. Ibid.

81. PBC (1993), Pakistan Banking Council.
82. SBP (1995), *Annual Report*, State Bank of Pakistan.
83. Ibid.
84. Pasha, H.A. & Wasti, S.A. (1993), 'Social Costs of University Closures', *The Pakistan Development Review* 32-4, Part II (Winter 1993), pp. 677–85.
85. National Assembly of Pakistan (1995), Replies to questions in the National Assembly of Pakistan by State Minister for Finance Shahabudin, Wednesday, 8 March 1995, Islamabad.
86. Ibid.
87. Ibid.
88. Ibid.
89. IBA (1995), *IBA Seminar Report*, Karachi, 11 April 1995.
90. Ibid.
91. World Bank (1999), *Household Savings in Pakistan*, by Dr. Ashfaque H. Khan and Dr. Zafar Moeen Nasir, Washington DC, July.
92. Ibid.
93. Government of Pakistan (1995), *Federal Bureau of Statistics*, August, 1996.
94. Government of Pakistan (1995), Ministry of Commerce.
95. Ibid.
96. Ibid.
97. *The News*, Wednesday, 2 August 1995, Lahore.
98. *The News*, Thursday, 13 July 1995, Lahore.
99. Government of Pakistan (1995), Central Board of Revenue.
100. Ibid.

10

COST-EFFECTIVE INDIGENOUS COMMUNITY POLICING MODEL[1]

Analysis of the impact of lawlessness on economic development in the previous chapters makes it clear that there exists a need for ensuring a system of law enforcement commensurate with the requirements of self-sustained economic growth. The police, being the agency responsible for prevention and detection of crime, should not only be efficient and accountable but also people friendly. Policing in all the four provinces of Pakistan, however, is governed by the Police Act (V) of 1861. This Act was aimed at administering a static, immobile and backward rural society living in villages and small towns. It envisages exercise of authority without local accountability. It presupposes a society without any constitution, without basic and fundamental rights, without organized public opinion and without mass media projecting and agitating the public interest.[2] Policing in the subcontinent was based on a paramilitary, paternalistic, colonial, empire-building and capitalistic rape of a colony. In Pakistan retrogressive steps with mounting distrust of the police and changes in recruitment policies with political considerations demoralized and frustrated the police personnel.

Policing in Pakistan has thus always faced a crisis of legitimacy. The public perceives the police as cruel, callous and corrupt while the police regard the public as illegitimate. This is a natural outcome not only of the colonial past but also of a tendency on part of successive dictatorial regimes to deviate from 'due process' to perpetuate their power. The legal principle of rule of law, which gives the practical expression to citizen's rights and obligations and determines the style of policing, was the first casualty.

The situation aggravated further in 1991 when rising incidents of breach of peace, violence, murder, kidnapping for ransom and robberies created a general sense of insecurity. Added to this were problems related to the fear of crime, public concern for law and order reflected in the print media and disappointment with police performance. It was in this background that I took over charge as the Deputy Inspector General of Police, Gujranwala Range, on 3 August 1991.

Realizing that immediate action was called for and law enforcement agencies could not operate in a vacuum, I adopted a strategy of policing by consultation and devised an indigenous, cost-effective model of community policing. This experiment (implemented during the period from 3 August 1991 to 1 August 1993) helped build up a reservoir of public support, punctuated by admiration hitherto unknown to the police. An integrated system envisaging multi-agency approach and broad-based consultation radically changed public perception of police performance, improved police morale, reduced fear of crime, and incidents of violence and created an environment congenial for effective interest identification, interest formulation, and interest integration. This chapter explains the basic concept of this model and Chapter 11 narrates the success story of its practical implementation.

Why Cost-effective Policing?

The police are responsible for the protection of life, liberty and property of citizens. For the performance of this basic function the resources of the police, in advanced countries, have always been quite substantial. Computerized data-bases covering a large variety of policing functions, especially incident logging, control and command operations, automatic fingerprint recognition with the ability to make a million comparisons in hours, helicopters and various types of photographic and video equipment are used by the police forces in these countries. Voluntary public resource-input has supplemented budgetary allocations.

The police in Pakistan, on the other hand, suffer from the limitations arising out of resource-content. Resource inadequacy, large population and budgetary constraints characterize the economy of the country. Not only is there a huge public debt and the concomitant debt servicing draining out the niggardly resources available with the exchequer, there is also rampant corruption found all over the country. The bad debts have crossed the one-hundred billion rupees mark. Exports, too, have not picked up and the inflow of Foreign Direct Investment (FDI) has almost dried up. The overall growth of the industrial sector, too, suffered a serious setback due to ethnic strife in Sindh. Agricultural sector has shown some progress but its overall thrust continues to remain traditional rather than dynamic. The economy has, in fact, lost buoyancy. The cost of controlling crime and conducting investigations is, however, colossal. There is, therefore, a need for not only a substantial increase in the budgetary allocation for the police but also adding to it the resource-input of the community. The development of the community's self-policing role ensures cost-effective policing because it augments limited police resources. Thus the addition of the community's resources to police resources definitely reduces the burden on the public exchequer and make the concept of police performance commensurate with the value for money thereby reducing overall policing costs a reality.

Role of Public

Issues pertaining to lawlessness, especially rising crime involving huge socio-economic costs, makes the anxiety of the people about the steady growth of crime and its intrusion into their lives understandable. The causes of crime are complex and multifarious. Everyone agrees that the criminal justice system (comprising the police, courts, prison and probation services, and the prosecution), on its own cannot hope to succeed in reversing the upward trend in crime figures. The underlying causes of crime lie within society itself, but if the concern of the public can be transferred into positive action then much can be achieved.

Within the criminal justice system, the police are basically responsible for the prevention and detection of crime implying, of course, the protection of life and property and the preservation of public peace. To perform these functions in accordance with the fundamental principles of 'consent and balance' and 'independence and accountability' police forces in advanced countries have evolved strategies ensuring close involvement of the public in their crime control functions. This is so because information flowing from the public to the police is of vital importance in the crime solving function of policing. If adequate information is provided to pinpoint the culprit fairly accurately, the crime will be resolved, if not it is almost certain not to be. This is borne out by various studies, whether conducted by observation,[3] analysis of records[4] or both.[5]

Not only does this pinpointing of the crucial importance of initial information emphasize the central role of the public in the clearing up of offences, but also the important part played by the uniform branch.[6] A high proportion of crimes were solved immediately because either the offenders were caught in the act, or were still at the scene of the crime when the police arrived, or their identity was given to the police by the victim or a witness.[7] Of the rest a high proportion were cleared up through questioning of offenders who admit other offences to be 'taken into consideration' (tic). Some studies suggest that as many as 40 per cent property offences are cleared in this way[8] although Steer and Bottomley and Coleman found a lower proportion of tics (20 and 25 per cent respectively).[9]

Thus the majority of offenders are detected in circumstances that do not involve the exercise of detective skills. The cases involving anything approximating 'real detective work' are about 25 per cent of Steer's sample, 23 per cent of Mawby's, and 13 per cent of Bottomley and Coleman's. But it may be added that 'although the police discover only a small proportion of offences they are often of a special kind, for example, some kind of drug offences which are unlikely ever to be reported by members of the public; motoring and other regulatory offences are also of this kind. And in dealing with organized professional crime, the police play a critically important role.'[10]

From these studies it may be safely said that where the community is supportive, police requests for members of the public who saw the incident concerned, or 'saw anything suspicious' to come forward, can be expected to yield results. In such a community the close relationship between the police and the public as regards the sharing of information and thus the likelihood of successful detection act as a deterrent upon the potential criminal. After the event, it is the same close sharing of information that will lead investigative policing to a likely successful conclusion.[11] The more the information the more the police can begin their investigation 'following actual leads and the less the recourse to stereotypes becomes the basis for starting investigation'.[12]

Since the adoption of 'policing by objectives' strategy and the Home Office Circular 114/83 (on Manpower, Effectiveness and Efficiency in the Police Service) the tendency in the police forces of England and Wales to give prominence to crime prevention through public involvement and community-based policing in setting goals and objectives is clearly discernible. This approach is backed at an institutional level by 'multi-agency' policing, crime prevention panels, and other police-initiated forums where the community's self-policing role has been developed. In addition, many forces, particularly the Metropolitan Police in the Newman years since his appointment in 1982, had also seen 'a greater media profile, with an enlargement of public relations department and the use of videos and glossy materials to get the police's message across'.[13]

Among the key devices for public involvement were consultative committees (with lay visitors reporting back to them), neighbourhood watch, volunteers, crime prevention panels, victim support schemes, greater use of the special constabulary (and attempts to recruit more blacks into it).

The 'multi-agency' approach involves police collaboration with other agencies, 'social, economic, cultural and educational' to develop solutions which address the root causes rather than the symptoms of crime. The assumption is that through better understanding of all the facts of any type of anti-social behaviour, the community, including the police, should be able to produce constructive, co-operative ventures to prevent or reduce the phenomenon, thus avoiding costly reactive policing.[14]

Various studies conducted in Pakistan, though limited in scope, do mirror a kind of 'conflict' and hostility between the police and the public. The reasons are not hard to find. When the people were fighting for their independence from a colonial rule, the police were used to subjugate them. The police in all the four provinces of Pakistan were thus policing without consent. Failure of the political institutions to develop in the aftermath of independence and break-down of the system at short intervals did not create conditions conducive for the legitimacy of the police. The situation, more or less, remains the same today. The community does not support the police because it sees them socially and politically oppressive and in no way fulfilling a protective role. The flow of information from the community to the police is most often involuntary. As a consequence, an important part of police activity aimed at obtaining information, comes to be regarded as the random harassment of the community at large, irrespective of involvement in crime. For efficiency, the necessary information has to be prised out of the community, often by force. This is done by the field officers either though a network of 'paid informers', payments being made out of money extracted from parties always willing to pay bribes to harass their opponents through the agency of the police or high profile activities such as stopping people randomly in the streets, raiding premises, taking people in for questioning, not on the basis of information already received, but as part of an attempt to secure information. This stop and search method creates deterrence and gives information at the expense of public alienation.

The pressure to solve crime is indeed very great. In the absence of any institutional framework of community policing or crime prevention through the willing co-operation of the public, smooth flow of information is replaced by arbitrariness. The result is criminal stereotypes, unscientific investigation, free use of preventive sections of law and a methodology incompatible with the dictates of democratic society. The convenience with which the magistracy can throw blame on the police often for collective or even individual failures, the appalling working conditions implying frustration and fatigue, the frequency of rebuke from the media, a willingness of the establishment to mistrust them and attempts by the rich and influential to claim immunity from the law, result in encouraging the police functionaries to ignore the need for a workable, open and co-operative attitude towards the public. In Pakistan, to use Lea and Young's phrase, police have become 'marginalized' from the community.[15]

It is against this background that the role of police in curbing crime becomes important. Generally speaking, internal groups and individuals either on their own or in collaboration commit crime with external interests, and the methods used by criminals are sometimes conventional and sometimes innovative. Thus, police administration is in constant need of reviewing its concepts and its operational techniques. However, in the ultimate analysis, police cannot cope effectively with culprits or solve crime mysteries without the willing and conscientious co-operation of the public at large.

Are police officials aware of the gravity of the crime situation in Pakistan? Have they ever thought of replacing the hatred against police by inspiring-confidence and respect? How far are they equipped to adjust to the requirements of fast-changing technological environment? These are some of the issues intended to be dealt with in this analysis. The idea is to present a policy package for improving police effectiveness in Pakistan. The proposed policy package is related to the totality of measures encompassing strategy and design for an effective and efficient police force in an emerging progressive and democratic set-up in the body-politic of Pakistan.

Pakistan's police administration is in urgent need of developing its own confidence building strategy in the light of our peculiar socio-cultural circumstances as well as successful crime control experiences of other countries. The rising crime wave in the country in early 1991 created a lot of embarrassment for the government and also a sense of insecurity in the minds of citizens and led to doubts about the competence of the police. This situation required not only organizational changes in police force but also positive interaction with the community.

It was in this background that the Gujranwala Range Police made a new crime control experiment. The Gujranwala Division contained more than ten million inhabitants and had been infested with heinous crime of all types. The basic approach of this experiment was voluntary involvement of local communities in crime control measures. It yielded highly satisfactory results. There was an appreciable fall in crimes of various types, particularly crime against property.

Before discussing the experiment in detail let us first examine the concept behind it.

Community Policing

Community policing implies control of crime with the willing support of public. It visualizes a police force, which tries to keep itself close to, and in tune with the communities it serves. It also assumes the presence of a conscientious public willing to identify itself with police action in providing peace and security to the citizens.

To enlist public support for police operations is not an easy task, especially because of their long standing reservations about the honesty and efficiency of the police. There is also the question of defining the term public, which apparently suggests the presence of a homogeneous community. This may or may not be true. Community policing is not an alternative to law enforcement but a condition for its success. It also implies willing support of public for police operations in controlling crime effectively.

The very phrase 'public support' suggests the presence of a homogeneous community. The assumption is difficult to sustain in reality. Even if it is true, feelings of support may not always run evenly within a group, but will probably rise and fall according to an individual's direct experience, word-of-mouth information and reports in print and electronic media. Other factors that may influence the nature and degree of co-operation, which individuals may extend to police in their investigation of a crime include visible effectiveness of police actions rather than mere assurances of safety, people's perception about police effectiveness and fairness based on their own personal experiences and identity and sharing of aspirations between the police and the community for curbing crime.

The identity factor is comparatively more important. It includes shared aspirations for the reduction of crime in general as well as specific to an area, and a mutual desire for improved quality of life. The extent to which an observer agrees with the police viewpoint will condition his perception of the fairness and legitimacy of police action. The police, on their part, must also identify themselves with the community's thinking. There must, additionally, be real attempts to become more effective; it is just not enough to be satisfied with publicizing the existing levels of effectiveness.

Explaining the community policing model in Devon and Cornwall police area, John Alderson, former Chief Constable of Devon and Cornwall Constabulary, described it as 'the foundation and spirit of preventive policing'. 'The concept', he wrote, 'acknowledges that policing generally in our time must seek a fresh ethical basis and come to rest on a form of social contract between (the) police and (the) public.' It also 'acknowledges', according to him, 'that police resources are finite and therefore too heavy a reliance on police power to solve basic social problems is unwise.'[16]

The essentials of effective public relationships by the police were outlined by Alderson in terms of identification of community policing with the basic preventive philosophy of the police with universal character, drawing of all localities into a dialogue on the nature of policing required, an analysis and propagation of crime patterns in public meetings, initiation and maintenance of a major police/public educational programme, posting of a significant proportion of beat strength as community constables, and finally, a co-operation between residents, voluntary and statutory bodies and the police to reduce fear of crime, and tension and to increase social concern including that for victims.[17]

It may, however, be mentioned that all such initiatives have limitations. A recent attack on community policing alleged that cops, in the garb of crime prevention officers, were acting in the front line of an intelligence system. They were, it was contended, not only watching crime but also watching very ordinary people in every day life. The result was that information about one in every four residents of a street was being collected.[18] In response, James Anderton, the Spokesman of the Association of Chief Police Officers, asserted that the neighbourhood watch scheme and preventive policing were designed to enable citizens to look after each other and provide the police with every bit of information to bring down crime. He also claimed a right to silence with regard to the police *modus operandi* of collecting and collating information.[19] Accordingly, a standard complaint is the lack of 'democratic control' of the police, which is often directed at community policing being an attempt at the surveillance and control of communities...under the guise of police offering advice and assistance...community policing offers no prospect of greater democratic control of the police and policing.[20] But it may be argued that such a reaction fails to take into account the purpose of policing. 'Policing can never operate entirely consensually—it is a mode of dealing with conflicts through the potential use of legitimate force.'[21]

There is no doubt that community consultation, recruitment from ethnic minority groups, crime prevention, community and race relations training, lay visiting schemes, educational programmes (such as Avon and Somerset Police Scheme for training young offenders as car mechanics) and co-operation with other agencies are initiatives which have, despite the criticisms from some quarters, definitely 'drawn the police into greater dialogue with the community than was formerly the practice'.[22]

Instruments of Community Participation

Under the prevailing law and order situation, it is the element of fear, which keeps people at a distance from the police. They are unwilling to provide information or help in the detection of a crime. On the other hand, delay in responding to calls in need and mishandling of cases by the police has created a distance between the police and the public.

If the police are able to remove fears by being helpful and careful in their relationship with citizens and are easily accessible in times of need and frequently visible, the chances are that people will involve themselves in the crime control tasks of the police. The police should, by their actions, demonstrate that they are accountable to and accountable for the people they serve. A country's socio-political framework consists of many elements. It is necessary to seek the co-operation of all these elements simultaneously and in an organized way.

Keeping in view our peculiar socio-cultural background, in my capacity as the Deputy Inspector General of Police of the Gujranwala Range, through broad-based consultation with a cross-section of society, I tried to evolve our own model of community policing. According to the consensus emerging from these discussions community participation in crime prevention can be elicited in the following ways:

Liaison with Elected Representatives

Part of keeping in tune with public sentiments in a democratic and complex society is interaction with its nominated or elected representatives like Members of National and Provincial Assemblies, Senators and Councillors. A close liaison between the police and public representatives is necessary to ensure their support in police operations and better understanding of problems relating to their constituents. Public representatives can play a significant role in bringing an end to old rivalries, which in many cases, result in an on-going series of murders and attempts to murder.

Role of Local Bodies

Local Bodies, in close collaboration with the police, can play a significant role in the improvement of traffic arrangements in urban areas and small towns by removing encroachments and providing proper stands for automobiles and slow moving vehicles and proper lighting in streets.

Police-Ulema Co-operation

In a country like ours, where sectarianism often assumes serious proportions, maintenance of peace, particularly during the month of Muharram, becomes a real test for the police. Special efforts are made to involve local religious bodies in peacekeeping efforts, including the formation of local peace committees comprising influential and respectable persons of various sects. The support of the 'ulema' can also be enlisted in crime prevention efforts and in educating the community to combat drug addiction and other social evils. This exercise of police-ulema co-operation needs to be further strengthened in preventing crimes of all kinds.

Neighbourhood Watch

This implies the establishment of a close and interactive relationship between policemen assigned to specific beats or rounds and citizens residing or working in such beat areas. This type of relationship creates a sense of responsibility and commitment in both parties and makes the area safe for commercial and residential purposes. The scope of neighbourhood watch can be widened to include formation of community liaison groups for determining public priorities, undertaking regular neighbourhood foot patrols, initiation of public awareness programmes through briefings on emergency telephone numbers, protection of personal possessions and motor vehicles, and prevention of the use and detection of unlicensed arms and provision of an ambulance service by the police.

Citizen-Police Advisory Councils

Citizen-Police Advisory Councils can be formed in order to provide an atmosphere of close co-operation between the police and citizens. These can help in conducting surveys aimed at evaluating public perception of crime seriousness and improving the work and image of the police.

Police Role in Hours of Trial

The police force can render help to citizens during emergencies such as floods and earthquakes. Thus, it not only protects the people against the ordinary acts of criminals but also renders them necessary help and assistance during natural calamities.

Improvement in Police Behaviour

The public's low esteem for the police is generally due to their officious behaviour. This is a legacy of the colonial days when the police in the subcontinent acted as a paramilitary force and policing was done to promote the empire-building objectives of the British colonialists. The police adopted offensive attitude towards the 'natives' and policemen came to be considered ill-mannered, corrupt and devoid of sympathy for their own countrymen.

However, because of the evoluting concepts of policing, a change in the behaviour of police is taking place. Emulating the examples of police martyrs and with public support and co-operation, an increasing number of police personnel are determined to gain a status of respect and honour in society through their good behaviour with the law abiding citizens. The police are adapting themselves to the new role of partners in law-enforcement rather than the sole enforcers of law. The perception is strengthening the philosophy of community policing.

Involvement of Schools

An important aspect of community policing is liaison between police officers and schools. This is crucial because police officers can offer guidance on the need to protect students from danger, be it road safety or drugs. The police can also make young people think constructively about the role of police in society. School children can be made aware of the hazards of drug addiction, responsibilities of civic nature, constructive role of police in society and measures to be adopted against social evils, like child abuse, through comprehensive programmes by holding talks, lectures, film shows, etc. in schools.

Courses on law and police can be introduced in schools curricula with a view to keeping young people away from crime by indoctrinating them with law-abiding attitudes and behaviour patterns. Talks and discussions on the electronic media by police and law enforcing officers can also bring the police close to young citizens.

Conclusion

The foregoing discussion envisages the role of community-based policing as part of an effective strategy of crime prevention. It emphasizes public participation in prevention and detection of crime through information and education for people and involvement of various segments of society in activities related to community safety. It also facilitates public identification with police tasks and ensures a greater degree of police responsiveness to public demands. Added to these positive trends is the addition of the resources of the community to the meagre resources of the police. The intertwined perception and action of the police and the public results in cost-effective policing which is a basic requirement of resource-poor economies like Pakistan.

NOTES

1. Parts of this chapter have been drawn from my book, *The Punjab Police in a Comparative Perspective* (1989), published by the Progressive Publishers, Lahore.
2. Government of Pakistan (1985), Aslam Hayat Police Committee Report, Islamabad, Ministry of the Interior, Government of Pakistan. Para 49 d, e, f.
3. Reiss, Jr., A.J. (1971), *The Police and the Public*, New Haven, Yale University Press. Chatterton, M. (1976), 'Police in Social Control', King, J. (ed.), *Control without Custody*, Cambridge, Institute of Criminology. Sanders, W. (1977), *Detective Work*, Glencoe, Free Press. Ericson, R. (1982), *Reproducing Order: A Study of Police Patrol Work*, Toronto, University of Toronto Press.
4. Mawby, R. (1979), *Policing the City*, Farnborough, Gower. Bottomley, A.K. and Coleman, C. (1981), *Understanding Crime Rates*, Farnborough, Gower. Burrows, J. and Tarling, R. (1982), *Clearing up Crime*, London, Home Office Research Unit. Mitchell, B. (1984), 'The Role of the Public' in *Criminal Detection Criminal Law Review*, August.
5. Greenwood, P., Chaiken, J., and Petersilia, J. (1977), *The Criminal Investigation* Process, Lexington, Mass., D.C. Health. Steer, D. (1980),

  Uncovering Crime, Royal Commission on Criminal Procedure, Study 7, London, H.M.S.O.

6. Reiner, R. (1986), *The Politics of the Police*, London, Wheatsheaf Books Ltd., Harvester Press, 1986.
7. 57 per cent in Steer's study and 62 per cent in Mawby's were solved in this way.
8. Mawby, R. (1979), *Policing the City*, Farnborough, Gower.
9. Steer, D.(1980), *Uncovering Crime*, Royal Commission on Criminal Procedure, Study 7, London, H.M.SO.
10. Ibid.
11. Lea, J. and Young, J. (1984), *What is to be done about Law and Order?* Harmondsworth, Penguin Books.
12. Ibid.
13. *Policing London* (1987), March/April, Vol. 4.
14. Metropolitan Police (1980), *Commissioner's Report 1980*, p. 8.
15. Lea, J. and Young, J. (1984), *What is to be done about Law and Order?* Harmondsworth, Penguin Books.
16. Alderson, J. (1981), 'Community Cops', Letter to the Editor, *New Society*, 207, London.
17. Ibid.
18. BBC Television (1987), Secret Society, BBC2 Television on 5 May 1987.
19. Ibid.
20. Gordon P. (1984), 'Community Policing: Towards the Local Police State', *Critical Social Policy*, 10, Summer.
21. Reiner, R. (1985-86), *The Politics of the Police*, London, Wheatsheaf Books Ltd., Harvester Press, 1986.
22. Baldwin, R. (1987), 'Why Accountability?' *British Journal of Criminology*, 27(1), pp. 97–105.

11

EXPERIMENT OF COST-EFFECTIVE POLICING IN GUJRANWALA

This chapter elaborates the main contours of the experiment of cost-effective policing in Gujranwala Range during the period from 3 August 1991 to 1 August 1993. While explaining the strategy of the experiment this chapter also mentions important case histories with a view to giving a clear idea of the outcome of the exercise. The success story of the implementation of this indigenous cost-effective community policing model can serve as a guide for policy-makers desiring to institutionalize this concept.

Features of the Experiment

The idea of introducing community policing has been present in the minds of police officers but it was put into practice, on experimental basis, only in August 1991 in the thickly populated administrative division of Gujranwala. This Division lies in the province of Punjab and is inhabited by more than 10 million people. It had remained infested with crimes of all types for a long period. With the involvement of community in anti-crimes operations, a significant reduction took place in unlawful activities. The main features of community policing, as in vogue in Gujranwala Division from 3 August 1991 to 1 August 1993, are as under:[1]

A system of police mobiles was introduced to provide service at the citizens' doorsteps within minutes of their call. For this purpose, a special telephonic facility was provided. Similarly, to improve police visibility and prevent crime, a squad of 120 motorcycles was raised. This helped in nabbing gangs of robbers. In order to prevent thefts and robberies in market places, market duty commandos were posted at critical spots. This not only made shopping safe and secure but also resulted in the reduction in incidents of eve teasing.

Police meetings with elected representatives became an important feature of community policing. These meetings helped to redress grievances and problems of the constituents of the public representatives. The elected representatives provided useful assistance in police developmental projects out of their discretionary funds. For instance, district local bodies made substantial contribution by way of financial aid to the families of eight police officials who laid down their lives in one of the bloodiest encounters with desperadoes at Ojala Kalan in February 1992. As a permanent tribute to the memory of these police officers and men, a library known as Shohada-e-Ojala Kalan Library was established in the Model Town Police Station, Gujranwala. Various organizations donated books to this library which gave the police station building the look of a social welfare centre and a place of tranquillity, safety, and peace.

In order to emphazise the need to observe traffic rules, the Gujranwala Police arranged a big rally in collaboration with children of various schools. Similarly, in order to create better understanding between the police and young citizens of Pakistan, lectures and film shows were arranged in educational institutions. Police officers also frequently participated in television programmes to answer questions from youngsters.

A Citizens-Police Advisory Council was set up. It provided for close co-operation between the police and the citizens. It educated the public in crime prevention measures and also helped in conducting surveys aimed at evaluating public perception of crime seriousness and the effectiveness of crime control measures. The survey results enabled the police to fix priorities to be adopted for crime control. For instance, a survey conducted during 1992 showed that criminal assaults on women topped the list of crimes which were considered most serious by the people, followed by dacoity and drug trafficking. The police objectives for the year 1993 were accordingly designed.

A Neighbourhood Watch Programme was started in Model Town 'A' Block of Gujranwala city. Local residents and the police worked out a *modus operandi* to launch joint drives against crime and enhance awareness of crime prevention measures. The Gujranwala police exhorted the people to use invisible security marking on their valuables and writing of registration numbers on the wind screens of their motor vehicles through sand blast technique as a protection measure.

The Neighbourhood Watch Programme produced positive results.[2] The Gujranwala Chamber of Commerce and Industry declared the in-charge of the Neighbourhood Watch Programme, DSP Mushtaq Hussain, as 'Policeman of the Year 1992' and awarded him a shield and a ticket for performing '*Umra*'. Regular meetings of police officials and the Chamber of Commercial and Industry helped improve mutual co-operation.

The Gujranwala Range Police rendered yeoman service during the 1992 floods by rescuing hundreds of stranded persons and providing them assistance in their hour of trial. In Gujrat District, one Sub-Inspector of Police saved at least 200 persons from drowning, acting alone with one boat. On receipt of information on 10 September 1992 that the water level was rising in the Chenab, Sub-Inspector Sultan Ahmed (who was then posted as Station House Officer of Police Station Jalalpur Jattan District Gujrat) immediately despatched rescue parties to the villages of Dhol, Chopala, Nat, Peer Bera, Marri Warriachan, Majoki, Pinyar, Bhelpur, Changawali, Kaan, Mohla, Lalooke,

Kotli Shahani, Shahbazpur, Nabipur, Noora Minrala, Pindi Jehani, Pindi Loharan, Mohata Sher Ali, Mohana Khas, and Mahiwal. The first task was to inform the villagers of the approaching calamity and to assist them in moving over to safe places. On 11 September 1992, at 9 a.m., noticing that village Pinyar was surrounded by water eight feet deep on all sides and about 200 stranded persons, including men, women and children, had taken refuge on trees and on roof-tops of houses which had not yet collapsed, the Sub-Inspector, with the assistance of Mujahid Kaleem, a local councillor, arranged a motor boat and immediately rushed to village Pinyar. Meanwhile, through a wireless message, he instructed the police party at Shahbazpur to arrange three manually operated boats. The needful was done and these boats were deployed to swiftly shift 150 persons (50 men, 60 women, 10 elderly persons and 30 children) to safe places.

This rescue operation had hardly been completed when information was received that about hundred persons were stranded in Chak Nabipur where all except three houses had collapsed. Sub-Inspector Sultan Ahmed, along-with ASI Ali Akbar, Head Constable Muhammad Qayyum and seven constables, left for Nabipur leaving another contingent to look after the evacuees from Pinyar. Nabipur presented a scene of complete devastation. Every house, which had remained intact, was full of water. All the stranded persons were shifted in three manually operated boats to safe places. This rescue operation was the outcome of the initiative and risk undertaken by the local police. On 16 September 1992, the then Prime Minister of Pakistan, Muhammad Nawaz Sharif, while touring the flood affected areas on a helicopter, landed at Pinyar. The flood affectees narrated to him the story of effective and efficient rescue operation launched by Sub-Inspector Sultan Ahmed and his colleagues. The public support, punctuated by a wave of admiration hitherto unknown for the police, deeply moved the Prime Minister of Pakistan who immediately announced the promotion of Sub-Inspector Sultan Ahmed to the rank of Inspector. Subsequently the Pakistan Television telecast his interview. This definitely helped improve the image of the Police.

In many cases large amounts of stolen money were recovered and returned to rightful owners. A perceptible change in the behavioural pattern of the police was also discernible. The Gujranwala Range Police adopted the motto of 'Truth and Integrity' and tried to gain a status of respect and honour through deeds of public service. On 6 January 1992, some unknown culprit stole away cash and prize bonds amounting to Rs 830,000 from a shop belonging to Abdul Wahid, a Cloth Merchant of Gujranwala, who lodged a complaint with the Kotwali Police Station, Gujranwala. On the night between 6/7 January 1992, Head Constable 1428 Muhammad Boota and Constable 1639 Muhammad Aslam were patrolling the Chohan Road when, at 2 a.m., they spotted a rickshaw coming from the direction of the Jinnah Road. They stopped the rickshaw and found one Zulfiqar alias Jappi, a Kashmiri resident of Bhatti Gate, Lahore, sitting in it. They checked his bag and found it containing cash and prize bonds. They interrogated Zulfiqar who confessed that he had stolen this amount from the shop of Abdul Wahid. He offered, at first, half of this amount and then the whole of it as bribe to both these police officials if they could let him off. Motivated and dutiful as they were, the police officials not only turned down the offer but also awoke the respectables of the area in whose presence the entire amount was counted which was Rs 830,000. The prize bonds' numbers also tallied with those reported by Abdul Wahid to have been stolen. I announced a reward of Rs 50,000 each for Head Constable Muhammad Boota and Constable Muhammad Aslam for their integrity, devotion to duty and adherence to professional ethics. It is worth mentioning that their salaries were Rs 2182 and Rs 2179 per month respectively. The entire stolen amount of money and prize bonds were returned by SSP Muhammad Iqbal and myself to the owner in a reception arranged in the honour of these two police officials by the Central Board of Tajiran (Merchants) in a local hotel. Tariq Aziz introduced them to the entire nation on the Pakistan Television Network through his popular programme, *Neelam Ghar*.

Once the police won its heart, the community itself cracked down on the criminals. To ensure protection of life, liberty and property of villagers, a village defence system involving constant foot patrol duties by various groups in selected villages, communication of important information regarding suspects, crime or possibility of crime to the police, protection of cattle through identification markings and active assistance in the apprehension of criminals and proclaimed offenders, was introduced. The result was that, in many cases, the villagers themselves either apprehended the dacoits or killed them in pitched battles. In the process, many villagers were injured or even made the supreme sacrifice of life, which was duly acknowledged by way of getting them duly rewarded either through the Government or the police budget. It will not be out of place to mention a few incidents of gallantry on the part of citizens.

i) On 1 September 1991 Muhammad Afzal Jat Gorraya, his father Nazir Ahmed and friends Nazar Muhammad and Muhammad Asghar, while proceeding to their village Bopora Kalan District Gujranwala on a *tonga* (a horse-driven vehicle) were waylaid by four armed persons, namely, Nizam alias Bali, Iftikhar Ahmed, Muhammad Sharif and Sakhawat alias Kaka. Muhammad Afzal and his companions jumped at the culprits who shot at Afzal and grievously injured him. Despite his injury Afzal and his feriends apprehended all the four criminals. Later Afzal succumbed to his injuries.

ii) On the night between 2/3 September 1991, three dacoits trespassed into the house of Muhammad Ashraf in Kot Noora (near Ghakkar), District Gujranwala. The inmates of the house resisted the attempt at robbery and raised a hue and cry. The dacoits opened fire and killed Ashraf and his brother. The neighbours, having heard the noise, surrounded the accused and returned the fire. As a consequence of the exchange of fire, two dacoits, namely, Mansha Masih and Boota Masih were killed on the spot and Abbas Masih was apprehended alive and handed over to the local police. The Government of the Punjab provided financial assistance of Rs 50,000/- to the affected family. In a meeting, covered by the Pakistan Television and the press, brave citizens were awarded cash rewards and certificates.

During the period of successive martial laws and autocratic governments, due to censorship on the publication of political news, the tendency of the print media to publish sensational crime-related news highlighting sexual crime, and projection in films of activities of robber-barons and their violent behaviour made a significant contribution to crime proliferation and marginalization of the police from the community. Respect for law and institutions of criminal justice administration gave way to 'criminal mentality'. The police were thus alienated from the public. It was, therefore, imperative to adopt a deliberate and sustained policy of media projection of police performance. This, of course, was to be accompanied by solid and tangible improvement in police effectiveness. In view of these considerations and in pursuance of the open media policy of the then Inspector General of the Punjab Police, interaction with journalists was further strengthened through the publication of a monthly police magazine *Police-ke-Shab-o-Roz*. Thus an attempt was made to enable various cross-sections of society to identify themselves with the police. Officials of all ranks were encouraged to write of their professional experiences. Internal information or policy matters, legal questions and regimental life, great deeds of police martyrs and their sense of sacrifice were also important subjects highlighted in the *Shab-o-Roz*. The police were able to gain public confidence, enhance their effectiveness and morale and inculcate a sense of self-esteem in their rank and file. Books written by police officials on professional subjects followed this for which due encouragement was given.

With the personal interest of the superintendents of police and through the co-operation of local influential persons, old enmities, wherein several persons had been killed on both sides, over a long period of time, culminated in truce and compromise, thereby putting an end to further loss of life. This was done through an informal revival of the *panchayat* system. For example, in village Batihanwala, District Narowal, twenty-five years old enmity existed between the Dogar and Jat groups over property and local political dominance. It resulted in the registration of at least twenty-six criminal cases in 1991 by both the parties. The local police, with the assistance of local respectable persons and public representatives, brought about reconciliation and compromise between the parties, thus bringing an era of enmity and turmoil to an end. Similarly, in the area of Police Station Subaz Pir, District Sialkot, two rival groups headed by Qamar-ud-Din and Iqbal Hussain, whose enmity had earlier resulted in a murder, were brought to the negotiating table and reconciliation and compromise was affected between them. Through all these measures, the criminals were isolated from the community and became an easy prey to the law enforcing agencies. Table 11.1 sums up the results achieved. This was positive development in crime prevention.

TABLE 11.1
Gujranwala Range (1992)
Old Enmities Culminating in Truce/Settlement

District	no. of parties/factions affected
Gujranwala	38
Gujrat	6
Sialkot	57
Narowal	3

Source: Nadeem, A.H., (1992) *Nazm-o-Nask Report (Annual Administration Report)*, Gujranwala Range, Gujranwala.

A new spirit of devotion to duty accompanied the public support and encouragement on part of the police officers and men. In their endeavour to eliminate crime and make people safe in every respect, police personnel in all the districts of Gujranwala Division, wrote, with their blood, a new chapter in valour and dedication to duty. In successive armed encounters with desperate criminals, twenty-two police officers and men laid down their lives. Criminals, too, met their end. These armed encounters symbolized unprecedented initiative, courage, vigour and determination on part of the valiant police officers and men. In face of dare-devil criminals, armed to the teeth, the police personnel did not hesitate to make even the supreme sacrifice of their lives. Here is a brief over-view of a few such incidents:

19 August 1991

Three proclaimed offenders, namely, Ijaz alias Jaji, Muhammad Sarwar alias Mitho and Shafqat alias Shakoo, with the intent to kill their opponents (who were under trial prisoners in police custody and had just come out of the Anti-Terrorist Court, Gujranwala to be escorted back to the jail), suddenly came out of a Toyota Corolla car and resorted to indiscriminate kalashnikov firing, thereby killing thirteen persons including seven of their opponents, one under-trial prisoner in a case unrelated to these parties, three passersby and two constables on duty, namely, Rafaqat Ali and Muhammad Aslam. Inspector Asif Ansari, too, received serious bullet injuries and fell down. At the main gate of the compound of the Anti-Terrorist Court, the three killers continued firing in the air to express their delight at the accomplishment of their task of killing their opponents. They snatched a Suzuki van, belonging to the WAPDA, and tried to make their escape driving through complicated streets and roads of Gujranwala city.

Inspector Arsalan Khan, SHO Civil Lines, Gujranwala, who happened to be on patrol, conveyed information of the occurrence on wireless network and himself started chasing the fleeing murderers on a motorcycle. I ordered the police mobiles to rise to the occasion and ensure apprehension of the criminals. Within minutes, the Gujranwala Police, including SSP Tariq Khosa, SP CIA, Mukhtar Gondal, SP Headquarters Khadim Hussain Bhatti, DSP CIA, DSP Saddar, DSP Civil Lines and

DSP Kamoki and their men, came into action. Meanwhile, Inspector Arsalan Khan conveyed a wireless message that the fleeing killers had crossed the Ferozewala Canal Bridge and were proceeding towards Muslim Chak. The police parties, adopting a well co-ordinated strategy, moved swiftly from different directions. The proclaimed offenders, having reached Muslim Chak, fired in the air to celebrate their success and continued towards Botala Sharm Singh.

The police went in hot pursuit. About one kilometre from Botala Sharm Singh, the accused abandoned the Suzuki van and tried to slip away through the rice fields. Meanwhile, the police had fully encircled them and were moving in from all four directions. The criminals, in a desperate attempt to escape, started spraying countless bullets at the police party causing injuries to Sub-Inspector Farooq Khan and Constable Muhammad Azad. The police returned the fire that resulted in the death of all the three killers. Scrutiny of record later showed that they were wanted in various serious criminal cases.

The entire episode ended within three hours of the commission of the barbaric act by the desperadoes. The prompt action, perseverance, valour and commitment to professional excellence not only restored public confidence in the police but also won them instantaneous praise from all sections of the community. The story of their efficiency was telecast not only by Pakistan Television but also by BBC, CNN, and the Voice of America.

31 October 1991

On this day, the police were engaged in three different armed encounters with proclaimed offenders and dangerous criminals in Sialkot and Gujranwala districts. In the area of Police Station Bombanwala, Inspector Aurangzeb, Sub-Inspector Syed Ijas Hussain Shah and his party challenged a dangerous criminal who fired at them and killed Sub-Inspector Syed Ijaz Hussain Shah on the spot. Constables Manzoor Hussain and Muhammad Sarwar, too, were injured. Despite having received bullet injuries, Constable Muhammad Sarwar, continued retaliatory firing, resulting in the death of the criminal.

In Gujranwala, in a raid conducted for the arrest of one Javed alias Jaida, involved in a double murder case, Inspector Muhammad Saleem Butt received bullet injuries in chest and rights arm. This armed encounter led to in the death of the murderer.

In Kamoki Circle, a proclaimed offender fired at the raiding police party deputed for his arrest. Police returned the fire that resulted in the death of the criminal.

19 February 1992

The Gujranwala Range police had been put on an alert following commission of a robbery at the District Council Check Post near Wazirabad and a bank dacoity at Gujranwala. Reportedly, three culprits, having committed these offences, had fled in a blue car. At 12:30 p.m., a blue car was seen near Manchar Chatta with three armed persons sitting in it. Having seen the police vehicle of Police Station Alipur, the suspicious car started proceeding towards Ahmad Nagar. SHO Alipur conveyed the information regarding the suspected car on wireless network. Accordingly SHO Ahmad Nagar, who was present at a police barrier set-up at Saroki Chowk, attempted to stop this car but the car broke the barrier, and moved towards Wazirabad at a very fast speed. DSP Wazirabad, Zamurd Khan, who was on his way back from Sambrial and Daska, directed the SHO of Police Stations Alipur and Ahmad Nagar to continue chasing the fleeing vehicle and himself took position on the Alipur Road. Having realized that it was almost impossible for them to reach the Grand Trunk Road, the culprits started moving towards Jandiala Dhabwala. DSP Wazirabad, Zamurd Khan, however, ensured that the gate on Sangowali Service Road was closed.

The criminals, having found the Sangowali Service Road closed, turned towards Kot Waris and came on the right bank of the Ojala Canal. They felt that the police had encircled them because the vehicle of DSP Wazirabad, Zamurd Khan, was right in front of them. The culprits immediately abandoned their vehicle. SHO Ghakkar, Muhammad Afzal, who had remained posted in Gujrat and had interrogated Afzal Fauji, immediately recognized the accused and asked him to surrender himself to the police. The accused responded with kalashnikov, and automatic rifle bursts thereby causing a serious head injury to DSP Zamurd Khan. Semi-unconscious, DSP Zamurd conveyed a wireless message that he had been injured. SHO Ghakkar immediately rushed towards the DSP's vehicle, picked him up on his back (who had by then lost consciousness), and directed Sub-Inspector Salabat Khan to carry him to the hospital.

Meanwhile, I had directed the ambulance and police reserves to move towards the spot. The criminals attempted to enter village Ojala Kalan but they found Sub-Inspector Farooq Khan and his party in the fields in front of them. They, therefore, entered Dera Inayat. As the distance between the criminals and the police party was narrowing down, they left Dera Inayat and managed to reach Dera Muhammad Ashraf. Having fortified themselves in a strategic position by removing a few bricks and having taken seven innocent persons, namely Nasreen, Chandi, Sonia (an infant), Safdar, Akbar, Barkat and Boota Masih as hostages, the desperadoes started a pitched battle with the police. Their relentless firing caused head injury to Sub-Inspector Farooq Khan and serious injuries to four other policemen. Despite heavy odds, the police remained undeterred. By this time, along with SSP Malik Muhammad Iqbal, DSP Gujranwala, Mushtaq Hussain, DSP Syed Zafar Abbas and DSP Yousaf Bajwa had reached the spot. I directed all concerned on wireless that, while returning fire, the safety of innocent hostages must be ensured. Meanwhile, on the loudspeaker of the village mosque, I asked the culprits to surrender to the police and assured them the safety of their lives. They, however, responded with renewed firing. I conveyed a wireless message to the Inspector General of Police, Sardar Muhammad Chaudhry, to send us an armoured car from Lahore. He personally began monitoring the arrangements for evacuation and treatment of the injured policemen.

Young men from Ojala Kalan, inspired as they were by the unprecedented gallantry of policemen, offered to fight the criminals with their licensed weapons. Keeping in view their safety, the offer was declined. But two persons, Nasrullah and Bashir Masih, did join the police party in the fight and sustained injuries. Having picked up the wireless messages, the Gujrat Police, under the command of SP Gujrat, Muhammad Masood Bangash, reached the spot. I directed them to cover the northern side of Dera Muhammad Ashraf.

The police were seriously handicapped on two counts. We had to ensure that the police firing, while making an attempt to evacuate injured policemen, did not hit any hostage. Fortified as they were, the criminals had caused great loss to the police. Despite heavy odds, police officers and men crawled through the fields and were able to evacuate the injured policemen including Sub-Inspector Farooq Khan and twenty-two others.[3] We rushed them in ambulances to the District Headquarters Hospital, Gujranwala.

Constable Muhammad Aslam 2981, from Wireless Staff, was supplying wireless sets to all commanders involved in the fight. Having distributed wireless sets to the police party in the northern and western sides, he was moving towards the eastern contingent when he was hit by the criminals and died on the spot.

At 6:30 p.m., the armoured car arrived from Lahore. SSP Muhammad Iqbal, together with two policemen, boarded it and launched a decisive direct assault at the fortified room from where the criminals, taking cover of innocent hostages, had been playing havoc for the last seven hours. Having seen the approaching armoured car, the desperadoes unleashed a rain of bullets. The police used teargas resulting in a big smokescreen making every thing invisible to hundreds of people who were witnessing the heroic police action from the Grand Trunk Road. The criminals, having removed more bricks from the north eastern wall of the entrenched room, jumped outside. Two of them, who were later on identified as Bashir Bhatti and Ahsan, were killed in the last fierce exchange of fire. As darkness had set in, visibility had become almost zero. The moment the police declared the death of two of the desperadoes, hundreds of people, who had been witnessing the fight, raising slogans of *Allah-o-Akbar* (Allah is Great), rushed towards Dera Muhammad Ashraf. The third accused, Afzal Fauji, taking advantage of the public euphoria, managed to slip away from the scene. The police had to stop firing due to the presence of a very big crowd of civilians. SSP Muhammad Iqbal went in to the room in the thick smoke caused by teargas shells, and rescued the innocent hostages. They were provided first aid and taken to Ojala Kalan. All of them were completely safe. They had not received even a scratch. The entire village, overwhelmed by the gallant action of the police resulting in safe release of hostages at the cost of their own lives, presented a scene of unprecedented appreciation for the police. The slogans of *Gujranwala Police Zindabad* (Long Live the Gujranwala Police) and expression of identification with police cause, were a visible demonstration of public support.

At about 8:30 p.m., Inspector General of Police, Sardar Muhammad Chaudhry, along with Deputy Inspector General of Police, Lahore Range, Rana Maqbool Ahmed, left Lahore for Gujranwala. SSP Malik Muhammad Iqbal and myself, handing over the operational command to SP CIA, Muhammad Anwar Virk, with the direction to trace out Afzal Fauji, left for the District Headquarters Hospital, Gujranwala. The Inspector General too arrived there. Words are simply too inadequate to describe fully the scene of public support and affection for the policemen at the District Headquarters Hospital. A large number of volunteers were donating blood for the injured policemen. Countless citizens, including public representatives, lawyers, journalists, representatives of welfare organizations, members of the Chamber of Industry and Commerce, students, teachers and businessmen were extending all kinds of help, financial, material and moral, to ensure proper treatment of the injured. The Medical Superintendent, Dr Mehboob Rabbani and specialists, Dr Arshad Chatta, Dr Asif Javed, Dr Iqbal Qadir and Dr Ashiq were providing treatment. Cases of serious injury were being referred to Lahore while others were operated upon locally.[3] The Lahore Police sent volunteer blood-donors to the Mayo Hospital and Kot Lakhpat Hospital where seriously injured police officers and men had been sent for the requisite surgical operations. The Inspector General of Police appreciated the courage, morale, bravery and dedication to duty of the part of the Gujranwala Range Police and directed the third accused, Afzal Fauji be traced and apprehended.

On 20 February 1991, I addressed a large press conference expressing our resolve to trace out and arrest the third criminal, Afzal Fauji. Mehar Muhammad Saleem, Member Provincial Assembly, Rana Saghir Ahmed, Chairman Gujranwala District Council, Babu Javed Ahmed, Mayor Gujranwala Municipal Corporation, Naveed Anwar Naveed, Secretary District Bar Association and Farooq Bhai, President Anjuman-e-Tajran (Haq Parast Group), also attended the press conference and offered all kinds of support to the Gujranwala Range Police. Mayor Gujranwala Municipal Corporation and Chairman Gujranwala District Council announced a donation of Rs 300,000 and Rs 600,000 each respectively for the families of police martyrs. The Government of the Punjab announced a financial assistance of Rs 300,000 each for police martyrs and Rs 150,000 for every injured policeman. The funeral of policemen, who had laid down their lives, was attended by thousands of persons including the Punjab Chief Minister, Ghulam Haider Wyne, Chief Secretary Punjab, Pervaiz Masood, Commissioner Gujranwala, Kamran Rasool, Deputy Commissioner Gujranwala, Khushnood Lashari, parliamentarians, members of District Council and Municipal Corporation, industrialists, businessmen and lawyers.

Continued strategic planning and ceaseless efforts facilitated inflow of correct information regarding the whereabouts of the third desperado, Afzal Fauji. He was seen going towards village Attlay Ghulam, in the jurisdiction of Police Station Sukheke, on 22 February 1991. The Hafizabad Police, under the command of ASP Ghulam Sarwar Jamali, immediately rushed to the spot. On his request, I directed a contingent of policemen from

Gujranwala to proceed to Attlay Ghulam. However, before the arrival of the reinforcement, the Hafizabad Police were engaged in a pitched battle initiated by Afzal Fauji. The exchange of fire, which continued for two hours, resulted in his death. His 7-mm rifle and cartridges were taken into possession. This brought to an end one of the bloodiest armed encounters in the history of the Punjab Police.

Talking to journalists at the Lahore Airport, the then Prime Minister of Pakistan, Muhammad Nawaz Sharif, described the supreme sacrifice of the police martyrs as unprecedented. He stated that it was a great example of complete devotion to duty. According to him, it was also a proof of ceaseless, uninterrupted and full-fledged campaign launched by the police against the criminals. In public meetings, press comments, statements of parliamentarians, both in the government and opposition, declamation contests and sports events arranged in their memory, the eight police martyrs of Ojala Kalan—Muhammad Farooq Khan, Muhammad Arshad, Muhammad Aslam, Muhammad Azam, Rana Iftikhar, Saifullah, Muhammad Afzal and Khudadad—were paid glowing tributes. They made the supreme sacrifice so that their countrymen could live in peace.

11 June 1992

It was the day of Eid-ul-Azha. In the early hours, Ghulam Shabbir Niazi, SHO Malakwal Police Station and Constable Gulzar Ahmed, were on patrol duty and attempted to stop three desperate criminals, who were in a car, at a police barrier. They resorted to indiscriminate firing causing serious injuries to both the police officials. Inspector Shabbir Niazi was taken to the Mayo Hospital, Lahore, where he succumbed to his injuries. When I had gone to see him in the hospital, forgetting his own pain and anguish, he told me, 'Sir, I am glad one of the accused persons, too, was killed when we returned the fire from the car of the accused persons. I was able to get hold of an identity card. This may help you in the arrest of the remaining accused persons.' A few minutes later, he died. Public support, emanating from the implementation of the principle of community policing, had brought a sea change in police culture. Neither injury nor death could stand in the way of dutiful police officials.

21 June 1992

On the way back from a court at Lalamusa, in an attempt to rescue a criminal from police custody, his companions attacked a van carrying under-trial prisoners. Their firing resulted in the death of Constable Jamshed Akhtar and injuries to Constable Zafar Iqbal. The accused ran away along with the rescued prisoner, Anwar, and a police rifle. The Gujrat police, under supervision of SP Muhammad Masood Bangash, came into action and, within three hours of the occurrence, after a fierce exchange of fire, resulting in the death of two accused persons and arrest of the third one, added a chapter to police effectiveness.

In a ceaseless fight against proclaimed offenders and dangerous criminals, Constables Ghazanfar Ali and Nowaiz Akhtar lost their lives on 21 July 1992 and 19 September 1992 at Gujranwala and Gujrat respectively. Similarly, on 20 September 1992 Inspector Umar Hayat, SHO Karianwala, who had, on 1 June 1992, won public acclaim for arresting a notorious gang of train dacoits and was awarded a gold medal by the local members of Provincial Assembly and District Council, Gujrat, in a public meeting at Malakpur Mirza, arrived at the Chenab Bridge to assist a police party engaged in an armed encounter with dangerous criminals. In the process he received fatal injuries. Just before his death, he spoke to SP Masood Bangash, 'Sir, I have laid down my life for honour of police uniform. Let us not allow any harm to come to this uniform.' On 25 October 1992, Sultan Ahmed Garah, SHO Sambrial, laid down his life in the performance of his duties.

The unprecedented sacrifices made by the Gujranwala Range Police helped change the negative thinking about police performance. Pakistan Television, in its programme, *Neelam Ghar*, on 19 April 1992, paid great tributes to the police martyrs of Gujranwala Range. Great thinkers and writers like Ashfaq Ahmed Khan, Dr Ghulam Murtaza and Nazir Ghazi, in the television Programme *Farz Shanasi* (Dedication to Duty) described the sense of sacrifice of policemen as an embodiment of love and affection for their countrymen. Superintendent of Police Khadim Hussain Bhatti, Saif-ur-Rehman Saifi, Khawaja Pervaiz and I wrote police songs eulogizing the bravery, dedication to duty and a firm commitment to service on the part of police martyrs. These songs were composed and sung by great singers like the melody queen Noor Jehan, Masood Rana, Rajab Ali, Shaukat Ali, Arif Lohar, Afshan and Amjad Hussain. The *Urdu Digest* and weekly *Zindagi* published details of the heroic incidents involving police officers and men from Gujranwala Range. The Government of the Punjab, declared the martyrs as alive in the spiritual sense, announced payment of full salary to their families till the time they would have normally retired.

Anti-Drug Education Awareness Project

The Gujranwala Range police launched their Anti-Drug Education Awareness Project on 9 June 1992 in Gujranwala. A special ward was reserved in the District Headquarters Hospital for free treatment of drug addicts. Co-operation was sought from the Health and Excise Departments of the Government of the Punjab, local philanthropists, the Citizen-Police Advisory Council, religious scholars, intellectuals, students, teachers, traders and medical experts. A register was maintained to record information regarding drug traffickers/dealers received from drug addicts by medical personnel. This enhanced the capability of the police to trace, apprehend and prosecute drug dealers. In 1992, 292 drug addicts were treated and rehabilitated. In a public meeting at Noshera Virkan, attended by journalists, police officers and prominent citizens, thirteen drug dealers from Chani Virkan and Dera Sachan, voluntarily and on oath on the Holy Quran, declared to give up the profession of drug dealing. This was a natural outcome of public pressure and the general awareness programme launched by the Gujranwala Police.

Similarly, free treatment of drug addicts, changed, amongst many others, the life of Nayyar Iqbal, a jeweller of Mohallah Shaheenabad of Gujranwala City. He was a drug addict since 1987 and had become a burden for his family. The treatment facility, provided by the Gujranwala Police, under its Anti-Drug Education Awareness Programme, changed him from an inactive and lethargic drug addict to a healthy young-man, fully involved in his profession and family.

Complaint Cell

To begin with, a Complaint Cell was established in the office of the Superintendent of Police, Sialkot. The objective primarily was to provide quick remedy to persons visiting his office. The other considerations of setting up this Cell were:

- The aggrieved persons appearing in the SP's office for the redress of their grievances were not properly honoured and attended to by the lower staff which certainly had a bearing on the image of the police.
- Since there was no officer present in the SP's office to attend to public grievances after office hours, people generally turned up at the residence of the Superintendent of Police to lodge complaints which quite often needed immediate response.
- Frequently, complaints requiring transfer of investigations presented by various persons were not based on genuine reasons. However, some Cell was certainly required to verify the nature of allegations and to remove the element of mistrust.

- In the absence of the Superintendent of Police from district headquarters, there was a need for a Cell dealing with all these matters because people were not generally willing to get their grievances handled at any other level.
- The Complaint Cell was also needed to take up matters for registration of cognizable cases not handled by respective police stations.

Three Inspectors, one ASI (Assistant Sub-Inspector) and four Constables were posted in the Complaint Cell.

The Complaint Cell functioned from 8.00 a.m. to 10.00 p.m. and officers performed duty on shift basis. The following types of complaints were handled by the Complaint Cell. Telephone calls received from the public for immediate police help were promptly responded to; officers were dispatched and grievances were resolved.

- On receipt of complaints about non-registration of any cognizable case, properly drafted complaints were sent to the police stations for registration and copies of FIRs (First Information Reports) were furnished to the complainants.
- Officers of the Complaint Cell also worked as arbitrators in certain civil matters with the assistance of the notables of the area as and when any aggrieved person lodged a request on compassionate grounds regarding civil disputes. However, only deserving cases were taken up and those, too, with the prior permission of the Superintendent of Police.
- There was a general tendency in Sialkot district to apply for transfer of investigation. The creation of the Complaint Cell helped a great deal in discouraging this trend. When some request based on the complaint about unfair investigation being carried out by the local staff was received, an officer of the complaint cell was dispatched to the respective village for examining the parties and the investigating officer. Conclusion about investigation was drawn at the spot and guidelines were issued for its finalization. In case of any subsequent complaint, the case could be re-examined in Superintendent of Police's Office. This *modus operandi* did

contribute to reducing the tendency for frequent requests for transfer of investigations.

- Matters concerning illegalities, manhandling, and misuse of official authority were also entrusted to the Complaint Cell because in these instances people expected a quick action.

- The Complaint Cell, with the passing of time, also assumed the role of collecting information about crime and criminals. This was mainly due to public trust and confidence which these officers gained with the passage of time and as a result of their fair working and aptitude towards social service.

This scheme was so successful that it was subsequently implemented in Gujranwala, Gujrat and Narowal districts. Generally, people reposed complete confidence in the scheme. They started sharing important information with police personnel which led to the resolution of many important cases. Consequently, the Complaint Cell helped in reducing the gap between the people and the police which is the crux of efficient and effective policing.

Back-up Support

The experiment in community policing in Gujranwala Range was backed up through the following measures designed to enhance professional effectiveness and efficiency of the police:

1. 'Policing by objectives' was introduced. As a result of the introduction of the concept of community policing, I met a cross-section of society in Gujranwala, Gujrat, Narowal and Sialkot districts. This cross section included, apart from public representatives, industrialists, traders representatives of local motor federations, ulema, students and lawyers. They were asked to identify their problems and suggest remedial measures. I also visited the District Councils, the District Bar Associations and the Chambers of Commerce and Industry in Gujranwala Division. Very useful suggestions were put forward and public

co-operation became available in a very short span of time. Part of the consultation process consisted of the meetings with the rank and file of the Gujranwala Range police. Everybody was free to put forward their viewpoint with candour and frankness. In the light of these suggestions a strategy of policing by objectives was introduced. Police objectives for the year 1992 were: improvement in police behaviour, recovery of unlicensed weapons, apprehension of proclaimed offenders, fight against drug trafficking, terrorism and public harassment through community consultation, facilitation of flow of information from the public to the police through voluntary community participation in urban and rural areas and improvement of traffic discipline in urban areas.

TABLE 11.2

Public Perception of Serious Crime: Results of Survey in Terms of Percentage of Sample Population

Priority in Terms of Seriousness

Category of Crime	1	2	3	4	5	6	7	8	9	10	11	12	13	14
						Per cent								
Dacoity	24	15	6	14	9	4	8	10	4	3	0	1	0	0
Kidnapping for Ransom	11	9	6	10	11	17	12	12	3	2	0	2	1	1
Fraud	6	2	4	4	2	0	4	3	5	6	6	14	10	27
Murder	19	6	6	8	7	13	6	9	7	9	2	2	1	1
Attempted Murder	5	7	3	5	13	13	15	6	6	7	9	4	0	1
Abduction of Women	10	12	25	12	9	8	7	4	1	3	2	2	2	0
Violation of Modesty of Women	17	23	13	9	8	7	6	7	5	0	2	2	1	1
Rape with Violence	38	18	14	11	5	3	5	2	3	0	0	1	0	0
Sale of Narcotics	20	13	7	15	16	13	5	6	5	2	0	0	0	0
Preaching Sectarian Hatred	5	8	7	5	2	6	12	9	12	8	12	5	14	2
Armed Robbery	4	6	1	0	2	1	1	4	6	10	18	15	19	10
Dealing in Fake Currency	7	1	7	1	4	3	5	10	11	10	12	11	13	4
Theft	4	6	1	2	1	1	0	8	0	8	10	15	19	25
Disturbance of Public Peace	5	4	0	2	1	2	5	8	8	18	8	8	11	0

Source: Nadeem, A.H., (1992) *Nazm-o-Nask Report (Annual Administration Report)*, Gujranwala Range, Gujranwala.

To determine police goals for the year 1993 a survey was conducted to ascertain public perception of crime seriousness.[4] Fourteen types of crime including dacoity, kidnapping for ransom, fraud, murder, attempted murder, abduction of women, violation of modesty of women, rape with violence, sale of narcotics, preaching sectarian hatred, armed robbery, dealing in fake currency, theft and disturbance of public peace were included in the questionnaire. A sample population of two hundred persons belonging to a cross section of society in the area of Model Town Police Station, Gujranwala, was asked to assign rating in terms of seriousness to all these offences.

According to survey results, 38 per cent of the respondents described rape with violence as the most serious crime. 24 per cent of sample population considered dacoity to be number one in seriousness. 20 per cent attached priority number one to murder while 17 per cent declared violation of modesty of women as the crime of utmost importance. The above table explains the priorities assigned to various offences in terms of seriousness by the sample population.

Accordingly, objectives of the Gujranwala Range Police for the year 1993 included crime prevention through community-based initiatives, protection of citizens against the drug menace, particularly by enhancing police efficiency with regard to apprehension of drug traffickers and follow-up of prosecution in courts, effective measures to eradicate crime against women and recovery of illicit weapons in conjunction with apprehension of proclaimed offenders, terrorists and anti-social elements, building up of police morale through inculcation of a sense of self-esteem and improvement in training and emphasis on social welfare role of the police under a motto of love, peace and service.

2. A circular order was issued on 3 August 1991 containing following instructions:

There would be no 'burking' of offences either by way of non-registration or minimization of offences.

Every Station House Officer would remain present in the premises of the police station daily from 4 p.m. to 6 p.m. to hear public complaints/grievances. In case of his absence the next senior most officer would perform this function.

Every Station House Officer would hold a fortnightly meeting with a cross-section of the community to determine their concerns and make efforts to attend to them.

The grievances of the downtrodden, the deprived and the indigent would be redressed on top-priority basis.

Every Station House Officer would hold a monthly meeting of subordinate investigating officers to review progress in under investigation cases and would issue necessary guidelines.

All first Information Reports would contain truth, nothing but the truth. In case the complainant did manage to fabricate truth, the investigation would be based on facts.

3. The crime situation in the Punjab and especially in the Gujranwala Range in 1990 and in the early months of 1991 was characterized by violence, lawlessness, dacoities, kidnapping for ransom and other heinous offences. In public perception, the police were unable to take action against influential warlords and criminals protected by them. To cope with the problems, in close collaboration with the divisional/district civil administration, an operation clean-up was launched on the night intervening 3/4 September 1991. 526 anti-social elements (including proclaimed offenders, protectors and patrons of dangerous criminals, dealers in narcotics/drug traffickers and gun-runners) were arrested. A huge quantity of various types of narcotics was seized and illicit arms and weapons were recovered. The immediate impact was a significant decrease in crime.

4. Simultaneously, steps were taken to narrow down the scope of discretion along with the tightening up of discipline. These measures were followed by briefings on professional matters.

5. The respective Central Investigation Agency (CIA) in Gujranwala, Gujrat, Narowal and Sialkot was reorganized. A mobile squad in each district consisting of a head proficient (alongwith a fingerprint kit), a photographer (having a camera), a video cameraman, in-charge of the Criminal Records Office (CRO) equipped with a video film containing particulars of notorious criminals, index cards and previous criminal records and an expert in footprints (*'khoji'*) ensured quick police response to incidents of crime. This arrangement was augmented by a system of surveillance of dangerous criminals set free after the expiry of their term of imprisonment or on acceptance of their bail bonds. In this connection, a close liaison with the prison service staff, procurement of necessary information from the jail records and communication thereof to the concerned police station were ensured. Lists of unidentified stolen property were updated and widely circulated to trace out the real owners. Protective measures against automobile theft included computerization of the particulars of vehicles stolen in the preceding five years, close liaison with the Excise and Taxation Officer in each district of the Range and launching of a sustained motivational campaign for general awareness about the marking of windscreens with the registration, chassis and engine numbers. Similar steps were taken by each district CIA to curb drug trafficking, apprehend proclaimed offenders and render assistance to police stations in the prevention and detection of crime.

Based on a scientific analysis of the strategy of criminals, a strategy for combating crime was devised. The net result was that fugitives were arrested even from Dubai and Saudi Arabia with the assistance of the Interpol. It will not be out of place to mention in detail, a case history of a proclaimed offender who was arrested from Dubai.

A notorious hired assassin and a proclaimed offender, Haroon alias Papu Butt, wanted by the Sialkot Police in various serious cases, apprehending his arrest, shifted his headquarters to Dubai. He would return to Sialkot under a fictitious name and passport, commit serious crime and go back to Dubai. Muhammad Ashraf

Marth Shaheed,[5] Superintendent of Police, Sialkot, was a thorough professional officer. He approached the Interpol for Papu's arrest but with no success because of several fictitious identities possessed by the criminal. To help the Interpol, he sent Inspector Tahir Mehmood to Dubai on 15 December 1991. Tahir Mehmood not only changed his own identity but also shaved off his moustache. He was soon able to cultivate reliable sources that would give him correct information about the whereabouts of Papu. On 24 December 1991, having received the information that Papu accused was busy listening to a song in a hotel, Inspector Tahir Mehmood reached there but the proclaimed offenders had left the hotel. Undeterred by this failure, Inspector Tahir Mehmood, continued his search in a professional manner. He would daily seek guidance from SP Muhammad Ashraf Marth on telephone. On 2 March 1992, with the assistance of the Interpol, Inspector Tahir Mehmood was able not only to arrest accused Papu but also to bring him back to Sialkot. This was an outcome of professionalism and devotion to duty on the part of late SP Muhammad Ashraf Marth and his team.

Strategies of Criminals and Police

To effectively implement the community policing model in Gujranwala Range, an analysis of the strategy adopted by criminals was carried out. The police officers, in successive discussion sessions, agreed that the criminals purported to isolate the police by bringing pressure on their working through Criminal Justice Administration System itself, by eliciting the support of electronic and print media, pressure and interest groups and public representatives in general. To avoid apprehension, they sought political patronage, cover of sectarian and student organizations and legal cover through writ petitions. It was also a unanimous conclusion of these discussions that the criminals not only tried to gain social respectability through ill-gotten wealth but were also better off as compared to the police in term of resources, mobility, arms and ammunition, initiative, planning, organization, co-ordination and financing.

Our analysis also indicated that the criminal was using the loopholes and inadequacies of Criminal Justice Administration to his own advantage by pitting one element of the system against the other. Drug money was being used to further weaken and bribe the system so as to create a sense of despondency and frustration amongst the members of the public with a view to alienating them from the law enforcing agencies.

In view of this analysis of the strategy adopted by the criminals, the Gujranwala Range Police evolved a strategy of crime control. The main objectives were to isolate the criminal and to neutralize the criminal propensities of the society, to destroy the criminal with the help and assistance of the community, society, public representatives and the government and to strengthen the moral fibre of the society by practising the tenets of righteousness and truth enshrined in Islamic teachings. Accordingly, measures were taken to de-link the criminal from political, sectarian and student cover. For this purpose, public opinion was mobilized and support of intelligentsia against the criminal was elicited. A close liaison amongst members of police force and other elements of Criminal Justice Administration System was constantly maintained to ensure a co-ordinated approach. Previously such elements were working at cross-purposes. Measures were adopted to solicit community support for controlling criminal propensities. These efforts were augmented by increasing police effectiveness through better training, use of latest techniques, procedures and equipment, better co-ordination with other Ranges, use of mass media to present realistic picture of crime, free registration of cases, investigation based on truth, co-operation of public representatives and ensuring follow up of prosecution process in courts.

The above mentioned measures were in addition to active role of the police in flood relief and rehabilitation, devising of operational plan to combat vehicles theft, computerization of data of stolen vehicles by Sialkot Police, video filming of scenes of crime by CIA Gujranwala, introduction of mobile patrol which reduced the reaction time, traffic control through a well-coordinated programme and publication of the '*Shab-o-Roz*' and the use of mass media by police officials for better projection of police viewpoint. Effective steps were also taken for increased activity of sports teams of the Gujranwala Range Police, projection of police heroes/'*shaheeds*', holding of seminars, and regular participation in periodic DIGs' Conferences to discuss professional issues. Furthermore, a comprehensive police welfare package was devised to build up motivation and morale.

The police made useful contribution in ensuring improvement in education environment in schools and colleges. The outcome was that the student community fully co-operated with the Gujranwala Range Police in implementing programmes aimed at drug control and road safety.

A close liaison with the medical community and lawyers helped improve medico-legal services and served as a check on the tendency of issuing medico-legal report on considerations of local political affiliation, faction-rivalries and clan (*biraderi*) pressure.

To streamline all police activities in a proper direction, a Five Year Plan (1991–1995) was prepared. The idea was to ensure planned modernization and development of the Gujranwala Range Police.

Conclusion

This chapter reinforces the conceptual framework explained in Chapter 10 by examining in detail the experiment of cost-effective policing made in Gujranwala Division during the period from 3 August 1991 to 1 August 1993. Having discussed factors of experiment, the chapter proceeds on to narrate the complaint cell, backup support, strategies of criminals and the police and implementation thereof. The idea behind all these measures was to prepare the police for meeting the challenges of the twenty-first century. For effective maintenance of order the police have the monopoly of the use of force. While emphasis was laid on the use of minimum force it was made clear to all police personnel that the minimum force did not mean 'no' use of force at all. Where inevitable, the force needed to be used with efficiency so that further loss in terms of injuries on both sides, i.e. the police and the protesters, could be averted. With this strategy, sectarian violence bordering on chaos, was effectively controlled, labour unrest, resulting in the blockade of the Grand Trunk Road was checked, peace was ensured during the Islamic month of 'Moharram', political and student-oriented demonstrations were effectively policed and order was ensured in sports-related activities.

Discipline on roads was ensured through improvement in the licensing system, observance of one-way traffic rules where applicable, removal of encroachments, affixation of reflectors on the rear of tractor-trolleys and balanced enforcement of traffic laws.

These back-up professional measures added credibility to community policing measures. The success story of this experiment helped improve police image and effectiveness.

NOTES

1. A documentary film, based on actual implementation of the programme of community policing and neighbourhood watch, was prepared under the title *'Bahmi Hifazat'* (Neighbourhood Watch) which is still available with me. It includes the following:

    Activities of the Citizen Police Advisory Council.

    Lectures delivered to women pertaining to home safety and upbringing of children as law-abiding citizens.

    Briefing given to school children on the role of police in society, police ranks, measures to protect oneself against opportunistic crime, road safety and implications of drug use.

    Marking of postcode with invisible pencil on valuable articles of household with a view to facilitating their identification in case of theft.

    Activities of street co-ordinators and steps to take neighbours into confidence while leaving home.

The marking of registration numbers on the windscreen of vehicles through the use of sandblast technique.

Implementation of the Anti-Drug Education Awareness Programme of the Gujranwala Range Police and free treatment of drug addicts.

Display of banners indicating the harm caused by narcotics.

Display of portraits and names of police martyrs and various activities aimed at highlighting the supreme sacrifices made by them in the line of duty.

Provision of free Ambulance Service to patients by the Model Town Police Station, Gujranwala.

Functioning of beat system in the Model Town area of Gujranwala.

Crime Reporting Centre established in the office of the Senior Superintendent of Police, Gujranwala and its functioning.

Police public liaison at the forum of the Gujranwala Chamber of Commerce and Industry.

Radio Programmes covering the briefing of school children and press reporters on the implementation of the Neighbourhood Watch Programme.

Interviews of the Inspector General of Police, Punjab, Commissioner, Gujranwala Division and the author on various aspects of the community policing programme of the Gujranwala Range Police.

Nishan-e-Azm (a memorial constructed to commemorate the sacrifices of police martyrs).

Proceedings of meetings aimed at raising police morale and expressing solidarity with the families of police martyrs.

2. The Neighbourhood Watch Programme was evaluated through scientifically conducted surveys. For details see Appendix 7.

3. The following police personnel were injured in the armed encounter at Ojala Kalan:

Zamurd Khan, Deputy Superintendent of Police
Muhammad Younas Butt, Sub-Inspector
Zulfiqar Ahmed Khan, Sub-Inspector
Faiz Ahmed, Assistant Sub-Inspector
Muhammad Ilyas, Assistant Sub-Inspector
Safdar Hussain, Head Constable 786
Muhammad Altaf, Constable 1412
Ghulam Ali, Constable 1050
Muhammad Abdullah, Constable 896
Muhammad Jamil Shahid, Constable 1847
Nasir Mahmood, Constable 207
Muhammad Jamil, Constable 2138
Shahid Moazzam, Constable 2045
Nasir Mahmood, Constable 455
Rafiq Hussain, Constable 395

Bashir Ahmed, Constable 1924
Manzoor Ahmed, Constable (Punjab Constabulary) 3114
Muhammad Arshad, Constable 1826
Muhammad Ashraf, Constable 90
Muhammad Siddique, Constable 1570
Muhammad Anwar, Constable 35
The following civilians were injured:
Nasrullah
Bashir

4. Nadeem, A.H., (1992), *Nazm-o-Nask* Report (*Annual Administration Report*), Gujranwala Range, Gujranwala, pp. 322–3.

5. As mentioned earlier in this book, Muhammad Ashraf Marth was a brilliant officer. While posted as the Senior Superintendent of Police in Multan in early 1997 he unearthed a group of terrorists who had stormed the Iranian Cultural Centre and killed the inmates. He also located all their links, financial resources, hit lists and equipment to jam police wireless sets. They threatened to kill him if he did not give up his hard pursuit of them. Subsequently, he was transferred to Gujranwala as the Senior Superintendent of Police. He continued his professional duty undeterred by threats. On 6 May 1997, he was gunned down by the terrorists in front of his official residence. He laid down his life in the line of duty.

12

IMPROVEMENT OF GENERAL CRIMINAL ADMINISTRATION SYSTEM

The aim of this chapter is to suggest short-term and long-term measures for improving general criminal administration system with a view to bringing it in conformity with the dictates of sustainable economic development. To fulfil this objective, it deals with changes that are required to make the criminal administration system people friendly, effective, efficient and accountable.

Four-Tier Network

The system of general criminal administration consists of a four-tier network, i.e. the judiciary, administration, police, and representative democratic institutions. It is important that these institutions should not act at cross-purposes. A co-ordinated, intertwined and integrated set-up for their smooth working needs to be evolved. This is because crime is a complex phenomenon and requires the whole-hearted involvement of the community as a whole. The strategy involved can be discussed both in terms of short- and long-term approaches.

Short-term Approach

In the short-term solution, no basic structural changes in the existing system of criminal administration are proposed. The thrust is at strengthening the existing system and bringing about a harmonious working relationship among the judiciary, administration, police, and representative democratic institutions.

Successive governments, in their eagerness to project themselves as proponents of development, kept eroding their own authority. Development plans categorized order maintenance and administration of criminal justice as non-developmental functions with low priority. Activities like family planning and management of nationalized banking and industrial units consumed a significant administrative energy and financial resources. Courtrooms, police stations and jails remained neglected. There was occasional increase, in police manpower and equipment. These measures were, however, *ad hoc* in nature and failed to correspond to the magnitude of the problem. Resource allocation and resource-content did not take into account the proper requirements of the police and crime increase.

TABLE 12.1

Budgetary Provisions for the Punjab Police in the Selected Years

Year	Punjab Budget (in million of Rs)	Police Budget (in million of Rs)	Police Budget as per cent of the Punjab budget
1947-8	207.4	24.7	11.00
1966-7	4077	127	3.10
1983-4	24012.9	789.7	3.29
1985-6	2567.91	994.5	3.87
1987-8	38806.6	1516.2	3.90
1989-90	42591.8	1648.4	3.87
1990-1	46720	2485.5	5.32
1991-2	55820	2762	4.95
1992-3	43615.86	3287.10	7.54
1993-4	49510	3897.46	7.87
1994-5	58219.43	4182.29	7.18
1995-6	68734.40	5107.25	7.43
1996-7	106340	5100	4.80
1997-8	121710	5720	4.71
1998-9	124610	6350	5.10
1999-2000	1314830	6950	5.29

Source: Finance Department, Government of the Punjab, Lahore.

This is indicated by the above table showing budgetary provisions for the Punjab Police in the years 1947–8, 1966–7, 1983–4, 1985–6, 1987–8, 1989–90, 1991–2, 1992–3, 1993–4, 1994–5, 1995–6, 1996–7, 1997–8, 1998–9 and 1999–2000. In contrast to the above meagre allocation of resources for the Punjab police, in England and Wales £ 2.9 billion are spent on the police each year compared to £ 1.1 billion in 1978–9. This represents an increase of 36 per cent in real terms.[1] The degree of relative neglect of the order maintenance machinery in the Punjab is further compounded by a highly unfavourable population—police man power ratio in comparison with England and Wales and Japan.

Police Population Ratio

The police population ratio has ranged between 1010 persons to 825 persons per policeman in the Punjab. This ratio is 427 persons per policeman in England and Wales and 555 persons in Japan.[2] Urbanization, hi-tech gadgetry available with criminals, organized crime, gun-running, drug mafia, foreign funded terrorism and exposure to foreign media and its impact have compounded the crime control problem. What is required is a massive effort on part of the government and society to cope with the challenge. The challenge is not yet insurmountable but the will of the government to act promptly and resolutely will salvage the situation.

Policing Style

Policing in Pakistan is conducted in a paramilitary fashion. Police officers are expected to perform some of the duties of a soldier and some aspects of the role of a police officer and inevitably fall between the two roles. It is, therefore, imperative to adopt a proper policing style. It will include the following:

Institutionalization of Community Policing

The recent community policing experiment (3 August 1991 to 1 August 1993) in Gujranwala Division needs to be introduced in other parts of Pakistan. Its results, combined with those of its replica in Dera Ghazi Khan (from 3 August 1993 to 4 April, 1994), show that it can provide a very effective response to the rising wave of crime in the country. Techniques of community policing may change from area to area but what is important is the development of a people-oriented police force, which commands respect and confidence of all segments of the society. Actually, it needs to be institutionalized. The Government of the Punjab did initiate in 1998 a process of police reforms though some of them had clear political connotations.[3] The institutionalization of community policing, in the real sense, is possible through the following measures:
- Community relations, aim and objectives: The primary aim of the community policing strategy in all the four provinces of Pakistan should be to deliver programmes, which meet operational and community expectations. For this purpose there is a need to develop a district based structure for community relations, which fosters a more responsive approach towards community groups. The idea is to improve the profile of police/community relations and to evolve a community safety programme (including both Community Relations and Crime Prevention activities).[4]
- Community participation: Community participation involves consultative groups, victim support schemes, crime presentation, exhibition and sports activities, interaction with the business community and distress telephone. The District Superintendents and the Sub-Divisional Police Officers should hold consultations with various groups. The groups should include elected and non-elected members from a cross-section of people. These groups should be constituted by the District Administration for their respective jurisdictions. At the same time, the government should provide funds for referring victims of crime—particularly burglary, theft or robbery—to groups of

volunteers who should help them in repairing psychological damage if any by the crime. Such volunteers may help the police in tracing the criminals. Furthermore, in each police station, in urban areas, an officer of the rank of Sub-Inspector with the assistance of an Assistant Sub-Inspector should visit shopping areas and advise people regarding preventive measures. He should also arrange neighbourhood watch where the citizens should co-operate with the police by keeping a watch on suspicious elements in the community and protecting each other's houses in their absence. These measures should be augmented by ensuring that various Station House Officers keep watch on the activities of street boys and bring to their parents' notice any deviant tendencies.

The Deputy Inspectors General and the Superintendents should be asked to hold regular meetings with the members of National and Provincial Assemblies, the Senators and the members of the local government of their areas. The police policies and problems should be brought to their notice. Similarly, the Sub-Divisional Police Officers should hold periodic meetings with the shopkeepers and business organizations within their jurisdiction. Attempts should be made to co-opt them in crime prevention.

To boost the above mentioned efforts, a two-digit distress telephone should be installed in all districts to attend to emergencies. Response time to distress calls will be reduced to restore public confidence.

A Sound Police-media Policy

The police are responsible for the protection of life, liberty and property of the citizens. For this purpose they have monopoly over legitimate coercive force which, though may not necessarily be used, yet is available for use when the circumstances so warrant. In the exercise of their deterrent function the police effectiveness and efficiency depend on their ability to obtain the acceptance and, if necessary, the support of majority of the different segments of the society. This, in turn, is shaped and modelled by the public image of police which, to a significant extent, is derived from the media presentation of policing. The image of the police reflected by the media is generally affected by the actualities of the police practice, but may not necessarily be a 'mirror-reflection' of the same. The industrial policy and political leanings of the media influence it. Nevertheless, a deliberate, planned and sustained public relations effort does quite often help the police in gaining a degree of public consent so vital for their success. This responsiveness to and concern for the media projection of the police—an important vehicle in the formulation of the public opinion—may be termed as the accountability of the police to the media. The media policy strategy must include:

Radio

Through radio programmes, large number of audience scattered throughout the country may be reached. All the DIGs (Deputy Inspectors General) and Superintendents of Police should maintain a close liaison with the Director of the nearest radio station. They must ensure participation of a maximum number of officers and men in radio programmes. In every district the anniversary of police martyrs needs to be commemorated. Special functions should be arranged to highlight their acts of valour. Police songs, paying tributes to them, should be widely circulated and their recorded cassettes be played. Proceedings of police functions held in the police lines on days of national importance (23 March, 14 August, 25 December, etc.) should be recorded and broadcast on the radio.

The Deputy Inspectors General and the District Superintendents of Police should ensure maximum participation of their officers and men in all types of radio programmes whether regular or especially arranged. For example:

- Broadcasting of interviews of officers and men involved in armed encounters with criminals, arrest of notorious gangs of outlaws and successful detection of difficult cases.
- Exchange of views with a cross-section of the community on matters pertaining to public perception of police working and the police views highlighting professional hazards and difficulties.
- Programmes arranged for housewives should include guidelines educating them on the subject of home security and protection against opportunistic crime.
- Police officers writing poetry should participate in *mushairas* and should not hesitate to disclose their police ranks.
- Audio cassettes of all radio programmes involving police officers and men should be prepared and sent to police training institutions. One copy should be sent to the Inspector General of Police. This aspect in the CPO (Central Police Office) can be looked after by the Assistant Inspector General (operations).
- Where the representatives of the radio are unable to cover an event, arrangements should be made for in-house recording.

In every district, selected men should be trained through the co-operation of the engineers of the Broadcasting Department so that they can undertake outdoor and indoor recording of quality fit for broadcasting. At the end of every quarter, all Range Deputy Inspectors General should send a detailed report to the Inspector General of Police mentioning various radio programmes in which police officers and men participated.

Television

Dissemination of information through the electronic media may go a long way in doing away with the monopoly of the print media in the field of crime reporting. This, however, will work if facts are reported about heinous crime and crime detection. One sided reporting of only crime detected will affect the credibility of the electronic media. Use can be made of programmes like the news, plays highlighting difficulties of police officers and men, Punjnad, Tariq Aziz Show, traffic and anti drug awareness programmes, educational programmes and programmes involving ladies and children. For this purpose, a special police committee headed by a Deputy Inspector General and three members including the Director Public Relations should hold regular/ periodic meetings with the Pakistan Television administration to evolve possible ways and means of improving police coverage.

The Print Media

The main principles of the media policy of the police should be openness and strict adherence to the truth as a means to sustain police credibility. This openness creates understanding and greater objectivity. The policy of openness, however, is subject to the constraints imposed by the need for natural justice in the disciplinary proceedings of the force and the requirements of the contempt law.

- Apart from the publication of a police magazine in every province, the respective Central Police Office and every district should publish a fortnightly/monthly newspaper (consisting of 12 pages of the size of *Time* magazine). The aim should be to reach a large audience and start a public debate about matters in which the police have a direct interest. This contribution is particularly important in such areas as public order, crimes of violence, and the increase in the use of firearms by both criminals and the police.
- Periodic publication of supplements in leading newspapers highlighting police performance and problems will go a long way in projecting proper police image.
- Presently the press is normally handled individually either at the Public Relations Officer level or by the individual officer. They do co-ordinate also but the required results are not obtained due to the fact that the department cannot refrain a

journalist from publishing distorted stories. It would be worthwhile if a legal officer may also be co-opted and used meaningfully in the set-up to deal with the media. His presence in the press briefing and advice to police officers prior to the briefing may go a long way in pre-empting subsequent legal complications. Legal officers may also be activated to challenge fabricated and slanderous reports appearing in the press. Desirability or otherwise of citing reporters as witnesses in sensational stories may also be examined. If they are cited as witnesses or complainants in sensational stories, the tendency to publish such stories will be discouraged.

In the same vein, legal approach may be used to forestall convening of such forums and gatherings where the intent is to malign the department. Similarly, libel proceedings may be initiated in deserving cases against defaulters. It has been generally seen that superior courts take a dim view of police behaviour largely due to the slant given to crime by the press. Whenever actual facts are brought to the notice of the courts, they always have taken a more realistic view. This affects the credibility of the press in the eyes of courts. Placing of actual facts before the courts cognizant of press stories in an organized and coherent way will improve the credibility of the police. This requires an institutionalized set-up.

- A medal and reward for the best investigative reporting will also go a long way in promoting amity between police personnel and media men.
- On the tactical side, three persons matter most as far as crime reporting is concerned. They are the crime reporter or correspondent, court reporter and shift in-charge or news editor. Proper respect and redress of their grievances and problems may go a long way in reducing bad publicity. This needs to be augmented by conducted tours of pressmen to police institutions to brief them about practical difficulties of the police.
- The police may evolve a system of issuing police accreditation cards for crime reporters.

- A system to brief the journalists regarding crime news should be evolved as an experiment in Lahore, Karachi, Peshawar, Quetta and Islamabad. The Public Relations Cell should be set up under an information office at the Central Police Office level. All serious crime reports or police performance of the day be faxed to this office daily by 5.00 pm and by 6.00 pm the newspapers should be briefed. All media men may be intimated to verify stories and gather information from this cell.

Crime Prevention Cell

This basis of good image is basically the way the individuals are dealt with by the police. The training must, therefore, emphasize courtesy and concern by operational officers. This, however, needs to be augmented by a deliberate public relations effort. For this purpose, it is proposed that a Crime Prevention Cell be set up in the office of the Inspector General of Police, under a Deputy Inspector General to be designated as the Deputy Inspector General Crime Prevention. The organizational chart of the proposed crime prevention cell has been given in Appendix 8. The Cell should arrange periodic seminars on policing, should have prepared videos, films and plays depicting the problems and lives of policemen and hold police-media talks at regular intervals.

- The work of the Crime Prevention Cell in the Central Police Office should be augmented by the posting of some officers of the rank of Assistant/Deputy Superintendent in each district as the Press Liaison Officer.
- The image building should be a collective and on-going effort. Periodic surveys should be conducted by the Crime Prevention Cell to measure the impact of its efforts.
- All these measures will succeed only if there is an effective follow up, technical inquiry and periodic review by

supervisory officers in relation to attitude and approach of individual officers.

It may, however, be pointed out that despite all these measures, it will not be possible for the police to have the support of all sections of the public. The public is not a homogeneous community. In every community there is concern for upright behaviour, efficiency and law enforcement, but one also finds compromised morality. These competing interests will have to be reconciled by working in close co-operation with the education department, the media, religious leaders and social welfare institutions. .

Revival of the '*Panchayat*' System

The restoration of *panchayats* can lift a great burden that the rural society has been carrying due to interminable delays and huge expenses involved in seeking justice even in small matters. In rural societies the more important cases relate to crimes involving property, cattle lifting, illicit weapons and minor disputes.

Crimes involving property primarily relate to burglary, theft and robbery. Cattle are a vital part of the village life and have always been subject to theft. Arms are needed to defend oneself against local enemies and are kept without licence if it cannot be obtained easily. Minor disputes occur over foul language, payments, eve-teasing, trespassing, etc. In all these cases, both parties have to suffer a great deal if either of them goes to the police. They realize that the punishment to the offender as well as the victim is far more than the offence justifies. They have to waste months even years while the case moves at a snail's pace, passing through investigations, court hearings and appeals.

If all these cases are handled by a *panchayat*, the situation will change dramatically. A *panchayat* meeting, with everybody present, can discuss all hard and circumstantial evidence in minute details and, keeping in view the traditions and social conditions, and come to a conclusion that will appear fair to everybody and give a judgement that will be acceptable to all.

Burden on the Police and the Judiciary

It is commonly known that there are neither enough policemen nor judges to deal with all cases speedily. The government cannot meet the requirement because of its limited resources and the great demand for development works. Therefore, it will be easier to meet the deficiency by reducing the workload rather than increasing the number of policemen and judges.

The handing over of less important cases to *panchayats* will allow more time and resources to the police to deal with serious crimes. Their efficiency will naturally improve when they have to deal with only about one-tenth of the cases. Consequently, crime control will be ensured, particularly in rural society, which is very conscious of its rather exaggerated sense of self-respect. Often clashes in rural areas are due to temporary burst of emotions and both sides are quite ready to patch up once they have cooled down. While the heat generated by emotions does not take long to dissipate, the case with the police does. It is after a great deal of loss of time, money and energy that the parties are able to get such a case settled at the investigation stage or during the court proceedings. However, a settlement will be a matter of a day or two if the matter goes to a *panchayat*, with the guilty party getting suitable punishment at the same time.

Arbitration at the Union Council Level

The Conciliation Court Ordinance, 1961 (as amended by Ordinance XVIII of 1982) was promulgated with view to entrusting certain disputes for decision at the Union Council Level by constituting courts headed by the Chairman of the Union Councils. Section 5 of the Ordinance explains that conciliation court shall consist of the chairman of the Union

Council and two representatives to be nominated by each of the parties to the dispute provided that one of the representatives so nominated shall be a member of the union council concerned.

Petty cases of both criminal and civil nature, which can be tried by the conciliation courts have been explained in the schedule to the Ordinance. The schedule has been bifurcated into two parts. Part I contains the offence which can be taken up by the conciliation court on the request of any of the parties, while it will take cognizance of a case falling in part II, if all the parties in the case agree to refer it to such court. A sample study of Union Councils Uggoki and Gohdpur (Sialkot District, 1991) was carried out which revealed that only seventeen and two cases respectively were instituted in these union councils in the year 1991, which were of civil nature. The general impression is that these courts are not functioning in a desirable manner, primarily due to some element of mistrust and partisan role of chairmen of Union Councils.

The ineffectiveness of these courts is adding to the work-load of police stations which are already facing great difficulties in the discharge of their official duties due to inadequate staff. Petty disputes sometimes culminate in serious offences. For the sake of giving strength to the decisions of these courts and to inspire confidence in the public, it is proposed that respective beat officer and revenue officer of the rank of *girdawar* may also be made ex-officio members of conciliation courts. This will help improve functioning of these courts, thereby relieving the police stations of unnecessary burden.

The Role of *'Numberdars/Chowkidars'*

The concept of village police officers requires activation of the role of *numberdar* and *chowkidar*. The *numberdar* should have a close link not only with the local union council but also with the police. He should monitor the working of the village *chowkidar*. The *chowkidar* should be required to co-ordinate his activities with the beat/zail officer of the police station and keep him informed about the presence of illicit arms, narcotics, suspicious characters and anti-social elements in his village. The *chowkidar* system has not been revived in its true spirit. The *chowkidar* should be paid out of the revenue fund and not from any other source.

Operational Police Schemes to Implement the Strategy of Crime Control

The strategy adopted by Sardar Muhammad Chaudhry, former Inspector General of the Punjab Police (from 20 June 1991 to 1 June 1993) provides food for thought. It may be emulated in all the provinces. One of the methods he employed effectively was to hold a series of conferences of Deputy Inspectors General of Police and other senior officer to discuss in depth the major issues and how to deal with them in the short as well as long term. The conferences were different in nature from the previous ones. The Inspector General did not give any stereotype orders or threats of punishment. Anybody could do that, he wanted his officers to apply their minds and come out with their best suggestions for solving the problems instead of merely obeying the orders of their superiors. He wanted this process to reach even the lowest levels of the force.

He started with conferences of Deputy Inspectors General and Senior Superintendents of Police at the provincial headquarters. These were followed by smaller ones at the range (divisional) headquarters where he would call at least half of the range Deputy Inspectors General of Police, Superintendents of Police of nearby districts and Deputy Superintendents of Police of the range along with relevant staff officers of the Central Police Office like Deputy Inspector General of Police (Crime Branch) and Director (Research and Development). Inspectors and selected Sub-Inspectors would also participate in those discussions.

The conference at the divisional headquarters would be enlarged the next day and held in a playground or parade ground so that the constabulary could also participate and give their observations and suggestions. The DIGS, SPs, DSPs, and SHOs were asked to hold such meetings on the same pattern in their own areas.

The proceedings were recorded and reported in detail in Urdu in the next issue of the monthly magazine of the range for the benefit of the entire force. The proceedings of the DIGs conferences at provincial headquarters were published in Urdu in *Muhafiz*, the Punjab police magazine for distribution among all policemen and officers of the departments related to criminal justice administration.

The provincial and other conferences were organized after brainstorming over many days to select subjects and issues. The officers would write papers on subjects of special interest to them. The detailed agenda and the papers were circulated in advance so that the participants could come fully prepared. The committees to monitor preparations were carefully constituted to ensure meaningful outcome. The items on agenda were mostly the practical problems faced by the police not only in the Punjab but also other parts of the country. For decades the successive governments and the senior command of the police had failed to attend to such professional matters. The long neglect had created a very serious situation not only regarding crime but also police management. Sardar Muhammad Chaudhary considered it his duty to not only attend to the neglected issues but also suggest realistic solutions with maximum participation from the highest to the lowest levels if the deteriorating trend in situation of loss had to be arrested. To broaden the scope of discussions and the flow of ideas, he would also invite senior officers from other provinces, Azad Kashmir and federal police agencies.

The conferences at the provincial level were attended by the Chief Secretary, Home Secretary, Law Secretary, Excise and Taxation Secretary, Advocate General and the Registrar of the High Court. The protocol was that the senior most among the participants would preside over the conference. At the divisional headquarters, the Commissioners, Deputy Commissioners and Sessions Judges would also attend and give their suggestions.

The same pattern was followed up to the lowest rung of criminal justice administrative machinery.

Long-term Solutions

Long-term solutions will include the preparation of Five-Year Plans (as was done in the Punjab in 1991–2) encompassing traffic management, training, transport and communications, arms modernization, modernization of equipment and logistic, constitution of a police technical cadre, modernization of investigative aids, detective training school, modern aid and equipment for scientific investigation, police buildings, manpower and morale, separation of investigation from watch and ward, strengthening of sub-divisional command, judicial lockups at sub-divisional level, induction at Sub-Inspector level with the minimum academic qualification of a graduate, encouragement of private detective and security agencies and police morale boosting. The details are as under:

Traffic Management

The total length of roads in the Punjab province, as it stood in 1990 is 27,566 kilometres as compared with 4305 kilometres in 1947. The following statement indicates traffic volume per 24 hours on various highways of the Punjab:

Lahore-Gujranwala GT Road

M/Cycle	Car	Wagon	Bus	Truck	Misc.
961	5785	2288	2529	2515	191

Traffic volume 24 hours = 15269

Lahore-Sheikhupura Road

M/Cycle	Car	Wagon	Bus	Truck	Misc.
848	1982	1072	975	1288	184

Traffic volume 24 hours = 6349

Lahore-Okara Multan Road

M/Cycle	Car	Wagon	Bus	Truck	Misc.
874	2961	818	1244	3870	686

Traffic volume 24 hours = 10453

Source: Highways Department, Government of the Punjab, Lahore 1990.

Keeping in view the road length and volume of traffic police kiosks on the pattern of police boxes in advanced countries need to be established. Police officers at police boxes will perform a wide range of activities such as patrolling their assigned jurisdiction to prevent crime and control traffic; providing crime prevention guidance and serving as a contact base between the police and travelling public. In urban areas broadcasting booths and free pattern information boards on highways, roadside radio rebroadcast system, ordinary and variable traffic signs should be used for traffic information dissemination. The information can be collected through vehicle detectors, TV cameras, helicopters, patrol cars and police motorcycles. In-built provision for Police Stations, Police Posts and Kiosks be made in all new projects of motorways, housing colonies, airports, parks, etc.

Training

The complex crime challenges posed by terrorism and organized crime call for proper training in anti-terrorism techniques. The Government of the Punjab, realizing the gravity of situation, established the Elite Police Training School at Lahore in 1997. This institution imparts training in techniques of combating terrorism and the Elite Police Force has played a pivotal role in curbing organized violent crime in the Punjab. It is proposed that all provinces should make similar arrangements.

Transport and Telecommunication

The importance of transport and telecommunications needs no emphasis for modern day policing. Whenever the fleet of transport or the equipment of telecommunications is provided, due importance is not attached to the factor of depreciation. As a result of this, after a period of four or five years, the whole fleet of transport reaches the stage of total breakdown. Thus, at the end of the brief period of ease, the situation becomes desperate and new efforts begin for a new fleet. Assuming the total life of a vehicle to be five years, it is suggested that 20 per cent of the supply of transport every year should be provided every year to keep the situation from deterioration. Similarly addition in telecommunication equipment, keeping in mind the depreciating factor, should also be added on yearly basis after every initial supply.

Arms Modernization

This is another sector in which the police force lags far behind the criminal, against whom it is supposed to run a crusade. The present day criminal is equipped not only with the sophisticated automatic small arms but also with deadly weapons like mortars, rocket launchers, and at times, with missiles and light artillery. In order to meet the challenge, there is an urgent need to equip the police force with modern matching weapons so that it can face the criminals with confidence.[5] It may, however, be added that for tear gas ammunition, instead of relying on foreign sources of supply, possibility of its manufacture by the Wah Industries needs to be explored. This will ensure not only uninterrupted supply but will also help save valuable foreign exchange.

Modernization of Equipment and Logistics

At present, the police are practically all brawn and no brain. The ratio of manpower to equipment is extremely low. As a result, almost everything is done by hand and thus the normal efficiency is very low. Modern equipment and aids are essential to bring the police out of the nineteenth century and improve their performance. A policeman in the field must have maximum support from his office, where computers and other facilities should be available. He himself should carry some of the elementary gadgets, like a pocket camera, tape-recorder, binoculars, etc. in addition to his arms. The equipment needed is of fairly common nature and does not involve any high degree of sophistication. Therefore, it will not be difficult to make full use of it.

Constitution of a Police Technical Cadre

There is need for introducing a technical cadre as an effective support unit. This will comprise technical supportive services working in the police department like computer personnel, wireless operators, mechanics, fax operators, photographers, forensic experts, etc. with or without police ranks.

Modernization of Investigative Aids

Forensic Science Laboratory and the Finger Print Bureau needs modern equipment, qualified staff and suitable building. The subject of Forensic Science is not taught at college/university level nor is there any institute of training for experts. Those joining the laboratory get on the job training. For the last twenty-three years, no expert has been sent abroad for higher studies in this science. In view of restricted promotion and lack of facilities, highly qualified people are reluctant to join and serve these institutions.

Detective Training School

Realizing the importance of scientific investigation, a Detective Training School was started in Lahore in 1967 to apprise the investigation officers of scientific methods of investigation and improve its standard. Subjects of forensic science, photography, criminology and fingerprints were included in the syllabus of scientific course of three months. Sub-Inspectors of police, from all over Pakistan, used to attend the course. Qualification of the course was included in the criteria for promotion from the rank of Sub-Inspector to Inspector. Establishment of a scientific institution was a good step to improve the scientific/detective knowledge of the investigating officers and meet the future requirements. The institution ceased to function in 1976. It is in the fitness of things to suggest its revival to impart necessary scientific training in this area of science.

Modern Aids and Equipment for Scientific Investigation

In addition to the increasing difficulty of criminal investigation due to it being spread over wide geographical areas and being committed with greater frequency and being committed in a sophisticated manner, efforts to track down criminals through the material evidence recovered from the scene of crime have often been hampered by the barriers of industrial mass production and distribution. On the other hand, investigation by questioning people in the vicinity of crime scene to obtain even the smallest scrap of information has become more difficult because helpful eyewitness information is seldom available in the urban area. Also, it has become increasingly difficult to obtain information or co-operation from a third person because of the indifference among citizens for the life of other people.

In view of these circumstances, the police need to strengthen capability for wide-area investigation by bolstering inter-provincial police co-operation in criminal investigations and improving wide-area alert systems in addition to the use of computers to control investigation information. The police should be provided with new equipment such as a system for automatically reading out the plate numbers of motor vehicles, and automatic fingerprint identification device. This is essential to strengthen and provide sophisticated investigation measure such as enabling the 'microscopic identification' of an extremely small amount of material evidence or minute material evidence left at the scene of crime. Measures need to be taken to strengthen police capability of international criminal investigation and encourage the use of police dogs in the identification process.

Automated Fingerprint Identification System, White Light Fingerprint Detection System, Fingerprint Identification Process, the process of car paint identification through colour value measurements, training and utilization of police dogs, instruments for identification, Reference Data Centre and equipment for lifting of foot prints are some of the technical aids which can be acquired over a period of time either through purchase or co-operation from friendly countries like Japan.

Police Buildings

Proper buildings, whether for offices or as living accommodation for officers and men, are another sector in which the police department presents a dismal and pathetic picture. Barracks and family quarters for men and officers are far below the required number worked out in the police rules. There are some dilapidated and dangerous buildings housing police stations and police posts, and in other cases, are functioning in rented buildings. In the Punjab alone, about 200 police stations are without proper lockups, of which the Lahore High Court has also taken a very serious view. The Punjab Constabulary Battalion Lines at various locations and Police Training Schools and Centres are also in dire need of these facilities. Last but not the least, each and every Police Lines needs a proper and well-equipped gymnasium to cater to the needs of unarmed combat, physical training and recreation of the Force.

The state of police buildings is miserable. Most of the constabulary does not have a proper roof over its head. They either live in dangerous buildings or under tents. Police Lockups are unsafe and at places are housed in rented accommodation. Sub-human working and living conditions are having a direct bearing on the efficiency and morale of the police force. This also lowers the image of the police in the eyes of the public with attendant disrespect for governmental authority exercised through police functionaries. An elaborate and immediate building programme for the above purposes needs to be undertaken.

Manpower

Due to increasing population, without the simultaneous increase in the police force, a huge shortfall has taken place. One glaring example of this is the shortage in the watch and ward and investigation staff of the police stations. The staff of police stations is determined in accordance with the Police Rule 2.2. The watch and ward staff is sanctioned for the urban police stations, i.e. for cities, towns and cantonments which have a population of more than 30,000. One constable is sanctioned for 450 inhabitants, one head constable is provided for every ten constables, one assistant sub-inspector to every five head constables and one sub-inspector to every hundred constables. According to the same police rules the watch and ward staff has to work in three shifts of eight hours each. Similarly, for investigation duties, one upper subordinate, i.e. sub-inspector/ assistant sub-inspector is sanctioned for every fifty registered cases along with two constables. Besides this, one upper subordinate is posted for 200 petty cases along with two constables. For the Punjab province, if requirement of one shift of watch and ward staff is worked out, it comes to: Inspectors/ 65, SIs/299 ASIs/1227, HCs/6734 and Constables/34,112. If we multiply it with three and add the shortage in investigation staff, a mammoth shortfall of 1051 SIs, 4249 ASIs, 21,900 Head Constables and 110,000 Constables is reached. However, keeping the resource constraints in mind, staff for only one shift needs to be provided. Requirements for each provincial police can be worked out accordingly.

Separation of Investigation from Watch and Ward

The separation already exists at the police station level. What is desired is the phased increase in the number of investigation officers of the rank of ASI (Assistant Sub-Inspector) and above since presently about 90 per cent of manpower comprises constabulary whose primary task is to perform watch and ward functions. Increased numerical strength and academic qualifications of investigating officers will go a long way in speedy investigation and submission of cases to courts.

Strengthening of Sub-Divisional Command

The weakest link in the police hierarchy is at the sub-divisional level. A Sub-Divisional Police Officer is supposed to supervise and manage at least three or four police stations. He is required to personally visit the scene of the crime in important cases. The staff support available to him consists mostly of only a reader and an assistant reader of the ranks of a Head Constable and a Constable respectively. In case of public disorder, out-break of violence or commission of heinous crime, he has to rely on the reserves available in the District Headquarters. The movement of reserves from the District Headquarters to the place of occurrence consumes a lot of time and prevents timely effective action at the Sub-divisional level. It will be in the fitness of things to propose that the idea of mini-district at the sub-divisional level be given a practical shape. Each sub-division should have mini police lines having at least two reserves of its own. The sub-divisional police officer should also have adequate staff support carefully worked out according to the volume of his work. He should have his own office establishment and adequate authority to control his subordinates.

Judicial Lock-Ups at the Sub-Divisional Level

The lack of adequate judicial lock-ups at the sub-divisional level poses a serious security problem at present. The prisoners are quite frequently waylaid by armed criminals on the way to courts. The need for adequate, secure and properly staffed judicial lockups at sub-divisional level is of paramout importance.

Induction at SI (Sub-Inspector) Level with Minimum Academic Qualification of a Graduate

This will bring in better stuff into the police, primarily tasked for investigation of complicated crimes both social as well as economic in nature.

Encouragement of Private Detectives and Security Agencies

Beside easing the burden of the police, such agencies will lend a helping hand to normal investigation agencies. They will bring fresh concepts and techniques of crime detection and control which may act as an example for normal investigation outfits.

Police Morale

Police morale is functionally related to measures undertaken by the government for the welfare and upkeep of police functionaries who are ready to lay down their lives for the protection of life, liberty and prosperity of the people. Factors such as hours of duty, rest days, conditions of service, working conditions and welfare aspects also need to be addressed. A survey of ninety police officials (including Inspectors, Sub-Inspectors and Assistant Sub-Inspectors) by a researcher of the Department of Sociology, University of Punjab, regarding security feelings and professional commitment resulted in the following observation:[6]

64.44 per cent felt insecure from the illegal transfer and or suspension caused by political influence; 50 per cent felt insecure from the suspected victimization of their high ups; 57.78 per cent did not feel secure with their monthly salary; 57.78 per cent did not feel secure with the provision of residential facilities provided by the department; a little less than one half of the respondents (47.78 per cent) felt insecurity for the future of their children in case of any accident during professional performance; majority of the respondents (52.22 per cent) did not feel secure from the sophisticated weapons possessed by the criminals; a substantial number of the respondents (47.78 per cent) realized that there was no guarantee of proper legal action against the accused.

It is obvious that in Pakistan, serious inadequacy of barrack accommodation, poor quality of both married and unmarried accommodation, serious inadequacy of medical cover for policemen and their families, long and tiring hours of duty and inadequate and delayed compensation for police officers killed/ disabled during encounters in the line of duty have an adverse effect on the personality and performance of the policemen. It goes without saying that all these factors are producing a 'dehumanizing effect' on policemen, making them 'rude, callous and culturally insensitive'. The government of the Punjab in 1988 adopted the following scheme of benefits for officers and men killed or injured in the line of duty:

a) Monetary compensation of Rs 300,000 to the families of police officials killed in armed encounters with criminals.
b) Grievous injury/incapacitation compensation of Rs 100,000.

Following additional proposals need consideration:
• A shift system on the pattern of the continental shift system (each shift of eight hours duration) be introduced in Pakistan. The gigantic expenditure involved may make its immediate materialization difficult. Until the time the shift system becomes a reality, an additional allowance to the extent of 20 per cent of pay be allowed to all ranks upto Inspector in lieu of overtime and for being on duty for twenty-four hours.
• There is no holiday for police officers in Pakistan. A weekly day off be given to all staff which can be managed by suitably rotating the staff.
• In case of death, the family of deceased police officer should be given:
  - a lump sum of Rs 500,000
  - monthly pension equivalent to the pay of the deceased upto the date on which he would have normally retired and thereafter a pension to his widow as would have accrued if he had been alive. (This has been introduced in the Punjab province since June 1992.)
• In case of disability, compensation may be given according to the following scale:
  - Rs 150,000 for major disability resulting in discontinuation of service.
  - Rs 30,000 for disability rendering a person unfit for field duty.
  - Rs 10,000 for other injuries.

It is worth pointing out that by the end of the year 2001, in the Punjab, in pursuance of the approval already granted by the competent authority, the compensation for the families of *shaheed* (killed) incapacitated police officials will be enhanced from Rs 300,000 and Rs 100,000 respectively to Rs 500,000 and Rs 200,000 respectively.

Beside measures cited above, there is a dire need for establishment of:
- Police hospitals in major cities on the pattern of CMH.

- Police public schools in all range headquarters. The education of the children of police officials is always neglected due to frequent transfers and is a source of constant worry for them. Such schools, moreover, will go a long way in fostering better police-public understanding.

Political Neutrality of Police Operations

The Aslam Hayat Police Committee, borrowing the idea of the Public Safety Commission from Japan, proposed that a Public Safety Commission be constituted to provide democratic control over the police at the provincial level and ensure political neutrality of all police operations.[7] The Commission, the committee proposed, will consist of:

(1) Minister in charge of Home Affairs as its ex-officio Chairman;

(2) Leader of the Opposition as member;

(3) Two members of the Provincial Assembly to be nominated by the Provincial Government on the advice of the Speaker;

(4) Four members to be nominated by the Chief Minister of the province after approval from the Assembly, as far as possible one each from amongst retired judges of the High Court, retired senior public administrators, eminent social scientists or academicians;

(5) The Inspector General of Police as Ex-officio Secretary.

The main functions of the Commission proposed by the Aslam Hayat Police Committee are:

• to inspect and report to the Provincial Assembly serious complaints of police excesses or persistent complaints of corruption against any district unit;

• to lay down broad police guidelines regarding service-oriented functions of the police; and

• to function as a forum of appeal for disposing of representations regarding victimization of officers refusing to obey illegal or irregular orders, if any, in the performance of their duties except those the remedies for which are otherwise provided under the law.[8]

Urban Policing

In large urban areas, several problems arising out of social tensions, greater opportunities for crime, and occasional spontaneous explosion of public disorder call for immediate response from the police at the operational levels and precise, comprehensive and prompt direction from the superior levels. There is seldom any time for discussion and debate and assessments and agreements. This can be achieved only when the police have a single chain of command, which performs the functions of decision-making and implementation. In large cities specially, these functions have to go together. It is therefore recommended that in Karachi, Lahore, Faisalabad, Rawalpindi, Multan, Gujranwala, Peshawar, Quetta and Hyderabad (with a population of more than 500,000) the system of Metropolitan Policing, as it exists in London and other Metropolitan areas of England and Wales, should be introduced. It is important that the Commissioner should be a police officer of adequate maturity, seniority and expertise. The Police Commissioner should have complete authority over his force and should be functionally autonomous.

This will require the replacement of the 1861 Police Act with a new Act. The new Act should provide for the metropolitan system in all the major cities mentioned above. The Ministry of Interior, Government of Pakistan, started considering the proposal of introducing metropolitan policing system in the major cities of Pakistan in January 2000.

Legal Aspects

Constitutional protection needs to be extended to all public servants, including public prosecutors. Furthermore, their selection should be made through the Public Service Commission. It is also in the fitness of things to propose that the mode of promotions of prosecutors be streamlined and the criteria of merit be strictly observed. The prosecutors/attorneys should have the same qualifications as those of the judges and be given the same emoluments and facilities. Simultaneously, the forensic and chemical laboratories need to be developed immediately to improve the quality of circumstantial evidence presented in the courts. The police should be encouraged to use fingerprints, footprints, photography and other scientific techniques. The eyewitnesses should be provided protection so that they are able to get their statement recorded without any fear. Enhanced penalties should be instituted to curb the prevalent practice of putting stock witnesses in the dock and filing fake sureties for bails. Last but not the least, cases should be quickly investigated and submitted to courts. The investigation officers should not be transferred too frequently.

Courts

It goes without saying that the judiciary should be separated from the executive at all levels in accordance with the constitutional provisions and the recent decision of the Supreme Court. The Supreme Court and the High Courts should handle the appointments, promotion and personal matters of the judiciary. All the appointments should be made on merit and through an apolitical forum. Service conditions of judges be improved and their emoluments increased to ensure that they do not fall prey to temptations. The retirement age of the judges of the Supreme Court and the High Courts should be the same.

The term that a number of people have used to capture the cluster of issues is governance. An essential component of governance is incentive compatibility, i.e. how can individual incentives be made to coincide with the public interest. In order to answer this question, one has to understand the structure of economic relationships, as well as the institutions and arrangements through which these relationships are governed. In the bureaucracy, things like supervision and monitoring, training, promotions and punishments, pay and perquisites govern these relations. Not enough attention has been given to these. Indeed, these issues are important even in discussing market signals especially when it comes to the informal sector. In Pakistan, economic relationships in the formal sector are governed through formal sector institutions including banks, auditors and government agencies, as well as access of the economic agents to the corridors of power. In the informal sector, by and large, it takes place through personal networks of family '*biraderi*', neighbourhood and the like. In order to make the informal sector more dynamic, one has to understand the basis upon which these informal institutions function, and the extent and limits of the co-operation they engender.

A very important point is the strengthening of the role, the autonomy, the independence and the integrity of judicial institutions in the country. The effectiveness of the lower courts is a major determinant to the enforceability of contracts as far as the small producer, such as one in the informal sector, is concerned. Since mutual co-operation is impossible without enforceable agreements, this determines the limits of mutual co-operation. At the moment, since the lower judiciary is overburdened (or because of other problems) it is not viewed by many as a reliable and speedy recourse. As a result, most small producers tend to limit their co-operation only to their personal networks. This creates a number of obstacles to improvements in efficiency in the informal sector.

Streamlining Procedures and Systems

The strengthening of the judiciary is a key to the continuation of the dynamism of the informal sector. In addition to this, a strong judiciary is vital to the creation of an atmosphere of stability and predictability in the absence of which economic agents cannot make long-term economic decisions. The creation of stability also requires respect for procedures in the government. It is correct that the uncertainty and unpredictability faced by the small producer is in large part because of arbitrary government policies. However, it may be added that it is because of the arbitrariness of the intervention, not because of the intervention itself. The arbitrariness of the government action should be reduced. However, this should happen not through the disappearance of the State but through the establishment of systems and procedures, through the provision of proper incentives to officials, through proper supervision and monitoring, and through better training and professionalism.

Prisons

Prisons in Pakistan are over-crowded. It is proposed that to reduce overcrowding in prisons, reports should be obtained regarding the offender's personality, family background, work record, his/her associates, etc. These reports may contain recommendations relating to suitability or otherwise of particular sentencing measures, although they should be intended only as a guide to the sentencing court. Apart from imprisonment, the following sentencing choices may be considered by the courts:

- Community services orders: a means of restitution to the community, which requires the offender to perform certain tasks for a prescribed duration.
- Probation: allowing the convicted person to remain at liberty but subject to certain conditions and restrictions. Such sentences may or may not involve supervision by a probation officer.
- Fines: primarily applied as penalties for relatively minor offences.

If sentenced to a prison term, the offender may be eligible for parole after serving a specific portion of the sentence. Parole is conditional release of a prisoner before serving the full sentence. The decision to grant parole should be generally made by a parole board.

These measures need to be strengthened through police cautioning of juvenile offenders and adoption of case screening practices. The sentencing policy must aim at reducing the excessively large number of remanded prisoners. At the same time, more separate jails should be built for juveniles and female convicts and steps should be taken to provide a healthy and reformative atmosphere in jails for the convicts. Excessive delays in the investigation and trial of cases must be minimized to reduce overcrowding in the prisons. There should be no special class available for the convicts in prisons. Time spent in jail during trial should be counted in the sentenced period. At present this provision is discretionary and it must be made mandatory.

There is no definite philosophy of imprisonment in Pakistan. It is not clear as to what is the objective of imprisonment vis-à-vis deterrence, retribution, reformation or incapacitation. We need to define our objectives and adopt a specific philosophy of punishment in accordance with our socio-economic and cultural environment. This, if done, will enhance effectiveness of the prison service and ensure a pragmatic sentencing policy. The strength of the prison service needs to be increased so that the personnel of the prison service escort the prisoners on judicial remand to courts. This will save police time and resources and they will be able to concentrate more on crime prevention and detection.

Medico-Legal Services

Medico-legal services should be improved by ensuring the issuance of medico legal certificates on merit. Those found guilty of issuing such certificates on considerations other than merit need to be made accountable through appropriate disciplinary measures.

Measures to Combat Terrorism

An important trend in the pattern of lawlessness over the past decade has been growth in the international dimension of crime. The criminal frequently seeks to use the separation of national jurisdictions to evade detection or punishment. The government should aim to ensure that there is no sanctuary for criminals by this means. Effective frontier controls should be maintained and full co-operation be given to international agencies and organizations to combat crime at this level. Wider arrangements for mutual assistance with other countries should be developed. Co-operation amongst democratic countries against terrorism is essential, not only in relation to improving physical security measures or the exchange of intelligence, but also in harmonizing political responses. A common approach is needed if State-sponsored terrorism is to be deterred. If terrorists win substantive concessions from a democratic government in one country, they are likely to give encouragement to terrorists in other countries. The government should take a lead in promoting discussion and co-operation at the international level.

Simultaneously, there is a need for evolving an appropriate response to the long-term changes in the economic structure of cities by helping to foster enterprise, encourage investment and create jobs. This response should also cater to social needs directly by supporting community and voluntary effort.

NOTES

1. Nadeem, A. H. (1989), *The Punjab Police in a Comparative Perspective*, Progressive Publishers, Zaildar Park, Ichhra, Lahore.
2. This information was collected from the Home Office, Government of the United Kingdom, Metropolitan Police, Tokyo and the Central Police Office, Punjab, Lahore in August 1991.
3. It is noteworthy that the Government of the Punjab constituted a Committee headed by Akhtar Mahmood, Member of the Provincial Assembly in December 1998 to suggest measures for making the Punjab Police people friendly, performance oriented and a symbol of peace and

respect rather than of oppression and torture. The Committee made the following recommendations:

Police constables should be imparted training of a very high standard to make them professionally sound and service-oriented. The recently started training of directly recruited Police Inspectors at the Police College, Sihala, may be adopted as a role model to be followed at other police training schools. Special efforts should be made for revamping of training institutions with a view to improving the existing training facilities and syllabus. The Inspector General of Police should arrange specialized refresher courses for staff in police stations.

As part of the process of cultural transformation, particularly at the police station level, two model police stations (one urban and one rural) should be established immediately in all the thirty-four districts of the Province. These police stations will serve as a role model in terms of performance and community satisfaction/participation. Selections of officers for posting in model police stations should be made very carefully. Proper equipment, transport, wireless sets and logistics should be provided to them. A package of incentives may also be worked out for the staff posted in such model police stations.

Neighbourhood watch schemes should be launched in urban residential localities. Public co-ordinators of the concerned residential area and beat officers should work together for ensuring peace and order in large cities. District Committees, comprising local Members of Provincial Assembly, District Superintendents of Police and Deputy Commissioners should select public co-ordinators of good reputation and integrity from amongst councillors and notables so that undesirable elements do not get access to police stations.

A core of young public volunteers, comprising college students and existing 'Police Qaomi Razakars' (civilian volunteers working for the police) should be raised in each district. They will work as additional police during emergencies, law and order situations during *muharram*, elections and natural calamities. This will help bridge the gap between police and the public. Existing system of Police Qaomi Razakars needs revamping.

Day and night shift duty officers in all police stations should deal with public complaints and redress their grievances.

Police cabins/contact points should be established in every urban locality at all important points especially commercial areas. This will ensure police presence and provide a general sense of security to the community against fear of crimes.

Police barriers should be removed from the cities. Mobile and random patrolling/checking should be made effective.

Frequent transfer of investigations should be discouraged. In order to ensure fair and just process of investigation, the following measures are recommended:

Insofar as possible, one investigation officer should be allowed to complete the investigation of a particular case. Transfer of investigation, if it is deemed essential, may be allowed for a maximum of three times, by Sub-Divisional Police Officers; Superintendents of Police and Range Deputy Inspectors General. For this purpose they will examine the record of the case in question and hear both the parties. It will be mandatory for all of them to record their reasons for transfer of investigation. In murder cases, an officer not below the rank of the Superintendent of Police will visit the scene of crime within twenty-four hours. The maximum period for completion of investigation should be fixed as one month.

Mandatory and legal requirements of timeframe for completion of investigations should be fulfilled. However, investigations should not prolong beyond one month.

Strict punitive action should be taken against the police officer responsible for conducting false and unfair investigation. Illegal or wrong arrest of any citizen, particularly in heinous cases, should result in dismissal of the officer affecting such arrest.

Every arrest under Section 54 of the Code of Criminal Procedure (1898) should be made with the prior approval of a gazetted police officer.

Investigation of blind murder cases, acts of terrorism and other heinous/ sensational cases should be assigned to District Central Intelligence Agency which should consist of a group of dedicated and honest police officers. Mobile crime laboratory should be raised in each district for reaching the scene of crime immediately and giving help in preserving the crime scene and carrying out the investigation on scientific lines.

Presently 80 per cent of Head Constables are performing mechanical duties. They are not performing the important task of investigation. Therefore, there is tremendous pressure on the limited number of Assistant Sub-Inspectors, Sub-Inspectors and Inspectors for investigation. The Committee recommended that the Head Constables, with minimum qualification of FA or equivalent, should also be authorized to investigate cases. An amendment in relevant Police Rules and the Code of Criminal Procedure (1898) was suggested to give effect to this recommendation.

The police should not interfere with non-cognizable offences. All matters pertaining to monetary transactions should be documented. Furthermore, all cases of quarrels need to be made cognizable. A special committee be constituted to examine the matter and make recommendations for necessary legislation. This committee should also suggest alternative remedies with a view to relieving the police of the burden of involvement in settling non-cognizable offences.

The Police Rules already provide for separation of watch and ward and investigation functions. However, practically, no such separation exists. To start with, watch and ward functions may be gradually separated from investigation in urban police stations.

District Superintendents of Police should, carefully, on the basis of professionalism and integrity, post Station House Officers. In case allegations against any Station House Officer are proven, he should be placed under suspension instead of mere transfer from his place of posting.

Weeding out of corrupt police officers/officials should be done in phases. To start with, Deputy Superintendents of Police and Inspectors with bad reputation should be sidelined immediately and debarred from field postings. District level committees, consisting of Members of Provincial Assembly, officials and respectable persons, should be constituted. They will identify corrupt police officials with a view to weeding them out of service.

Complaints of corruption and high-handedness against police officials should be accorded highest priority. Monitoring of the functioning of police force at District level should be streamlined and made effective.

Police officials are presently performing duties almost round the clock. They need rest as is allowed to other government servants. Therefore, shift system of 12-hours needs to be introduced. The beginning should be made with urban police stations.

Promotion examination of constables should be very fair and centrally organized to ensure standardization. The Constables who qualify the promotion examination should be promoted as Head Constables as soon as possible.

Direct recruitment of policemen should be made at three levels only i.e. Constable, Sub-Inspector and Assistant Superintendent of Police. The rank of Assistant Sub-Inspector may be declared a promotion rank by doing away with 25 per cent quota for direct recruitment. Direct recruitment in the rank of Sub-Inspector should be restricted to 25 per cent of total posts. Necessary amendment in Police Rules should be made to give effect to these recommendations.

Basic educational qualification for Constables needs to be raised to Intermediate level instead of Matriculation. Boards constituted at District level purely on merit should recruit Constables.

The Committee felt that in sectarian and ethnic cases, statements made under Section 161 Code of Criminal Procedure (1898) before a gazetted police officer be made admissible in evidence before a court of law. However, it was recommended that a sub-committee on legislation be constituted to review this in the light of decision given by the Supreme Court of Pakistan in a recent case holding that the statement recorded before a police officer could not be accepted as a piece of evidence in the court.

Panchayat Committees at electoral ward level, institution of honorary magistrates and reconciliation courts be revived/constituted for resolution of petty disputes and summary trial of non-cognizable cases with a view to ensuring immediate disposal of such matters.

Short-term and long-term plans be evolved for construction of police station buildings with a visible change in their design to cater for modern-day requirements such as a reception/complaint counters, briefing rooms, etc. Preference should be given to construction of barracks and family quarters to provide residential facilities to police officials. To begin with, at least 2 per cent of the total outlay of Annual Development Plan should be earmarked for police buildings.

The competent authority should appoint a Standing Commission on Police for constant monitoring and evaluation of their performance. A Member of the Provincial Assembly may head the Commission. Other members of the Standing Commission will include retired judges, an eminent lawyer, a professor, the provincial Home Secretary and the Inspector General of Police, Punjab. The commission should constantly evolve policies related with policing matters and act as an accountability commission on behalf of the public. The secretariat support may be provided by the Inspector General of Police, Punjab. The commission shall report directly to the head of the Provincial Government.

Gallantry awards QMP (Quaid-e-Azam Police Medal) and PPM (President's Police Medal) should carry a monthly allowance of Rs 3000.

A Committee headed by Talib Hussain, Member Provincial Assembly, had already submitted its recommendations on the issue of review of salary structure for Constables and Head-Constables. This Committee recommended that the recommendations made by the aforesaid Committee might be adopted. The salary structure up to the rank of Inspector be reviewed with a view to providing appropriate relief package to police officials.

4. The tasks required to achieve these key objectives of community policing will involve the need for designing performance indicators to encourage activities aimed at developing a positive role for respective provincial police forces in the community, providing training to meet the defined needs of those officers who have daily contact with the community and developing existing and creating new avenues of co-operation with the community through the establishment of appropriate district level liaison groups to streamline police involvement with members of various interest groups.

5. At present, the personal weapon for the Constable and the Head Constable is the rifle (.30 or 7.62 mm) while the upper subordinates are authorized to carry a six-shot revolver. Gazzetted officers can equip themselves with either a pistol or a revolver, at their own expense.

A police officer in the field is called upon these days to deal with criminals who are armed with sophisticated and deadly automatic weapons like Mouzers and Kalashnikovs. In almost 95 per cent of the cases, a police officer has to tackle such criminals in crowded or built-up areas. For this purpose, he needs a weapon, which can be pulled out immediately, and is capable of being used at short range and in crowded localities. The rifle is a long-range weapon, is heavy and cumbersome. It is impossible to use it with speed and accuracy at close quarters and in congested areas. Resultantly, the police fail to effectively counter the criminals during commission of serious crime. They are unable to return the fire from the outlaws due to sheer unsuitability of the weapon carried by them. Heavy causalities are being suffered by the police at the hands of the criminals merely for want of a proper weapon to combat them.

All over the world, policemen of all ranks use automatic pistols as their personal weapon. This is the weapon which has been found ideally suited to the nature of operational duties required to be performed by the police, in their day to day functioning. It is light, can be carried in a side holster with uniform or in a concealed manner in plain clothes in an under-arm holster, and is a safe and effective short-range hand-gun which can be used in crowded areas with maximum possible safety for innocent citizens who may otherwise be seriously injured or killed as a result of cross firing between the police and criminals.

6. Ahmad, R. I. (1988), 'Security Feelings and Professional Commitment of Police Officers', a thesis submitted to the Department of Sociology, University of the Punjab, Lahore, pp. 71–2 (unpublished).

7. Government of Pakistan (1985), *The Aslam Hayat Police Committee (1985) Report*, Islamabad, Ministry of the Interior, Government of Pakistan, Para 60.

8. The Government of General Pervez Musharraf, after assuming power on 12 October 1999, constituted focal groups under the Ministry of Interior to consider possibility of constituting a National Public Safety Commission. The Federal Cabinet, in its meeting held on 11 April 2001, took the following decisions to improve the quality of policing in the country:

a) An independent Public Safety Commission to be established at the national level to insulate the police from extraneous interference and to ensure political neutrality of its operations.

b) The Provincial Governments to establish Provincial Public Safety Commissions.

c) Independent police forces to be established in the capital city districts of Islamabad, Karachi, Lahore, Peshawar and Quetta.

d) A Police Complaints Authority to be established in each province and for the Federal Capital Territory.

e) An independent Prosecution Service to be established in each province, as also in relation to the police law enforcement agencies of Federal Government.

f) A Criminal Justice Co-ordination Committee to be established in each district headed by the District and Sessions Judge.

g) The police force in each district to be organized on functional basis.

13

CONCLUSION

The primary functions of a modern democratic state including the protection of life, liberty and property of its citizens and improvement in the overall quality of life implying maintenance of rule of law and ensuing economic development are interdependent and mutually supportive. Crime is a major problem of national and international dimensions. In certain cases it affects political, economic, social and cultural development of nations and obstructs the protection of human rights, fundamental freedoms and peace, stability and security.

Organized crimes, economic crimes and terrorism and insurgency do derail the process of economic development and their impact transcends national boundaries. This has led to the realization of the need for international co-ordination and co-operation culminating in the adoption of practically oriented bilateral and multi-lateral model treaties designed to improve crime prevention and criminal justice administration.

Though no economic progress is possible in a state of chaos, disorder or absence of the rule of law, only recently it has been realized that economic development does not merely denote a relentless pursuit of a higher Gross National Product (GNP). Economists like Paul Streeten, focusing on human development and North, emphasizing the critical role of maintenance of the rule of law in the institutional setting, do imply that economic development includes an improvement in the quality of life, which cannot be achieved in a state of anarchy and crime-ridden society.

Lawlessness in Pakistan is characterized by political pattern, socio-economic lawlessness and crime. All these aspects have assumed gigantic proportions over the past few decades. Considered in the theoretical context and political overtones of lawlessness, the present state of virtual anarchy in Pakistan is an outcome of multiplicity of factors including tolerance and acceptance of lawlessness resulting from the abrogation of the 1956 constitution, glorification of crime, erosion of patriotism, moral breakdown, immoral and illegitimate governance, decadence of the educational system, media madness, population explosion, haphazard process of urbanization, unemployment, social injustice, sectarian bigotry, transborder troubles, internal terrorism, loss of national honour and self-esteem, tempting evacuee property, dichotomy of laws in settled and tribal areas, misuse of police force by successive governments, marginalization of the police from the public, removal of organized public support system, introduction of basic democracy, demolition of criminal justice system, illegal immigrants and refugee dens, repudiation of the concept of Pakistan, drug menace, kalashnikov syndrome, ethnic issues and their exploitation, extension of patronage to criminals by a multiplicity of political, religious, feudal, ethnic and linguistic organizations and influential personalities, etc.

Economic development and law and order are interconnected and interdependent. It is possible to delineate the relationship between law and order and economic development both at the macro-economic and micro-economic levels. Law and order can be considered as an implicit assumption in the classical theories of growth, Spengler's analysis of civil and political order and the Rostowian model of growth.

Attempts have been made to establish linkages between law and order and economic development. The fundamental reality becomes absolutely clear that the law and order situation is the primary cause of macro-economic instability, which is reflected in fluctuation and variations in prices, production of goods and services and other related economic variables. On the contrary, a country having no law and order problem gets the benefits of macro-economic stability and sustainable economic growth.

Likewise, strategies of economic development pertaining to urbanization and social sectors like health, housing and education or even growth-rate oriented policies with a perception of inequality in the distribution of income adversely affect crime prevention and criminal justice issues.

The socio-economic costs of lawlessness in Pakistan have been colossal. Socio-economic lawlessness, political pattern of flouting the constitution and laws and an incessant wave of terrorism, violence and organized crime bordering on a state of virtual anarchy, particularly in Karachi, have substantially affected the economic performance of Pakistan. The empirical evidence is available in the shape of trends emerging in the relationship between law and order and economic indicators like the rates of growth of the Gross National Product (GDP), manufacturing sector and agriculture along with the rate of inflation and unemployment. These indicators have been considered in their historical perspective. Their movement has taken place in a positive or negative direction depending on the relative stability or instability in law and order condition during the timeframe taken into consideration. Further empirical evidence of the intimate relationship between the law and order situation and economic performance in the context of Pakistan is available in the form of the bearish behaviour of the Karachi Stock Exchange, in response to violence and political instability in specific time series substantiated by that of the Lahore Stock Exchange in response to strike calls, the shortfall in revenue collection in a milieu of lawlessness, non-recovery of stuck-up loans, social cost of university closure, sick units, size of black economy, dwindling national savings, imports-exports gap, budget deficit, capital flight (particularly that of portfolio investment), the activity at the Karachi Port Trust and the loss in insurance premium. This evidence is further reinforced by references to tax-culture, assets of some drug barons and other related information given in the appendices. As a consequence of operation of these factors, the economy is struggling with macro-economic imbalances, severe strains on external accounts and a significant savings-investment gap. In the absence of reasonable macro-economic stability, financial liberalization has resulted in destabilizing capital flows, high interest rates and capital distress.

The administrative response to lawlessness in Sindh was found by first deploying the army and then giving police powers to the Rangers. The police, too, follow generally a paramilitary strategy of combating violence and crime. These measures have failed to achieve the desired results. The net outcome of the deployment of the army was a debilitating stalemate, perception of temporary relief being allowed to become a substitute for a longer-term cure, inability of the army operation to deal with issues relating to socio-economic discontent and politico-ethnic tension, the removal of pressure on the government to seek ways of political accommodation, infiltration of the virus of corruption within the army as a consequence of the performance of civilian duty, incidence of actual or perceived excesses on the part of law-enforcing agencies including the Army, Rangers and the Police and active involvement and visibility of the army in civilian affairs. Thus the strategy adopted to control lawlessness has proved to be counter productive. There is, therefore, a need for a sound strategy of controlling lawlessness (for details see Appendix 9).

What the criminal justice system can, and ought to do, is to deliver justice. To hold individuals responsible for their actions is a worthy goal. However, the criminal justice system is failing to achieve this. A criminal justice system that lets the guilty off scot-free because of considerations resulting from a culture of socio-economic and political lawlessness and soaring crimes protecting the influential, the rich and the powerful leaves witnesses and victims more bruised than they did after the original offence, treats those convicted of serious crimes more lavishly than the victims, and wrongfully convicts the innocent while failing to convict the guilty is not serving justice.

A sound strategy for the criminal justice system should follow an agenda encompassing the maintenance and encouragement of public confidence in the criminal justice system, the search for greater efficiency and effectiveness and the retention of the proper balance between the rights of the citizen and the needs of the community as a whole. The role of the police, the courts, the prison and probation services, the medico-legal facility and the prosecution is of crucial importance. Nevertheless the police set the legal process into motion immediately after the occurrence of an offence. They are also mainly responsible for crime prevention and enforcement of laws. The criminal justice system does not operate in a vacuum. The drive to halt the rise in crime depends to a large extent on the climate created by the standards of behaviour observed by individual citizens; the degree of responsibility accepted by parents, the standards and values disseminated in schools; and the image of acceptable behaviour presented by the media. The components of the criminal justice system react to, and are themselves affected by the wider social context in which they operate. As the police hold the front line against crime and disorder, attempts have been made in advanced countries to combat crime through a strategy known as 'community policing.'

Good Governance

The issues of governance, corruption and poverty remain fundamental to Pakistan's economy. Pakistan has once again survived a difficult economic crisis but it still faces very serious problems of poverty, slow growth and vulnerability in the balance of payments. Underlying most of the economic problems faced by Pakistan is the 'crisis of governance'. This is contributing to the recent slowdown of economic growth and increase in poverty. Corruption, a manifestation of poor governance is, hurting the economy by raising transaction costs and heightening uncertainty. There is need to place considerable emphasis on making the accountability process transparent and objective by establishing an autonomous, non-political agency to investigate cases of corruption. The various suggestions for the resolution of these problems deserve serious and urgent consideration by the government; inattention to these could jeopardize the economic reform programme the government maintains it is committed to. The most stubborn problem in Pakistan's macro-economic and structural reforms is the long-term failure of fiscal revenues to rise as a share of GDP. The prime reason for this has been lax adherence to the rule of law in collecting taxes, bank loans and power tariffs. Poor governance has also led to inefficient use of public funds. It is more than apparent that thefts of electricity, overstaffing, inefficiency and poor bill collection have brought WAPDA (Water and Power Development Authority) and KESC (Karachi Electric Supply Company) to the brink of collapse.

In the financial sector, the stock of non-performing loans grew by 600 per cent between end-June 1989 to end-June 1998 when they stood at Rs 146 billion.[1] Over the years, there has been widespread political interference in both lending and loan recovery—or rather the lack of it—by banks. On the taxation side, a complex tax regime, a narrow tax base, an inequitable tax burden, weak tax administration, widespread tax evasion and rapid growth of a tax-free informal sector in the economy can be identified as the major but unresolved problems. The fall in the tax-GDP ratio from 14 per cent to 9 per cent is cause for grave concern.

Another problem area is official credibility and investor confidence. Although Pakistan has managed to deal with the immediate crisis, its credibility with the multi-nationals, officials and private creditors and investors has been seriously damaged. This is reflected in the recent down grading of Pakistan by international rating agencies leading to loss in investor confidence, lower domestic investment and private remittances and a rise in the cost of external financing. Unless the government rebuilds its credibility in international financial markets and implements policies to strengthen the balance of payments position by higher growth of exports and larger inflows of foreign private capital, Pakistan will again run into serious balance of payments difficulties when normal debt-serving resumes. The implementation of a reform agenda needs strong political will and commitment. It is also obvious that the opposition to this, which will inevitably come from vested interests, ought to be surmounted. The resolution of the problems of poor governance, corruption and poverty can be postponed only at the risk of further compounding the economic crisis.

What we really need is: (i) debate on the overall socio-economic development issues that will help evolve a consensus on the policies to be pursued; (ii) formulation of integrated and meaningful policies focused on short- and long-term implications and future plans of action; (iii) social sector development; (iv) a participatory socio-economic development approach; (v) law and order; (vi) political stability; (vii) a reformed electoral system; (viii) employment promotion and manpower development; (ix) an institutional mechanism ensuring greater co-operation and integration of policy makers and policies with the target groups and different actors involved in the process; and (x) a transparent mechanism of accountability of the public servants and public representatives.

This brings us to the most vital question of repeated interruptions in governance under a valid democratic constitution. One major cause of lawlessness has been a tendency of deviation from the constitutional process. This is a position no different from other new democracies facing challenges of internal subversion and external threats. For good governance this trend needs to be checked through a stable civilian structure, tightening up of discipline in all the services of the State and improving their training, emphasizing the importance of conflict resolution through institutionalization.

Improvement in General Administration

A very simple example of this can be taken from the income tax structures. Schedule II of the Income Tax Act, which lists the exemptions to taxable income, contains a large number of exemptions granted to individuals by name. This kind of an arbitrary exercise of policy provides an incentive not towards efficiency but towards the manipulation of the system. It also creates uncertainty for individual competitions, since no one knows who will receive the exemption tomorrow. Governmental procedures must be clarified and streamlined, not that there should be no income tax, or that the income tax officer or the finance minister should be replaced by robots with no discretionary powers whatsoever. In addition to this, a strong judiciary is vital to the creation of an atmosphere of stability and predictability in the absence of which economic agents cannot make long-term economic decisions. The creation of stability also requires respect for procedures in the government. It is correct, as Papanek implies, that the uncertainty and unpredictability faced by the small producer is in large part because of arbitrary government policies but it is because of the arbitrariness of the intervention, not because of the intervention itself. The arbitrariness of the government action should be reduced. However, this should happen not through the disappearance of the State but through the establishment of systems and procedures, through the provision of proper incentives to officials, through proper supervision and monitoring, and through better training and professionalism.

The policy prescriptions that emerge out of this focus on incentive compatibility include the following:
- decentralization;
- the establishment of participatory institutions both political and economic;
- the strengthening of the judiciary; and
- administrative reform including the improvement of incentives to the bureaucracy.

Measures for Macro-Economic Stability

For achieving the above mentioned objectives, macro-economic stability needs to be ensured through the implementation of following recommendations:
• The first thing is to arrange a wholesale debt-equity swap and to put our assets in the international market as shares

thereby reducing our liabilities as being done by many other countries. We need not worry about who would buy our assets as ownership concept is diffusing these days. In the interest of broadening the tax base and ensuring a sound taxation system, it is in the fitness of things to recommend the imposition and proper collection of tax on the income from the agricultural sector. This sector has the potential to contribute at least 4 to 5 per cent of the GDP which comes to around Rs 100 billion per year.[2] Furthermore, aggressive land reforms should be carried out in the country, which are imperative to develop a progressive society.

- The time has come to change the feudal system in which some families dominate the whole society; where governments come in power just to dispense patronage to these people. We should now start debating these land reforms and tax on the agricultural sector.

- There is also a dire need to reduce the defence expenditure. Both India and Pakistan, combined, have spent $20 billion a year on their armies. Countries within the fold of SAARC (South Asian Association of Regional Countries) could decide to reduce military expenditure by 5 per cent every year not only to curtail expenditure under this head but also to avoid military imbalance in the region provided all the countries do it together. Whether we want to educate our people, provide them drinkable water or spend heavily on defence is the choice we have to make.

- We need a fair taxation system with a minimum discretion system, with minimum discretionary element and maximum computerization to run the country's economy. The present system has become a kind of joke in which we are piling up taxes upon taxes with no substantial returns. No government can run the economic system effectively if it confronts the business community or industrialists.

National Policy for Criminal Justice Administration

We often talk of national policies for economic development, trade, education, health and labour. It is high time that, in view of the rapidly changing economic and technological fronts, which require a crime-free atmosphere, we should also give an urgent thought to the formulation of a National Criminal Justice Administration Policy. This is because no economic development is possible in the absence of the rule of law. The proposed policy should include appropriate measures for achieving public confidence, greater effectiveness and efficiency for the police service, prosecution agency, courts, prisons and medico-legal services. The idea should be to strike a balance between the needs of the community and rights of individual citizens. To begin with, the following recommendations, given under the following appropriate heads, need to be included in the proposed package of a National Criminal Justice Administration Policy:

Improvement of Criminal Justice System

In an earlier work, I had presented a concept of a developmental approach to policing as against the traditional approach henceforth applied.[3] The traditional approach to policing concentrated on isolating the crime control function from the courts and liberal grant of bail, prolonged and procrastinated trials, low conviction rates, a large number of pending files in the courts, inadequate punishments and cumbersome procedures of civil and criminal law with consequent loss of faith in the judicial system were not given due attention. There were occasional increases in police manpower and equipment but the thrust of the traditional approach was an incessant rhetoric of police-magistracy co-operation and an amplification of the thesis of police excesses, inefficiency and corruption without considering the limitations imposed on policing by a retrogressive crimino-legal system as a whole. The develop-

mental approach, wherein lies the hope for improving police
effectiveness has remained unarticulated, because it was rarely,
if ever, considered in policy terms. The five basic propositions
underlying the developmental approach are:

- The police function is distinguished from all others in the
  field of public protection and public safety by its reliance
  upon the minimum and not the maximum use of force, its
  necessary subordination to the decrees of the courts, its
  strict adherence to the essential rule of law, and its
  attachment to the concept of human rights.
- The discretionary police use of power for crime control
  and imposing reasonable order involves the art of
  compulsion by personal persuasion through which the
  police endeavour to reflect the will of the people. They
  prevent crime, detect offences, maintain order and keep
  the peace. They do not administer justice, deny civil
  liberties, engage in reprisals or terrorize communities. They
  should not be used as sticks to thrash opponents of the
  well-to-do and the influential into submission.
- The above-mentioned functions can be performed by a
  police force having a self-contained organizational
  structure where there is no distortion of command and no
  dilution of accountability.
- For the achievement of these goals, formal intervention is
  required in the shape of an overhauling of laws and
  procedures relating to the system of criminal administration.
- The intervention must be bold and decisive. It should give
  the democratic national interest a definite preference over
  the minority group interests of any class of civil servants,
  howsoever strong the lobby may be.

Having outlined the salient features of the developmental
approach, it is in the fitness of things to consider ways and
means of improving police effectiveness in Pakistan. This can
be done with reference to solutions to the problems pertaining
to law enforcement.

The short-term approach to the problem does not envisage any change in the basic structure of the existing system of criminal administration. What is required is the strengthening of the existing system through a well co-ordinated, properly-outlined and clearly defined strategy of harmonious working relationship among the judiciary, administration, police and democratic institutions. Apart from the provision of adequate resources to the police institutionalization of community policing involving effective public participation through various techniques of consultation, a balanced media policy, revival of the *panchayat* system, conferences of police officers at the provincial and district levels with meaningful agenda on the lines of the experiment made in the Punjab during the period from 20 June 1991 to 1 June 1993 can go a long way in preserving the rule of law and ensuring an environment conducive to economic development.

The long-term approach consists of a multiplicity of measures. These will include, of course, all fields of police activities like traffic management, training, transport and communications, arms modernization, modernization of equipment and logistic, constitution of a police technical cadre, modernization of investigative aids, detective training school, modern aid and equipment for scientific investigation, police buildings, manpower and morale, separation of investigation from watch and ward, strengthening of sub-divisional command, judicial lockups at sub-divisional level, induction at Sub-Inspector level with minimum academic qualification of a graduate, encouragement of private detective and security agencies and boosting of police morale. A proper strategy to achieve tangible results in all these fields should encompass the fixation of priorities in scientifically prepared Five Year Plans on the pattern of the experiment the Punjab police had undertaken in 1991–92.

NOTES

1. World Bank Report (1999).
2. Haq, M. (1995), Speech delivered in a reception given by industrialists in honour of Dr Mehboob-ul-Haq, Karachi, 29 August 1995.
3. Nadeem, A.H. (1989), *The Punjab Police in a Comparative Perspective*, Lahore, Progressive Publishers.

APPENDIX 1

Law and Order Computable General Equilibrium Model Developed for the Present Study

Association of growth targets with political stability and social sectors

The purpose of this book has been to examine the relationship between law and order and economic development both at the macro-economic and micro-economic levels. Having clarified the concepts of 'law and order' and 'economic development' in conjunction with the determinants of economic development important linkages between law and order and economic development have been identified both in the context of macro as well as micro-economic frameworks. The growth and investment targets will have to be associated with political stability and improved law and order situation. Furthermore, strategies of economic development pertaining to urbanization and social sectors (e.g. housing, education, health) or physical growth leading to a perception of inequality in the distribution of resources caused socialization-related problems and adversely affected crime prevention and criminal justice issues. The situation in Pakistan reflects haphazard urbanization and poor conditions in social sectors.

Quantitative measurement of linkage between law and order and economic development

No attempt has been made so far to quantitatively measure linkage between law and order and economic development.

Modified structuralist CGE model of linkages between law and order and economic development

There are many models but perhaps a model on the lines of Computable General Equilibrium would appear to be more appropriate. We shall call it Modified Structuralist CGE Model of Linkages between Law and Order and Economic Development.

Explanation of modified structuralist CGE model of linkages between law and order and economic development

Before we explain the Modified Structuralist CGE Model, it is pertinent to present the outline of a prototype and standard structuralist CGE Model. This summarizes the major linkages and determinants of production, exports, imports, consumption demand, investment demand, labour supply, labour demand, saving and investment (demand and supply) functions along with basic identities of prices, labour income, capital income and government income, etc.

Structural CGE Model

Real Flows

(1) $X(L^D, V^D. K^D)$ production

(2) $X(E.D^S)$ export transformation

(3) $Q^D(M, D^D)$ import aggregation

(4) $M/D^S = f1 (P^E, P^D)$

(5) $E/D^S = F_e (P^E, P^D)$ export supply

(6) $C^D(P^q, C)$ consumption demand

(7) $Z^D (P^q, Z)$ investment demand

(8) $V^D (R, W, P^q, P)$ intermediate demand

(9) $Q^D = C^D + Z^D + V + G^D$ total demand for composite good

(10) $L^S (W, P^q)$ labour supply

(11) $L^D(R, W, P^q, P^k)$ labour demand price

(12) $K^D (R, W, P^q, P^k)$ capital demand Real System Constraints

(13) $D^D - D^S = 0$ product market

(14) $L^D - L^S = 0$ labour market

(15) $K^D - K^S = 0$ capital market

Nominal Flows

(16) $Y^L = W. L^S.(I - T^L)$ labour income

(17) $Y^K = R. K^S (1^K)$ capital income

(18) $Y^S = T^L.W.L^S + T^K.R.K^S$ government income

(19) $C (Y^L, Y^K)$ consumption function

(20) $S^P = Y^L + Y^K - C$ private saving

(21) $M = P^{SM}$, M dollar imports

(22) $E = P^{SE}$, E dollar exports price equations

(23) $P^m = r, P^{Sm}$ import price

(24) $P^e = r, P^{Se}$ export price

(25) $P^q (P^M, P^D)$ composite

(26) $P^x (P^e, P^d)$ output price Nominal System Constraints

(27) $S^P + S^G r. B - Z = 0$ savings investment

(28) $Y^s - P^q, G^D S^G = 0$ government balance

(29) $M - E = B$ balance of trade

(30) $F3 (P^d, P^m, P^e, W) = P$ numeraire

Accounting Identities

(31) $P^x, X = P^e, E + P^d, D^s$ value of output = value of sales

(32) $P^Q, Q^d = P^m, M + P^d, D^d$ value of composite goods = absorption

(33) $P^x, X = W, L^d + R, K^D + P^q, V^D$ value of sales = value of inputs

(34) $P^q, C^D = C$ consumption demand = expenditure

(35) $P^q, Z^D = Z$ investment demand = expenditure

Endogenous Variables

X = aggregate output

D^s = supply of domestic output

D^D = demand for domestic output

E = exports

M = imports

Q^D = composite good demand

V^D = intermediate demand

L^s = labour supply

K^D = capital demand

C^D = real consumption

Z^D = real investment

Y^L = nominal income

Y^K = capital income

Endogenous Variables, cont.

M = dollar value of imports

E = dollar value of exports

P^m = domestic price of imports

P^e = domestic price of exports

P^x = price of aggregate output

P^d = price of domestic sales

P^q = price of composite goods

W = wage of labour

R = rental rate of capital

r = exchange rate

Y^G = government income

S^P = private savings

S^G = government savings

C = nominal consumption

Z = nominal investment

Exogenous Variables

G^D = real government demand

K^s = aggregate capital supply

T^L = tax rate on labour income

T^K = tax rate on capital income

B = balance of trade (in dollars)

P^{Sm} world price of imports

P^{Se} world price of exports

P = numeraire price index.

The disequilibrium generated in the labour and capital markets is subsequently picked up by the real sector causing changes in the output mix, export sector and import requirements per equations (1), (2) and (3). This causes further chain reactions in other sectors affecting demand for consumption, investment and intermediate goods. The system then finds a new equilibrium with changes brought about in the labour and capital incomes, and government income as shown in equations (16), (17) and (18). Finally, the price profile of imports, exports and intermediate products undergoes a change which affects public sector balance, trade balance and so on. These changes are measurable in terms of equations (24) to (30).

Basic Thesis

We have further established the thesis that Law and Order and economic development are closely related and there is a two-way cause and effect relationship between these two major variables of political economy. With a view to capturing the impact of Law and Order on various economic sectors and sub-sectors, we present below a modified structuralist CGE Model incorporating the specific variables depicting the Law and Order conditions in the country and the associated changes originating therefrom.

Ingredients

The first step in this direction is the identification of a Law and Order variable, i.e., $\emptyset^c$ which is the composite index of political economy of Law and Order conditions prevailing in a country over a specific period of time. The composite index is the weighted index of the major Law and Order variables such as the phenomenon of war ($\emptyset^w$), the emergence of internal political changes/upheavals/protests etc. ($\emptyset^p$), the phenomenon of strikes ($\emptyset^s$) which may be national, regional or sector-wise (such as strike of the transport sector), ethnic and religious conflicts ($\emptyset^e$) and finally the miscellaneous factors causing Law and Order situations which are depicted in the symbol ($\emptyset^m$). These variables of Law and Order situation are weighted by intensities such as α^1, α^2, α^3, α^4, and α^5 respectively indicating the relative effectiveness (intensity) of the specific stimuli of Law and Order situation for the macro-economic variables and sectors.

In the light of above, we can define the composite index of Law and Order situation i.e., $\emptyset^c$ as following:

$$\emptyset^c = \alpha^1\emptyset^w + \alpha^2\emptyset^p + \alpha^3\emptyset^s + \alpha^4\emptyset^e + \alpha^5\emptyset^m$$

The first component $\alpha^1 \emptyset^w$ on the right hand side of the equation is the multiplicand of (w, i.e. the Law and Order conditions resulting from War, and (the intensity co-efficient) α^1, the degree of impact of the war on the national economy. The magnitude of $\emptyset^w$ would be determined by factors such as the intensity, duration and the coverage (people and areas affected by the war, weapons used, size and strength of the armies engaged in the conflict, etc.), while α^1 would be determined by the internal strength of the economic system and the 'morale' of the people etc. On a prior basis, it can be concluded that larger the magnitude of $\emptyset^w$, larger would be its effects on the economic system and thus larger the magnitude of α^1, given other factors as constant. In other words, the parameter of α^1 would be influenced not only by the economic resilience and viability of a country and the common response of the affected people, but also by the magnitude of $\emptyset^w$ itself. Ceteris paribus, larger the size of $\emptyset^w$, larger would be the size of α^1.

There is thus a close correlation between $\emptyset^w$ (the occurrence and spread of war conditions) and α^1 (the impact of war on the national economy). At the same time, for an inherently weak economy, α^1 would be large suggesting that the economy has limited capacity to absorb the adverse effects of the war with the result that the ongoing process of economic development would be undermined in a substantive manner. Similarly, if the war is being fought on a massive scale involving large-scale resources, manpower, etc., its implications for growth and welfare would be serious and far-reaching.

The above outlined rationale about the determinants of α^1, $\emptyset^w$ and then $\alpha^1 \emptyset^w$ can be extended to other components of $\emptyset^c$ and $\alpha^2 \emptyset^p$, $\alpha^3 \emptyset^s$ and so on. In a nutshell, we can suggest that intensity coefficients such as α^2, α^3, etc. are influenced on the one hand by their qualifying (associated) variables such as $\emptyset^p$, $\emptyset^s$ and so on, and on the other by the internal dynamism of the economic and social system, built-in strength of the people and the political framework of the country concerned.

Modifications

The relevance of the composite Law and Order index requires that the traditional structuralist CGE Model earlier presented be modified to accommodate the effects of Law and Order situation in a country.

Accordingly, the modified model is given in the forthcoming table. The main characteristic of the Modified Structuralist Law and Order-Development CGE model is that it does not disturb the major identities of the basic structuralist CGE model such as prices, savings, etc. but highlights the modified production, consumption and investment functions by incorporation of the composite index for a Law and Order variable, namely $Ø^c$. The variable of $Ø^c$ is further differentiated in terms of direct and indirect effects of Law and Order on various economic sectors as well as strong and weak effects. This suggests that the Law and Order conditions can have immediate, instantaneous, strong and direct effects on economic sectors such as production, exports, consumption, savings, etc., and the Law and Order conditions can effect these variables in an indirect, and weak way. Hence $Ø^c$ can be further differentiated in terms of the following:

$Ø^c$ .sd = Strong and direct effects of Law and Order on the macro and micro economic variables.

$Ø^c$ .wd = Weak, but direct effects.

$Ø^c$. si = Strong but indirect effects on the economy.

$Ø^c$ .wi = Weak but indirect effects on the economy.

The differentiation is important in order to focus on the specific sector-wise implications of various sources of Law and Order conditions of a country.

Of particular significance is the estimation of the index of $Ø^c$, i.e., composite Law and Order index which should be prepared after selecting a year in a country which is (quite) normal from the point of view of Law and Order conditions, which would be characterized by situations such as absence of war, a minimal of political changes, strikes or ethnic, religious conflicts, etc. Indeed, much of future research would concentrate upon giving specific values to α^1, α^2, etc., as well as $Ø^W$, $Ø^P$, etc. However, our present model being a path breaker in this domain, could lay down the foundations for future research and could provide guidelines for the Third Generation modelling incorporating all the variables originating from the political set-up of a country, especially the Law and Order conditions.

Equations

The modified structuralist CGE Model linking Law and Order and economic development is discussed below briefly:

a) The production function, i.e. equation (1) has been modified to include $\emptyset^c$ .sd and $\emptyset^c$ .si indicating that Law and Order can have strong and direct effects on the output of our economy as well as indirect effects.

b) The export transformation function has been modified to include the new variable $\emptyset^c$ .si implying that Law and Order condition can have strong but indirect affect on the export behaviour. However, the second term within the export transformation function includes $\emptyset^c$ .sd because in case the Law and Order situation is concentrated say in the major export harbour, the export performance of the country will be adversely affected by such a localized strike.

c) In equation 3, the inclusion of $\emptyset^c$ .si again indicates the strong but indirect affects of Law and Order condition on imports of a country. The basic premise is that foreign exporters would be affected indirectly (though strongly) from a Law and Order situation of the home country.

d) The equation (4) represents changes in demand for imports as affected by Law and situations. It incorporates $\emptyset^c$ si, as the demand for imports is likely to be affected indirectly by Law and Order condition.

e) The export supply function is modified with inclusion of ($\emptyset^c$ sd and $\emptyset^c$ si depending upon the specific condition whether the Law and Order situation is specific to an export sector such a textile or is of general nature.

f) In equation (6) the consumption demand now includes $\emptyset^c$ sd as well of $\emptyset^c$ mi. This is to take into account some of the immediate and direct effects of Law and Order situation on consumption behaviour as well as the indirect long-term effects of Law and Order condition.

g) Equation (7) showing investment demand has been modified to include all the possible stimuli, strong, mild, direct and indirect. The rationale for this modification is based on the fact that investment is highly sensitive to Law and Order factors and is affected through multiple channels both direct and indirect.

h) Equation (8) has been modified including $\emptyset^c$ sd, $\emptyset^c$ si, $\emptyset^c$ wi to incorporate the direct, and indirect effects of the Law and Order condition on economic variables both strong and weak.

The other equation could be explained in the similar manner.

Assumptions

The modified structuralist CGE Model linking Law and Order and economic development is based on the following important assumptions:

   a) There exists a positive relation between law and order situation and socio-economic indicators in a general sense, though in some cases it may not be true.
   b) Index weights are determined on the basis of frequency of particular types of disturbance-creating factors.

Modified Structuralist Law and Order and Economic Development CGE Model

(1)	$X(L^D, V^D, K^D, \emptyset^c$ sd, $\emptyset^c$ si$)$	production
(2)	$X(E.D^S, \emptyset^c$ sd, $\emptyset^c$ si$)$	export transformation
(3)	$Q^D (M, D^D, \emptyset^c$ si$)$	import aggregation
(4)	$M/D^D = fl(P^m, P^d, P^c si)$	import demand
(5)	$E/D^S = f2 (P^e, P^d, \emptyset^c$ sd, $\emptyset^c$ si$)$	export supply
(6)	$C^d(P^q, C, \emptyset^c$ sd, (c si, $\emptyset^c$ wi$)$	consumption demand
(7)	$Z^d(P^q, Z,$ (c sd, (c si, $\emptyset^c$ wi$)$	investment demand
(8)	$V^d(R, W, P^q, Px,$ (c sd, $\emptyset^c$ si, $\emptyset^c$ wi$)$	intermediate demand
(9)	$Q^D = C^D + Z^D + V^D + G^D$	total demand for composite good
(10)	$L^S(W, P^q, \emptyset^c$ sd, $\emptyset^c$ .si$)$	labour supply
(11)	$L^D(R, W, O^q, P^X, \emptyset^c$ sd, $\emptyset^c$ si$)$	labour demand
(12)	$K^D(R, W, P^q, P^x,$ (c sd, $\emptyset^c$ si$)$	capital demand

Real System Constraints

(13)	$D^D - D^S = O$	product market
(14)	$L^D - L^S = O$	labour market
(15)	$K^D - K^S = O$	capital market

Nominal Flows

(16)	$Y^L = W.L^S .(I - T^L, \emptyset^c$ sd, $\emptyset^c$ si, $\emptyset^c$ wi$)$	labour income
(17)	$Y^k = R. K^s (T^k \emptyset^c$ sd, $\emptyset^c$ si, $\emptyset^c$ .wi$)$	capital income
(18)	$1Y^G = T^L .W. L^S + T^K R.K^S.$ ($\emptyset^c$ sd, $\emptyset^c$ si, $\emptyset^c$ wd, $\emptyset^c$ wi$)$	government income

(19) $C(Y^L, Y^K, \emptyset^c \text{ sd}, \emptyset^c \text{ si}, \emptyset^c \text{ wi})$ consumption function

(20) $S^p = Y^L + Y^K - C,$

    $(\emptyset^c \text{ sd}, \emptyset^c .\text{si}, \emptyset^c \text{ wi})$ private saving

(21) $M = P^{\$m}, M$ dollar imports

(22) $E = P^{\$m}, E$ dollar exports

Price Equation

(23) $P^m = r, P^{\$m}$ import price

(24) $P^e = r, P^{\$e}$ export price

(25) $P^q (P^m, P^d)$ composite price

(26) $P^X (P^e, P^d)$ output price

National System Constraints

(27) $S^p + S^G r. B - Z = 0$ saving investment

(28) $G - P^q, G^d S^G = 0$ government balance

(29) $M - E = B$ balance of trade

(30) $f_3 (P^d, P^m, P^e, W) = P$ numeraire

Accounting Identities

(31) $P^X, X = P^e, E + P^d, D^S$ value of output = value of sales

(32) $P^q, Q^D = P^m, M + P^d, D^D$ value of composite goods = absorption

(33) $P^X X = W, L^D + R, K^D + P^q, VD$ value of sales = value of inputs

(34) $P^q, C^D = C$ consumption demand = expenditure

(35) $P^q, Z^D = Z$ investment demand = expenditure

Endogenous variables

X = aggregate output
D^S = supply of domestic output
D^D = demand for domestic output
E = exports
M = imports
Q^D = composite good demand
V^D = intermediate demand
L^S = labour supply
L^D = labour demand
K^D = capital demand
C^D = real consumption
Z^D = real investment
Y^L = nominal income
Y^K = capital income

Endogenous variables, cont.

M = dollar value of imports
E = dollar value of exports
P^m = domestic price of imports
P^e = domestic price of imports
P^X = price of aggregate output
P^d = price of domestic sales
P^q = price of composite good
W = wage of labour
R = rental rate of capital
r = exchange rate
Y^G = government income
S^P = private savings
S^G = government savings
C = nominal consumption
Z = nominal investment

Exogenous variables

$\emptyset^c$ = Composite Index of Law and Order conditions
G^D = real government demand   B = balance of trade (in dollars)
K^S = aggregate capital supply $P^{\$M}$ = world price of imports
T^L = tax rate of labour income $P^{\$E}$ = world price of exports
T^K = tax rate of capital income   P = numeraire price index

Conclusion

The basic thesis of the Modified Structuralist CGE Model of Linkages between Law and Order and Economic Development is that Law and Order and economic development are closely related and there is a two-way cause and effect relationship between these two major variables of political economy. It also incorporates the specific variables depicting the Law and Order conditions in a country and the associated changes originating therefrom.

APPENDIX 2

Political Pattern

Since the achievement of sovereign statehood, Pakistan has had to traverse an arduous path in the quest of a democratic order. Moves towards democratic rule have been more an aberration rather than the norm. Pakistan's normal political pattern has been marked by intolerance of dissent and an authoritarian streak with institutions being the biggest casualty.

Mass Agitation

1951   Bengali Language Movement.
        Language problems became quite sensitive in Pakistan immediately after independence. In 1951 the movement for making Bengali one of the national languages gained momentum. It created a lot of heat and led to widespread disturbances.

1953   Anti-Qadiani Movement.
        Mainly concentrated in the Punjab, the Anti-Qadiani Movement had countrywide impact. The pressure on law enforcing agencies was tremendous.

1968–69 Anti-Ayub Movement.
        A sense of deprivation resulting from a perception of inequalities in the distribution of income, a system of indirect elections and complete control of all institutions by a powerful bureaucratic elite made the masses rise up against Ayub Khan's regime. This happened in 1968–69 when a decade of reforms was being celebrated. In all these years of unrest, the police had to face angry and frustrated mobs who were baton-charged and fired upon under the orders of the civil servants.

1971 Bangladesh Movement.
In the aftermath of the 1970 elections and perception of unfair treatment of Bengalis with regard to their share in political and economic power, Pakistan suffered on account of the civil war followed by aggression by India in 1971 leading to the separation of East Pakistan. A new country by the name of Bangladesh came into existence.

1972 Urdu Language Movement.
It was a movement launched by Urdu-speaking people in Sindh. As a consequence thereof, the schism between new and old Sindhis assumed dangerous proportions.

1974 Anti-Qadiani Movement.
The demand by religious parties to declare Qadianis a minority resulted in widespread riots. The Qadianis were consequently declared a minority.

1977 The PNA Movement.
The Pakistan National Alliance consisted of right-wing parties opposed to the Pakistan People's Party government. The alleged rigging of the 1977 elections by the ruling party led to countrywide protests, marches and riots. As a consequence thereof, General Ziaul Haq assumed power and marital law was declared in the country. The constitution was suspended.

1983 The MRD Movement.
The effort by the Martial Law regime to perpetuate itself made the political forces come together. They launched a movement known as the Movement for the Restoration of Democracy (MRD) which was punctuated not only by demonstrations and voluntary arrests but also by rioting, subversion and underground activities. The result was that terrorism emerged in Pakistan and took a dangerous form in 1986, 1987 and 1988. Even now it remains a serious threat to peace in Pakistan.

1986 Terrorist Activities.

1987 Terrorist Activities.

1988 Terrorist Activities/Political Crisis.

1992–93 Long March and Political Agitation.
On 18 November 1992 the Pakistan People's Party arranged a Long March against the government of the Pakistan Muslim League. In the subsequent developments, the 1993 elections took place resulting in the formation of the government by the Pakistan People's Party.

Martial Law

With intervals, the country remained under Martial Law for a considerable length of time.

Military Actions/State Repression

1958   Balochistan.
1961   Dir-Bajaur (NWFP).
1968   Balochistan.
1971   East Pakistan.
1973   Balochistan.
1983   Sindh.
1989   Pucca Qilla Operation/Karachi.
1990   Benazir Bhutto's Government dismissed.
1992   Military Action in Sindh.
1993   Violence in Karachi.
1994   Killings in Karachi on a massive scale.
1995   Killings in Karachi continued along side dialogues between the MQM(A) and the government. Both presented their demands and counter demands. Various strike calls and unending bloodshed.

Abortive Coups/Conspiracies

1951   Pindi Conspiracy Case.
1966   Agartala Conspiracy Case.
1973   Attock Conspiracy Case I.
1975   Hyderabad Conspiracy Case.
1980   Maj.-Gen. (Retd.) Tajammul Hussain Affair.
1984   Attock Conspiracy Case II.
1995   Arrest of over thirty army officers including a 2-star general for their abortive attempt to capture the military headquarters in the name of their version of an Islamic revolution.

Political Parties Banned

1954   Communist Party of Pakistan.
1958   All parties banned (lifted in 1962).
1963   Jamaat-e-Islami (lifted by court action).
1971   Awami League.
        National Awami League Party (lifted in 1972).
1975   National Awami Party (revived under new name).
1979   All parties banned (lifted in 1985).

United Fronts

1954   Jugto Front (East Bengal).
1963   National Democratic Front (NDF).
1964–65   Combined Opposition Parties (COP).
1967–69   Pakistan Democratic Movement (PDM).
           Democratic Action Committee (DAC).
1973   United Democratic Front (UDF).
1977   Pakistan National Alliance (PNA).
1981   Movement for Restoration of Democracy (MRD).
1988   Islami Jamhuri Ittehad (IJI).
1993   People's Democratic Front (PDF).

Election Results

1951   Punjab rigged.
1954   East Bengal victorious Jugto Front dismissed within three
           months.
1959   Pakistan's first general elections scheduled for March pre-
           empted by October, 1958 coup.
1965   Entire electoral process rigged with franchise allowed only
           to 80,000 people out of 100 million population.
1971   Awami League, federal majority party, banned and crushed
           via military action.
1973   In Balochistan, NAP-JUI majority parties coalition dismissed,
           military action followed.
1977   Results nullified because of alleged partial rigging of polls.
1977–79   Twice postponed.

1985   Non-party polls.

1988   Smooth transfer of power.

1990   Dissolution of the PPP Government and controversial elections.

1993   Ishaq-Nawaz Sharif conflict; elections of 1993 under the auspices of the armed forces.

1994   Provincial Government of NWFP was removed through the suspension of the NWFP Assembly under a Presidential order.

1995   Imposition of the Governor's Rule in the Punjab. Change of government as a result of changing loyalties of the Members of the Provincial Assembly. A contest for number games by the government and the opposition through the use of all types of means.

Major Court Constitutional Decisions

1953   Supreme Court upholds dismissal of the Constituent Assembly.

1959   Supreme Court legitimizes Marital Law in 'Dosso Case'.

1972   Supreme Court declares Yahya Khan's Martial Law illegal in 'Asma Jilani Case'.

1975   Supreme Court upholds government ban on NAP.

1977   (May) Lahore High Court declares Bhutto's limited Martial Law as illegal.

1977   (November) Supreme Court legitimizes Martial Law under 'Doctrine of Necessity'.

1988   Supreme Court declares the dissolution of Assemblies by General Ziaul Haq (after his death) as illegal but allows fresh elections.

1993   Supreme Court declares dissolution of Assemblies by Ishaq Khan as illegal.

1997   Supreme Court declares dissolution of Assemblies by Farooq Khan Leghari as justified.

1997   Decisions of higher courts indicating complete difference of opinion on constitutional matters culminating in declaring the appointment of Sajjad Ali Shah as Chief Justice of Pakistan as unconstitutional, illegal and contrary to the decision of Supreme Court in case of Al-Jehad Trust v. Federation of Pakistan PLD 1996 SC324.

2000   Supreme Court upholds the military coup of 1999 and grants a three year's tenure to the Chief Executive with the power to amend the constitution.

Background and Removal of Rulers

1951	Liaquat Ali Khan	Politician	Assassination.
1953	Khwaja Nazimuddin	Politician	Dismissed despite a parliamentary majority.
1954	Ghulam Mohammad	Bureaucrat	Paralysis.
1955	Mohd. Ali Bogra	Bureaucrat	Intrigue.
1956	Ch. Mohammad Ali	Bureaucrat	Infighting.
1969	Ayub Khan	Army	Agitation followed by coup.
1971	Yahya Khan	Army	Forced resignation following Dhaka debacle.
1977	Zulfikar Ali Bhutto	Politician	Agitation followed by coup.
1988	Ziaul Haq	Army	Mysterious Accident.
1990	Benazir Bhutto	Politician	Dissolution of the National Assembly by the President under pressure from the armed forces.
1993	Nawaz Sharif	Politician	Dissolution of the National Assembly after the Prime Minister's resignation through mediation done by the armed forces.
1996	Benazir Bhutto	Politician	Dissolution of the National Assembly and dismissal of the Government of Prime Minister Benazir Bhutto on 5 November 1996 by President Farooq Ahmad

			Khan Leghari on charges of corruption, economic mismanagement and unsatisfactory law and order. The armed forces were used to implement the presidential order.
1997	Farooq Ahmed Khan Leghari	Politician	Resigned from the post of the President of Pakistan in the aftermath of a dispute between the Executive and the Supreme Court Chief Justice Sajjad Ali Shah whose appointment was held by the Court to be irregular. The President sided with Sajjad Ali Shah.
1999	Nawaz Sharif	Politicial	Military coup on 12 October 1999.

APPENDIX 3

Tax Culture

The Income Tax Eastern Zone, headed by Regional Commissioner, Sheikh Muhammad Munir, recently prepared a collection chart of major business centers, shopping plazas and commercial markets in Lahore, Kasur, Sheikhupura, etc. The chart makes interesting reading. For instance, out of all Anarkali traders, only ten declare that their annual income in the fiscal year 1994–95 exceeded Rs 200,000. No matter how sympathetic someone is to the traders' cause, he would find it hard to swallow this bit of 'revealing' information. Observers place the average income of an ordinary Anarkali vender at Rs 80,000 to 200,000.

Continuing in the same pattern, there are twelve cases where the Anarkali traders have shown their income to be between Rs 150,000 to Rs 200,000. According to the tax collection record, there are only 178 returns where the traders have assessed their income to be between Rs 50,000 to Rs 100,000. Lying at the bottom of the tax-payment table are 1240 traders who have declared their annual income to be below Rs 50,000. It comes to about Rs 4000 per month.

The situation at Brandreth Road is the same. Here we have the biggest tools and automobile spare parts market of the country, housing goods worth billions of rupees but what do they pay the government. There are only four Branderth Road traders who, tax records say, have shown the 'courage' to declare their annual income for 1994–95 to be over Rs 200,000. There are nine returns where the traders have declared their annual income to be between Rs 150,000 and 200,000 and thirty-four instances where the income has been shown to be between Rs 100,000 to Rs 150,000. A total of 167 returns give the income of the tax-payer to be between Rs 50,000 and Rs 100,000 while 484 Brandreth Road traders paid less than Rs 50,000 in twelve months.

The total income tax collection from Anarkali and Branderth Road is Rs 3.303 million and Rs 2.448 million respectively.

Moving on to the big wholesale market in Lahore, the annual collection from Akbari Mandi is Rs 1.448 million. Only two shopkeepers appear on record with declaration that their annual income exceeds Rs 200,000 and 12 others who declare that their income is between Rs 150,000 to Rs 200,000. Like the Anarkali and Brandreth Road traders, the majority (492) of Akbari Mandi traders also show their annual income to be below Rs 50,000. Another 116 traders bracket themselves among those earning Rs 50,000 to 100,000 each year while twenty-two claim their income to be between Rs 100,000 and Rs 150,000.

Records say that 1642 traders filed returns for the fiscal year 1994–95 from Azam Cloth Market. Five of them show earning exceeding Rs 200,000, twenty declare their income to be Rs 150,000 to Rs 200,000 and sixty fall in the 100,000 to 150,000 category. Another 293 submit returns with an income between 50,000 and 100,000 and the rest (398) claim that they earned less than Rs 50,000 during the period.

The chart shows that the total income tax collection from Urdu Bazar is Rs 3.125 million, with a total of 1400 returns. Six of these returns show the income of the tax payer in excess of Rs 200,000, and eight between Rs 150,000 to Rs 200,000. As many as 1080 declarations show the income to be below Rs 50,000, while in 152 instances the earnings are placed between Rs 50,000 to Rs 100,000.

The total income tax collection from Hall Road is Rs 2.582 million. The break-up is: Total returns -1189; Over Rs 2,00,000-2; Rs 150,000 to 200,000 -14; 100,000 to 150,000 -48; Below 50,000 -951.

Of the 879 returns filed by Shah Alam Market traders, 653 show their income to be less than Rs 50,000. In 174 cases, the declaration is of Rs 50,000 to Rs 100,000, while 36 claim their income to be between Rs 100,000 and Rs 150,000. There are only 12 returns in which the income has been put at Rs 200,000, and in eight cases it exceeds Rs 200,000.

But the goldsmiths of Suha Bazaar (gold market) take the cake. Take a look at the records and you will find that not a single one of them earns in excess of Rs 200,000. And we are talking about income per year and not per month. As many as 148 Suha Bazar's returns show an earning of less than Rs 50,000, 42 between Rs 50,000–100,000 and 20 between Rs 1,000,000–150,000. Only four goldsmiths declare their income to be in the 150,000–200,000 range. And with that we return to the streets of protest.

(Source: *The News*, Friday, 29 September 1995.)

The feudal lords who acquire membership of the National and Provincial Assemblies by spending, on an average, five million rupees and Rs 3 million respectively, are reported to have collectively paid only Rs 3 million as wealth tax. This is ironically equal to the amount that a candidate spends on electioneering for a seat in the provincial assembly. The statistics mentioned in the official CBR's Directory of Tax Payers 1993–94 published in *The News*, Friday, 15 September 1995, provides interesting information about the holders of high offices, legislators, those managing corporate business and salaried people regarding their declared income, assessed income and the amount of tax paid by them.

APPENDIX 4

Tracing/Freezing of Drug Assets by Anti-Narcotics Force (ANF) during the Period 1994–95

Sr.No	Name of Drug Barons	Value of Assets	
		in million US $	in million Pak Rs
1.	Mirza Muhammad Iqbal Baig	21.8	700
2.	Asif Ali Khan	0.46	15
3.	Tasnim Jalal Goraya	0.62	20
4.	Munawar Hussain Munj (MNA)	1.56	50
5.	Sardar Gujjar	0.62	20
6.	Sharaf-ud-Din Sheikh	3.37	108
7.	Fahim Babar	0.62	20
8.	Meahaise Family	0.93	30
9.	Haji Ayub Afridi	27.6	886
10.	Anwar Khattak	36.8	1180
11.	Ashraf Rana	1.48	47.6
12.	Daud Jatt	10.031	321
13.	Luqman Palari	0.2	6.4
14.	Hakim Ali Khoso	0.46	15.0
15.	Amir Ali Moosa	0.40	13
16.	Dawood Khan Pathan	0.79	27.8
17.	Muhammad Iqbal Soudagar	0.0062	0.2
18.	Ch. Muhammad Shafi	0.56	18
19.	Syed Zulfiqar Ali Shah	0.10	3.5
20.	Haji Habibullah	4.68	150
21.	Sakhi Dost Jan Notazai (MPA Balochistan)	2	70
	Total	**115.0872**	**3701.5**

Source: ANF, 1995.

APPENDIX 5

List of Sectarian Organizations

a)	Sipah-e-Sahaba Pakistan (SSP)	Sunni (Deobandi)
b)	Sawad-e-Azam Ahle Sunnat	Deobandi
c)	Tehrik Nifaz-e-Fiqah-e-Jaffria (TNFJ) Sajid Shia Naqvi Group	
d)	Tehirk Nifaz-e-Fiqah-e-Jaffria (TNFJ) Hamid Shia Moosvi Group	
e)	Tehrik Haq Char Yar	Deobandi/Wahabi
f)	Majlis Tahaffaz Khatam-e-Nabuwat	Sunni
g)	Muttahidda Shariat Mahaz	Sunni
h)	Anjuman-e-Farooqia	Sunni
i)	Jamaat Ahle Sunnat	Sunni
j)	Jamiat Ulema-e-Islam	Sunni/Barelvi
k)	Jamiat Ulema-e-Pakistan	Deobandi
l)	Jamiat Ahle Hadith	Wahabi
m)	Al-Badar Federation	Sunni
n)	Tauhidi Group	Wahabi
o)	Jamaat Mujahideen Pakistan	Deobandi
p)	Immamia Organization	Shia
q)	Imamia Students Organization	Shia Militant
r)	Alamdar Students Organization	Wings of TNFJ
s)	Abuzar Ghaffari Group	Naqvi Group
t)	Mukhtar Force	Shia (Militant Wings of TNFJ Moosvi Group)
u)	Wafaq Ulema-Shia	Shia (Affiliated with TNFJ)
v)	Sipah-e-Muhammad	Shia (Militant Group)
w)	Tehrik-e-Nifaz Shariat-e-Muhammadi	Sunni-Active in Malakand Division
x)	Lashkar-e-Jhangvi	Deobandi (A militant offshoot of SSP)

APPENDIX 6

Important Tribal Feuds in Balochistan

Bugti vs Bugti: A political tussle between the Kalpar Bugtis and Raheja Bugtis led by Nawab Akbar Bugti turned into a blood feud. The Kalpars left the area and are now trying to resettle in Sui. The Kalpars are also supported by some of the Massori Bugtis.

Bugti vs Raisani: Apparently there was no direct dispute between the two tribes. The clash between the Bugti and Raisani tribals in the city in 1994 created strong tension between these tribes, culminating into the clash at Sariab Road on 27 August 1994, leaving nine dead and several injured.

Bugti vs Mazari: The feud erupted over the ownership of sand dunes in the border of Punjab and Balochistan near Kashmore. The two sides attacked each other on several occasions and many precious lives were lost.

Raisani vs Rind: The feud dates back to the murder of some Jatois (a clan of the Rind tribe) on the eve of the local bodies elections 1979. Tribesmen from both sides have clashed on several occasions since then. Nawab Ghous Bakhsh Raisani, a leading tribal and political figure of the province, was also murdered during these clashes.

Rind vs Rind: The dispute is between the families of Sardar Yar Muhammad Rind, an MNA representing JWP (Jamhoori Watan Party), and the late Sardar Taj Muhammad Rind.

Hameedzai vs Ghaibzai: Both are branches of Achakzai tribe. They entered into the blood feud after the murder of Haji Muhammad Khan Ghaibzai. Gulistan, the native area of Achakzai, has been ruined due to the use of lethal weaponry during the clashes that often take place.

Magsi vs Magsi: Mainly a family dispute between the families of Nawab Zulfiqar Ali Khan Magsi. Over twenty persons were killed when Nawab Zuliqar Ali Magsi's caravan was ambushed near Panjuk in Jhal Magsi district when he was proceeding to file nomination papers for the October 1993 elections.

Raisani vs Domki: There was no dispute between these tribes until recently but the Sariab Road clash on 27 August 1994 pitched them against each other, when the two sons of Sardar Chakar Khan Domki were killed.

Marri vs Marri: The differences between the Bijarani and Gizini branches of the Marri tribes erupted during their self-exile to Afghanistan. The Bijaranis are no longer loyal to Nawab Khair Bakhsh Marri and their tug of war over the financial benefits from the Kohlu area continues.

Nasir vs Tareen: Additional Deputy Commissioner, Pishin was killed near Ziarat; Senator Sardar Yaqub Khan Nasir was accused in this case.

Sulemankhel vs Mandokhel: The tribes have a dispute over some land in Sambaza, north of Zhob. Several clashes have taken place between the two tribes. The Sulemankhels are not allowed to enter Zhob.

APPENDIX 7

Evaluation of Community Policing Experiment

Technique of Evaluation

Having discussed the community policing experiment and the strategy of its implementation in the Gujranwala Range, we now weigh it in terms of evaluation with reference to results achieved. The Neighbourhood Watch Programme was launched in the 'A' Block of Model Town, Gujranwala, on 20 June 1992. It was preceded by a survey in the area to get information about public perception of their social responsibilities, security needs, fear of crime, police legitimacy and other related issues. Based on the same questions, a second survey was conducted in January 1993, i.e. six months after the launching of the neighbourhood watch programme. Both the surveys were held under the auspices of the Citizen Police Advisory Council to ensure impartiality and credibility. A comparison of the findings of the two surveys indicates the degree of success of the neighbourhood watch in the achievement of its perceived goals.

Neighbourhood Watch Programme

Aims and Objectives

The aims and objectives of the above mentioned Neighbourhood Watch Programme are outlined as under:
- To reduce the opportunity for crime.
- To improve police-public relations and communication.
- To inculcate security consciousness through a general awareness about legal rights of citizens, road safety, traffic laws and ways to protect oneself against crime.

- To launch an anti-drug education awareness project with a view to rehabilitating drug addicts and prosecuting drug dealers/traffickers.
- To engender community spirit.

Strategy

Following are the main contours of the strategy adopted for the implementation of the neighbourhood watch:
- 'A' Block Model town was divided into five beats.
- On foot beat patrol was introduced.
- Greater co-ordination of beat officers with the personnel of the Civil Defence, Police Quami Razakars and the street/*mohalla* co-ordinators.
- Corner meetings by the respective beat officers to promote consultation.
- A Citizen Police Advisory Council was set up.
- Seminars, meetings, lectures and rallies involving children, housewives and common citizens with a view to promoting awareness about
    i)   Road Safety;
    ii) Protection against opportunistic crime;
    iii) Responsibilities of citizens;
    iv) Police role in society; and
    v)   Civic responsibility to obey the law of the land.
- Marking on valuables of the residential address/postcode by a marker of invisible ink to facilitate their identification in the event of theft through the use of the ultra-violet light.
- Marking of the registration, engine and chassis numbers on the windscreens of automobiles through the sand blast technique to ensure protection against theft.
- Verification of antecedents of domestic servants ensured.
- 'Rights of Neighbours', 'How to Save Yourself from Crime', 'Your Basic Rights' and 'Hazards of Drug Addiction' were the topics regarding which sign boards and pamphlets were distributed.
- Introduction of the police ambulances service.
- Revival of '*chowkidara*' system in streets, localities and markets.
- Periodic review of the programme in the meetings of the Citizen Police Advisory Council.
- For elimination of dug trafficking and addiction ADEAP (Anti Drug Education Awareness Project) was launched.

- Police officers and men were encouraged to write books, articles, true crime stories based on their personal experience and poems designed to boost up the morale of the Force.
- Campaign against sectarianism, meaningless old rivalries, drugs and social vices.
- Police songs eulogizing the great deeds of police officials and men were composed and played in market places, vehicles and public gatherings.

Results of Surveys

Following are the details of the surveys:

1) Are you satisfied with the system of police patrolling?

	June 1992	January 1993
Not Satisfied	90 per cent	1 per cent
Satisfied	3 per cent	92 per cent
Indifferent	7 per cent	1 per cent
Partially satisfied	-	6 per cent

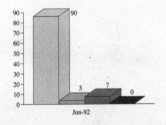
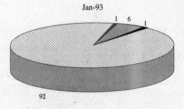

2) Whenever you leave your home, do you entrust it to be looked after
   by your neighbour?

Yes   11 per cent 94 per cent
Occasionally   19 per cent   2 per cent
Never   70 per cent   4 per cent

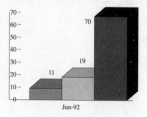

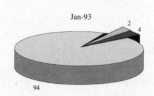

3) Do you always lock your vehicle ?

Yes   26 per cent 99 per cent
Occasionally   33 per cent   –
Always forget to lock the vehicle   5 per cent   1 per cent

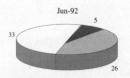

4) Do you keep a watch on the habits/conduct of the friends of your children and acquaintances?

No	81 per cent	4 per cent
Occasionally	13 per cent	-
Did not answer this question	-	5 per cent
Keep a watch on the habits of own children	6 per cent	88 per cent
Keep a watch on friends' habits	-	3 per cent

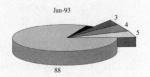

5) Are you aware of your child's performance in the school?

Yes	43 per cent	87 per cent
Occasionally yes	41 per cent	4 per cent
Do not have time to do so	16 per cent	4 per cent
Did not answer this question	-	5 per cent

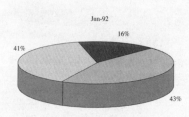

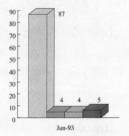

6. Have you noted down the telephone of police emergency/your police station?

No	73 per cent	6 per cent
Yes	11 per cent	92 per cent
Only know one number	16 per cent	2 per cent

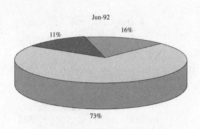
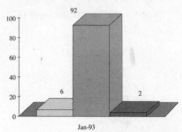

7) Do you know it is your legal right to obtain a copy of the FIR registered by you?

Yes	49 per cent	93 per cent
No	36 per cent	4 per cent
Is it possible?	15 per cent	3 per cent

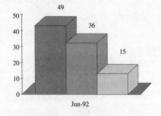
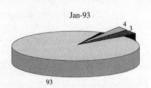

8) Do you resent/dislike being stopped by the police at their check post?

Yes	70 per cent	12 per cent
Occasionally resent it	21 per cent	7 per cent
Do not mind	9 per cent	81 per cent

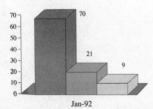
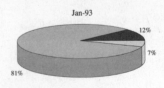

9) Are you afraid of criminals and crime?

Yes   72 per cent   25 per cent
Occasionally scared   13 per cent   8 per cent
Not scared   15 per cent   67 per cent

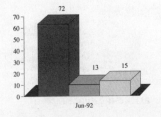

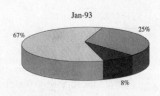

10) Are you satisfied with the performance of the courts?

Yes   26 per cent   Question was not
Partially satisfied   29 per cent   included in this
Not satisfied   45 per cent   survey.

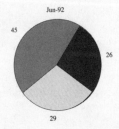

11) Do you feel yourself to be safe in your home?

Yes   3 per cent   79 perc ent
Partially safe   7 per cent   8 per cent
Do not feel safe   90 per cent   13 per cent

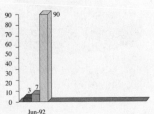

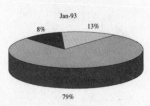

12) Are you satisfied with police performance?

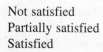

Not satisfied   77 per cent   12 per cent
Partially satisfied   17 per cent   8 per cent
Satisfied   6 per cent   80 per cent

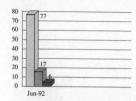

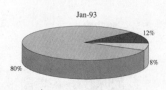

13) Are you keeping a watch-man in the marketing place?

Yes   90 per cent   98 per cent
No   10 per cent   2 per cent

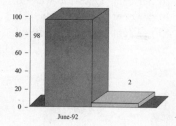

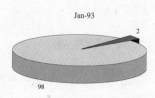

13 a)   Are you keeping a watch-man in the residential area?

Yes   44 per cent   84 per cent
No   56 per cent   16 per cent

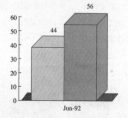

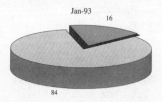

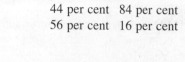

Social Attitude

14) In case you see a crime being committed will you report it to the Police?

	Previous (June 1992)	Latest (January 1993)
Will report	13 per cent	91 per cent
Will hesitate to report	11 per cent	4 per cent
Will not report	76 per cent	5 per cent

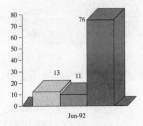
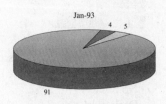

15) Will you give evidence against a criminal/bad character or a 'goonda'?

No	95 per cent	11 per cent
May think about it	–	2 per cent
If pertains to myself Yes	5 per cent	87 per cent

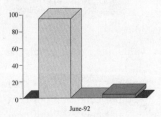
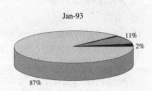

16) Will you use your licensed weapon in the apprehension of a criminal?

No	86 per cent	8 per cent
May do so	5 per cent	7 per cent
In case the crime is committed against respondent's own person Yes	9 per cent	85 per cent

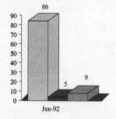

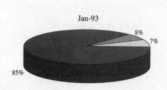

17) In case a dacoity takes place in your neighbour's house will you make an attempt to get hold of the offender?

No	53 per cent	1 per cent
Definitely Yes	-	94 per cent
Will inform the police	17 per cent	5 per cent
Will depend on circumstances	30 per cent	-

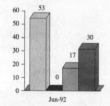

18) Are you in favour of keeping your valuables, gold jewelry in banks/lockers?

Yes	69 per cent	97 per cent
Not Necessarily	22 per cent	1 per cent
Even banks are not safe	9 per cent	2 per cent

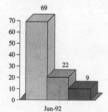

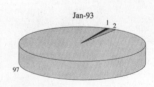

19) Would you like your possessions to be marked by the pencil of invisible writing with a view to facilitating their identification through the use of ultra violet light in case of theft?

Yes	37 per cent	99 per cent
Not sure	42 per cent	1 per cent
No	21 per cent	0

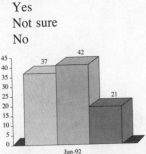

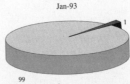

Jan-93

20) Have you rented your house or a portion thereof to a person whose antecedents you do not know?

Yes	44 per cent	9 per cent
Know something about them	20 per cent	1 per cent
No	25 per cent	44 per cent
Irrelevant Question	9	46

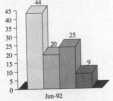

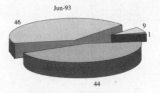

Jun-93

21) Are you in favour of aimless roaming about in the streets after 12'O Clock at night?

There should be a check	48 per cent	89 per cent
There should be a check when needed	44 per cent	2 per cent
No need	8 per cent	9 per cent

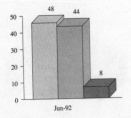

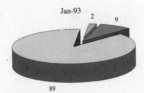

Jan-93

22) Housewives: When the bell rings do you open the door without verifying the antecedents of the caller?

Often it so happens	76 per cent	10 per cent
Occasionally yes	3 per cent	2 per cent
Not at all	65 per cent	88 per cent

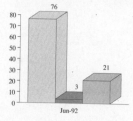

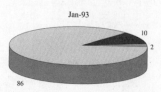

23) Do you keep your outer electricity bulb on at night?

No	86 per cent	10 per cent
Yes	3 per cent	86 per cent
Occasionally yes	–	4 per cent
Street light is there	7 per cent	–

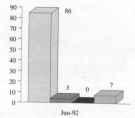

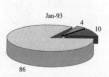

24) Are you in favour of boycott of drug-dealers/traffickers?

Yes	89 per cent	98 per cent
Partial boycott	6 per cent	–
No	5 per cent	2 per cent

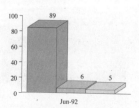

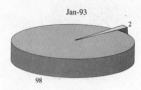

25) Have you made a report/memorandum of the registration no., chassis no. and engine no. of your automobiles?

No	39 per cent	9 per cent
Yes	42 per cent	89 per cent
May do so	19 per cent	2 per cent

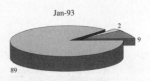

26) Do you know that the Station House Officer (SHO) of your police station is bound to be present in the police station from 4 pm to 6 pm daily to hear public complaints?

Do not know	83 per cent	10 per cent
Yes I know	17 per cent	85 per cent
Not sure	-	5 per cent

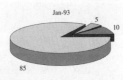

27) Are you sure that if someone gives information to the police under a promise of anonymity the police will honour their commitment?

Complete faith in the police	11 per cent	80 per cent
Do not trust the police in this context	83 per cent	9 percent
Partial confidence in the police	6 per cent	11 per cent

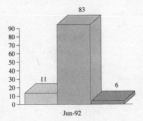
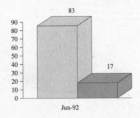

28) Would you like to be an eye-witness in an incident taking place in your presence?

No	87 per cent	13 per cent
May be	3 per cent	11 per cent
Yes	10 per cent	76 per cent

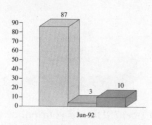 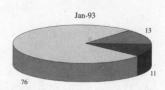

29) Are you satisfied with the present method of giving evidence?

No	87 per cent	23 per cent
To some extent	3 per cent	17 per cent
Completely satisfied	10 per cent	60 per cent

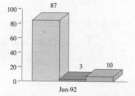 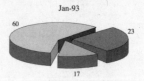

30) If you are a complainant in a case will you get the FIR registered based on truth and the actual facts of the case?

Yes	79 per cent	95 per cent
Depends on circumstances	21 per cent	3 per cent
No	–	2 per cent

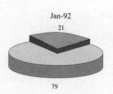 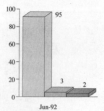

Cost-Benefit Perspective

Looking at the experiment from the perspective of costs and benefits it is worthwhile pointing out that the important items of expenditure were as under:

Items	Cost in Rupees	Met by
10 Security Markers at the rate of Rs 450 per marker	4500]	Donated by the Scotland Constabulary through Bashir Maan, former Member Police Committee, Glasgow
Ultra Violet Light Tube	2525]	
Advertisements		
Preparation of films/ documentaries	150,000]	
Leaflets, pamphlets, newsletters etc.	70,000]	Citizen Police Advisory Council
Marking of registration, chassis and engine particulars on windscreen of Vehicles	50 per vehicle	Individuals concerned
Magazine per issue	40,000	Advertisements
Reward to citizens	30,000	Police Budget
Expenditure on the treatment of a drug addict	10,000	Philanthropists/ Citizen Police Advisory Council
Police Ambulance Service (running expenditure)	10,000	Police Budget

The impact in terms of reduction in over all recorded crime in 1992 as compared with the previous years provides evidence of the success of the experiment. However, of more importance was the reduction in fear of crime, enhanced police legitimacy and the emergence of community spirit to fight crime collectively.

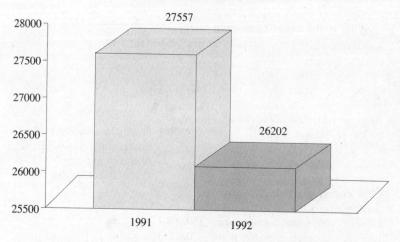

Source: Nadeem, A.H., (1992) *Nazm-o-Nask Report* (Annual Administration Report),
Gujranwala Range, Gujranwala.

This evaluation of community policing experiment in Gujranwala
Range indicates the intrinsic benefits in terms of increased involvement
of the police into wider community development and creation of new
avenues of co-operation and communication with public and private
organizations. The strategy involved is a recipe for the improved profile
of police/community relations. It was instrumental in developing a
community safety programme in collaboration with other agencies.
The experiment not only developed a structure for community relations
but also fostered a more responsive approach to community groups,
thereby reducing fear and improving quality of life.

APPENDIX 8
Proposed Crime Prevention CELL

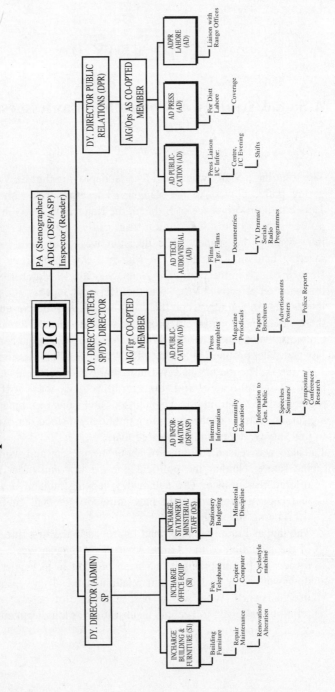

APPENDIX 9

A Sound Strategy of Controlling Lawlessness

The solution in Sindh was found by first deploying the Army and then giving police powers to the Rangers. The army was withdrawn in 1994 but to restore peace in Karachi, the Rangers were given policing power which includes conducting raids, making arrests and interrogating the suspect. The decision was taken at a high level meeting held in Karachi on 18 March 1995, with Prime Minister Benazir Bhutto in the chair (*The News*, Sunday, 19 March 1995). Was this solution effective? What was the degree of success in combating lawlessness in Karachi when the Army was deployed? For answers to these questions it will be appropriate to refer to the Human Rights Commission of Pakistan which conducted a survey on the handling of law and order problem in Sindh (HRCP, Fact Finding Mission Report, June 1994). The inquiry had its limitation. Nevertheless, its coverage, both geographically and demographically, was sufficiently representative to permit broad conclusions and a few recommendations.

Certain features of the prevailing public mind stood out. According to this survey, it generally appeared that:

1. There was reason for concern about the present and worry about the future. Neither the political nor the law and order situation offered reassurance. The authorities, lacking both in imagination and capacity for any bold new initiative, seemed captive to a debilitating stalemate.

2. The law and order situation had improved in the first three months of the induction of the Army. After that a plateau was reached in respect of the problems it had been brought in to tackle, while a downward slide had begun in relation to the ills its coming had itself spawned. What was at best a measure of purely temporary relief was allowed to become a substitute for long-term cure.

3. Both dacoity and acts of urban disruption and terrorism in Sindh were factors of socio-economic discontent. An Army operation by itself could not eliminate them, it could only drive them into animate suspension. While the dacoits were still biding their time, the urban militants were already making a comeback in defiance of the Army's presence. If one was sustained by a quiet feudal support system, the other was driven on political and emotional impulse and thrived on activism.

4. Army intervention did nothing to ease the politico-ethnic tension. It only hardened the divide. MQM was convinced that the action was aimed at crushing it. Sindhi nationalists saw it as serving to throttle popular aspiration. To both, the Army seemed to have delayed any redressive advance over their respective grievances. The intervention therefore had led in part to an intensification of the militants on each side, rendering a political resolution certainly no easier today than it was two years ago. Also, one thing that the Army's fathering of an MQM spilt did do was to start off a portentous process of blood-letting within MQM.

5. Because of the intervention, the government felt relieved of the pressure to seek ways of political accommodation with rival elements in the province. It resorted instead to such methods to cover its flanks and reinforce itself as making expedient appointments in administration, judiciary and local government, pressurizing individual critics and opponents, and drawing upon pockets of extra-political support. This widened the political fissure. It also diminished its ability to appropriately deal with powerful feudal and *patharidars*. (One specific instance of government's self-serving acts frequently pointed out was the transfer of Justice Anwar Nasir Zahid from the High Court to the Shariat Court. This was one issue on which all sections were of one opinion—they all regretted the change. Many thought that it was done because the Army wanted it.)

6. Two years of civilian duty had caused the virus of corruption to become widely spread within the Army. There were few that were believed to have escaped the infection.

7. Incidence of excesses committed by or attributed to the Army and the police or the clutch of their subsidiary agencies had diminished over the past several months but it still occurred and the restraint was not uniform. From public humiliation to torture to outright killing, it took many forms. It was a reminder that the order had not changed.

8. The role of the Army according to official claims was progressively being reduced. But its visibility and even active involvement in the cities had not much diminished.

From the above report of the Human Rights Commission of Pakistan, it is obvious that mere deployment of the Army or the Rangers cannot adequately ensure a sound administration of criminal justice. Rather it is counter productive. There is, therefore, a need for a sound strategy of controlling lawlessness. The strategy so devised should ideally encompass the following principles:

1. The central objective of government's strategy for the criminal justice system should be to sustain the rule of law by preventing crime wherever possible; by detecting the culprit when crimes are committed; by convicting the guilty and acquitting the innocent; by dealing firmly, adequately and sensibly with those found guilty; and by giving proper effect to the sentences or orders which are imposed. At the heart of the strategy, there are three underlying themes — the maintenance and encouragement of public confidence in the criminal justice system; the search for greater efficiency and effectiveness; and the retention of the proper balance between the rights of the citizen and the needs of the community as a whole.

2. The strategy should be concerned particularly with the police, the courts, the prison and probation services and the prosecution. The 'formal' criminal justice system — the processes of detection, prosecution and sentencing and the effect of the penalties imposed is crucial in deterring potential offenders, in protecting society from its most dangerous members and in giving help to those offenders who are willing and able to benefit from it. It must show society's disapproval of criminal activity and secure public confidence that justice is done and seen to be done. Without that confidence, the rule of law will lose respect with damaging effects on the individual communities who suffer from crime and on citizens who feel threatened by it and might otherwise be tempted to take the law into their own hands.

3. Experience in recent years has shown not only the importance of public confidence in the criminal justice system but also the system's limitations. Crime is a widespread, intractable and complex phenomenon for which no simple 'causes' can be proved. It has been rising steadily in Pakistan. Similar rises have taken place in other countries since 1947. Its incidence is commonly associated

with the presence of wider social problems such as a weakening of the family and a decline in standards of conduct and respect for authority. It follows that there are no simple 'solutions' to the problem of crime as such and that crime cannot be overcome and the needs of the victim cannot adequately be met through the operation of the criminal justice system alone. That system can only react after the crime has taken place. Wider social policies, for example for education, housing, employment and support for the family, must also play a part. Special attention must be given to providing help for victims. The problems and the means of dealing with them will be different in different areas and for different individuals.

4. The government's strategy for dealing with crime should have five main elements:
   a) Promoting action to prevent crime.
   b) Providing the criminal justice services, such as police, prisons and probation, with the extra resources they need to meet the increasing demands made on them.
   c) Strengthening the powers of the police and the courts while maintaining the necessary safeguards for the individual.
   d) Improving the efficiency and effectiveness of all parts of the criminal justice system.
   e) Providing more effective support and increased reassurance for the victims of crime.

The above mentioned programme is not static. In the light of experience, it needs constant strengthening. There is a need to evolve a sound strategy of combating the problem of lawlessness in Pakistan. The strategy so devised should be commensurate with the requirements of sustainable economic development.

BIBLIOGRAPHY

Ahmad, R. (1993), Book Review on 'Development Economics—A New Paradigm', *Pakistan Banker*, magazine of the Punjab Bank, July–December 1993.

Ahmad, R. I. (1988), 'Security Feelings and Professional Commitment of Police Officers', a Thesis submitted to the Department of Sociology, University of the Punjab, Lahore, pp. 71–2 (unpublished).

Ali, A. (1994), 'The Bloodiest year for Karachiities', Lahore, *The News*, 26 November.

Asian Survey Vol. XXX, No. 5, May 1990.

Auolakh, A.M.A. (1999), *Prison Administration in Pakistan*, S and S Publishers, Urdu Bazar, Lahore, pp. 245–6.

Baldwin, R. (1987), 'Why Accountability?' *British Journal of Criminology* 27(1), pp. 97–105.

Banking Council of Pakistan.

BBC Television (1987), *Secret Society*, BBC2 Television on 5 May 1987.

Becker, H. (1973), *Labelling Theory Reconsidered*, New York, Free Press.

Bernard, T. (1990), 'Angry Aggression Among the "Truly Disadvantaged"', *Criminology* 28, 1, pp. 73–93.

Blumstein, A., Cohen, J., Roth, J. and Visher, C. (1986), *Criminal Careers and 'Career Criminals'*, Washington, DC, National Academy Press.

Bottomley, A.K. and Coleman, C. (1981), *Understanding Crime Rates*, Farnborough, Gower.

Braithwaite, J. (1989), *Crime, Shame, and Reintegration*, Cambridge, Cambridge University Press.

Burgess, R. and Draper, P. (1989), 'The Explanation of Family Violence: the Role of Biological, Behavioral and Cultural Selection', in L. Ohlin and M. Tonry, eds., *Family Violence*, Chicago, III: University of Chicago Press.

Burrows, J. and Tarling, R. (1982), *Clearing up Crime*, London, Home Office Research Unit.

Central Board of Revenue, 1995.

Central Police Office, Karachi (1994), *Official Data.*

Central Police Offices of Lahore, Karachi, Peshawar, Quetta and Islamabad.

CESDHA (1982), 'The Social Impact of Major Development Measures on Specific Population Groups', pp. 37, 47, 54 and 56, Draft Paper.

Clavey, T. (1995), 'Terrorism', Article published in the *Los Angeles Times* reproduced in the *News International*, 20 April 1995, Lahore.

CPO Karachi (1994).

CPO Peshawer (1994).

CRG (1995), Survey Report by Control Risks Groups, *British Consultancy.*

Crime Branch of Sindh Police (1999), *Official Data*, received vide Memo No. CB-SO/99/1287-92/Karachi, dated 17 July 1999.

Crime Branch of the NWFP Police (1999).

Crime Branch of the Punjab Police (1999).

Crime Branch, Karachi (1999).

Crime Branch, Quetta, 1999.

Crimes Investigation Department of the Punjab Police (1999), *Official Record*, Lahore.

David, P. (1979), *Sociologia Criminal Juvenil.* Ed. Depalma, Buenos Aires, 1979, p. 139.

David, P. (1981), *The World of the Undocumented Migrant*, with M. Lucero Palma, Universidad Autonoma Ciudad Juarez, Juarez, Mexico, 1981 (in press).

Davidoff, L., and Greenhorn, M. (1991), 'Violent Crime in England and Wales', Paper presented at the British Criminology Conference, York.

Duncan, C. (1987), 'Viewpoint—Reasonable Force', 14 July. 10.30 p.m., London, ITV.

Duncan, E. (1989), *Breaking the Curfew: A Political Journey through Pakistan*, London, Penguin Group.

Ercelawn, Aly and Nauman, M. (1996), 'Restructuring Water and Sewerage Services in Karachi: Citizens' Consent or Coercion', paper presented at the seminar on *Citizens' Role in the Governance of Karachi*, 20–30 November 1996.

Farrington, D. (1989), 'Early Predictors of Adolescent Aggression and Adult Violence', in *Violence and Victims*, 4: 307–31.

Farrington, D. (1991), 'Childhood Aggression and Adult Violence: Early Precursors and Later Life Outcomes', in D. Pepler and K.

Rubin, eds., *The Development and Treatment of Childhood Aggression*, Hillsdale, NJ, Erlbaum.

Field, S. (1990), *Trends in Crime and Their Interpretation*, London, HMSO.

FPCCI (1994), *Analysis of Stocks*, Report, Federation of Pakistan Chambers of Commerce and Industry, November.

Gauhar, A. (1995), Observations made in an article published in *The Nation*, Wednesday, 28 June 1995.

Gartner, R. (1990), 'The Victims of Homicide', *American Sociological Review* 55, 1, pp. 92–107.

Gordon P. (1984), 'Community Policing: Towards the Local Police State', *Critical Social Policy* 10, Summer.

Government of Pakistan (1985), *Aslam Hayat Police Committee Report*, Islamabad, Ministry of the Interior, Government of Pakistan.

Government of Pakistan (1995), Central Board of Revenue, Islamabad.

Government of Pakistan (1995), Establishment Division, Islamabad.

Government of Pakistan (1995), Federal Bureau of Statistics, August, 1995.

Government of Pakistan (1995), Ministry of Commerce.

Government of Pakistan (1998–99), Economic Survey, 1998–99. Finance Division, Economic Adviser's Wing, Islamabad.

Government of Sindh (1995), *Minutes of the Meeting Chaired by the Prime Minister*, March 1995, Karachi, Home Department.

Greenwood, P., Chaiken, J., and Petersilia, J. (1977), *The Criminal Investigation Process*, Lexington, Mass., DC Health.

Griffiths, D. (1995), 'Monitoring International Money Laundering', *The U.N. Conference on Crime*, 9 May, Cairo

Hanmer, J. Radford, J., and Stanko, E. (1989), *Women, Policing and Male Violence: An International Perspective*, London, Routledge.

Scully, D. (1990), *Understanding Sexual Violence*, London, Harper Collins.

Dobash, R. E., and Dobash, R. D. (1992), *Women, Violence, and Social Change*, London, Routledge.

Haq, M. (1995), Speech delivered in a reception given by industrialists in honour of Dr Mehboob-ul-Haq, Karachi, 29 August 1995.

———— (1997), *Human Development in South Asia*, Oxford University Press, Karachi.

Hasan, A. (1998), 'Introduction' in Akhtar Hameed Khan's book, *Orangi Pilot Project: Reminiscences and Reflections*, Oxford University Press, Karachi.

Hasan, A. (1992), *Seven Reports on Housing*, OPP-RTI, Karachi, p. 17.

Hassan, A. (1999), 'Pakistan's Debt Problem: Its Changing Nature and Growing Gravity', Paper presented at the 15th Annual Conference of the Pakistan Society of Development Economists, 6 November, Islamabad.

Highways Department, Government of the Punjab, Lahore 1990.

Horiuchi, K. (1995), 'Overview of Mutual Assistance and Extradition Issues', (The) Joint Seminar on Contemporary Issues Concerning Criminal Justice—A Comparative Perspective, 12–16 March, Rawalpindi.

Hussain, M., (1990), *Pakistan's Politics—The Zia Years*, Lahore, Progressive Publishers, Zaildar Park, Ichra.

IBA (1995), IBA Seminar Report, Karachi, 11 April 1995.

India Today (1995), *The Transparency International Survey*, quoted in the 15 July issue.

J.N. (1978), *Report on the World Social Situation*, p. 35.

KCCI (1995), *Survey Report, 1995*, The Research Cell, Karachi Chamber of Commerce and Industry.

KCCI (1995), *A Study on Production Losses During the Past Six Months*, Karachi Chamber of Commerce and Industry, Economic Wing, July 1995.

Kemal, A. R. (1987), 'Pakistan's Experience in Employment and Manpower Planning', in R. Amjad (ed.): *Human Resource Planning, The Asian Experience*, New Delhi, ARTEP.

———— (1994), 'Structural Adjustment, Employment, Income Distribution and Poverty', *Pakistan Development Review* Vol. 33, no. 4, 1994.

Khan, A.H. (1998), *Orangi Pilot Project: Reminiscences and Reflections*, Oxford University Press, Karachi, pp. xix–xx.

Khan, M. Abbas (1996), *Problems of Law and Order and Police Reforms*, IGP's Briefing to the Prime Minister of Pakistan, 7 February.

Khan, Shahrukh, R. and Aftab, S. (1996), 'Structural Adjustment, Labour and the Poor in Pakistan', mimeo, Pakistan Institute of Labour Education and Research, Karachi, 1996.

KSE (1994), *Daily Situation Report*, Karachi Stock Exchange, 21 November 1994.

KSE (1995), *Daily Situation Report*, Karachi Stock Exchange, 7 April 1995.

KSE (1995), *Daily Situation Report*, Karachi Stock Exchange, 10 April 1995.

KSE (1995), *Daily Situation Report*, Karachi Stock Exchange, 24 April 1995.

KSE (1995), *Daily Situation Report*, Karachi Stock Exchange, 28 June 1995.

KSE (1995), *Daily Situation Report*, Karachi Stock Exchange, 29 June 1995.

KSE (1995), *Daily Situation Report*, Karachi Stock Exchange, 17 July 1995.

KSE (1995), Interview with Nadim Ahmad Siddiq and Khadim Ali Shah Bukhari.

KSE (1995), *Daily Situation Report*, Karachi Stock Exchange, 17 July 1995.

KSE (1995), *Bulletin*, Karachi Stock Exchange, July 1995.

Lamb, C. (1991), *Waiting for Allah: Pakistan's Struggle for Democracy*, New Delhi, Penguin Books.

Iderson, J. (1981), 'Community Cops', Letter to the Editor, *New Society* 207, London.

Lea, J. and Young, J. (1984), *What is to be done about Law and Order?* Harmondsworth, Penguin Books.

Levi, M. (1997), 'Violent Crime', *The Oxford Handbook of Criminology*, Clarendon Press, Oxford, pp. 841–82.

London Metropolitan Police (1980), *Commissioner's Report 1980*, p. 8.

Mahmood, Z. and Nazli, H. (1996), 'Estimates of Unrecorded Accumulation of Private Foreign Assets', (unpublished) PIDE, Islamabad.

Mawby, R. (1979), *Policing the City*, Farnborough, Gower.

McClintock, D. 'General Report on the Criminological Aspects', pp. 17 and 19 in *Cities and Criminality*, 10th International Congress of Social Defence.

Meier, G.M. and Baldwin, R. (1972), *Economic Development: Theory, History, Policy*, Charles E. Tuttle Company, Tokyo, Asia Edition.

(The) *Muslim*, Tuesday, 23 January 1990, Islamabad.

Nadeem, A. H. (1989), *The Punjab Police in a Comparative Perspective*, Progressive Publishers, Zaildar Park, Ichhra, Lahore.

——— (1992), *Nazm-o-Nask Report* (Urdu), (*Annual Administration Report*), Gujranwala Range, Gujranwala, pp. 322–3.

Nadeem, M. (2000), 'Foreign Investment Nosedives', *The News*, Friday, 14 January 2000, Lahore.

Naqvi, N. H. (1993), 'Modern Development Thinking Areas of Global Consensus', *Pakistan Banker*, Magazine of the Bank of Punjab, January–June 1993, Lahore, p. 47.

The Nation, Wednesday, 28 June 1995, Lahore.

(The) Nation, Friday, 19 July 1991, Lahore.

(The) Nation, Thursday, 25 January 1990, Lahore.

National Assembly of Pakistan (1995), Replies to questions in the National Assembly of Pakistan by State Minister for Finance Shahabudin, Wednesday, 8 March 1995, Islamabad.

New York Times, 9 March 1995, New York.

News Journal (1999), *The News Investor's Business and Financial Journal*, June, 1999, p. 2.

(The) News, Monday, 17 July 1995, Lahore.

(The) News, Sunday, 16 April 1995, Lahore.

(The) News, Thursday 22 June, 1995, Lahore.

(The) News, Thursday, 13 April 1995, Lahore.

(The) News, Thursday, 13 July 1995, Lahore.

(The) News, Thursday, 2 July 1995, Lahore.

(The) News, Thursday, 20 April 1995, Lahore.

(The) News, Thursday, 22 June 1995, Lahore.

(The) News, Thursday, 29 June 1995, Lahore.

(The) News, Tuesday, 27 June 1995, Lahore.

(The) News, Tuesday, 27 June 1995, Lahore.

(The) News, Wednesday, 2 August 1995, Lahore.

(The) News, Wednesday, 28 June 1995, Lahore.

(The) News, Wednesday, 30 June 1999, Statement of Minister for Information, Mushahid Hussain Syed in the Senate.

North, Douglass, C. (1991), *Institutions, Institutional Change and Economic Performance*, Cambridge University Press.

Oscar, N. (1972), *Defensible Space: Crime Prevention Through Urban Design*, New York, Macmillan, 1972.

Pakistan Administrative Staff College (1994), *Law and Order Report of Group 'A' of the 61st National Management Course*, 1994, Lahore.

Pakistan and Gulf Economist (1995), Report on Karachi, March.

Pakistan Banking Council 1993.

Papanek, Gustav F. (1987), *Lectures on Growth, Equity and the Political Process: Lessons from Southern Asia*, Pakistan Institute for Development Economics (PIDE), Islamabad.

Pasha, H.A. & Wasti, S.A. (1993), 'Social Costs of University Closures', *The Pakistan Development Review* 32–4 Part II (Winter 1993), pp. 677–85

PBC (1993), Pakistan Banking Council.

Pharmaceutical Association of Pakistan (1999), 'Market Survey' (unpublished), Lahore.

Police Bureau of Research, Ministry of Interior, Government of Pakistan.

Policing London (1987), March/April, Vol. 4.

Population Census (1998), Planning and Development Division, Islamabad.

Preale (1976), *The Employment Problem in Latin America. Facts, Outlooks and Policies,* Santiago, 1976.

—————— *(1979), Growth, Employment and Basic Needs in Latin America and the Caribbean*, Report of the Director General to the 11th Conference of American States, Geneva, ILO, p. 6.

PTC (1995), *Briefing*, The Pakistan Telecommunication Corporation, Karachi.

Recorder, 18 July 1995.

Reiner, R. (1986), *The Politics of the Police*, London, Wheatsheaf Books Ltd., Harvester Press, 1986.

Reiner, R. (1992), *The Politics of the Police*, 2nd edn., Hemel Hempstead edition Wheatsheaf.

Skogan, W. (1990), *The Police and Public in England and Wales*, A British Crime Survey Report, London, HMSO.

Which (1990), 'The Police', in *Which?* May, pp. 258–61.

Reiss, Jr., A.J. (1986), *Communities and Crime*, University of Chicago Press.

Rostow, W. (1971), *Politics and the Stages of Growth*, Cambridge University Press.

Sahibzada, M.H. (1997), *Poverty Alleviation in Pakistan: Present Scenario and Future Strategy*, Institute of Policy Studies and Friedrich Ebert Stiftung, Karachi.

Sanders, W. (1979), *Detective Work*, Glencoe, Free Press.

Savona, E. (1995), 'Criminal Syndicates', The U.N. Conference on Crime, 9 May, Cairo.

Sayeed, Asad and Ghaus, A. (1996), 'Has Poverty Returned to Pakistan?' mimeo, Social Policy and Development Centre, Karachi, 1996.

SBP (1995), *Annual Report*, State Bank of Pakistan.

Special Branch, Punjab, *Special Branch Report*, 1994, Lahore.

Special Branch, (1999), *District/Sect-wise Details of Deeni Madaris*, Directorate of Research and Reference, Special Branch, Punjab Police, Lahore, February 1999.

Spengler, J. (1949), *Theories of Socio-economic Growth: Problems in the Study of Economic Growth*, National Bureau of Economic Research, July 1949.

State Bank of Pakistan (1992), *Bulletin*, February and December, Karachi 1992.

———— (1995), *Bulletin*, Karachi, June, July and August 1995.

———— (1995), *Bulletin*, Karachi, September 1995.

Steer, D. (1980), *Uncovering Crime*, Royal Commission on Criminal Procedure, Study 7, London, HMSO.

Streeten, P. (1995), 'Development Ideas in Historical Perspective: The New Interest in Development', Quaid-e-Azam Lecture at the Eleventh Annual General Meeting of Pakistan Institute of Development Economics, 18 to 21 April, Islamabad.

The Europa World Year Book 1995, Vol. I and II.

Time Magazine, 12 March 1990, USA.

Toch, H. (1969), *Violent Men*, Harmondsworth, Penguin.

Transparency International Index, World Bank.

UNDP (1999), *Human Development Report 1999*, launched at the UN Information Centre, Islamabad, on 16 July 1999.

United Nations (1978), *Report on the World Social Situation*, p. 33.

Wilson, J., and Herrnstein, R. (1985), *Crime and Human Nature*, New York, Simon and Schuster.

Wolfgang, M., and Ferracuti, F. (1967), *The Subculture of Violence*, London, Tavistock.

World Bank (1993), *World Development Report*.

———— (1998/99), *World Development Report*.

———— (1978), *World Development Report*, 1978.

———— (1979), *World Development Report*, 1979, p. 81.

———— (1999), *Household Savings in Pakistan* by Dr Ashfaque H. H. Khan and Dr Zafar Moeen Nasir, Washington DC, July.

World Bank Report, 1991.

World Development Report, 1993.

Zaidi, S.A. (1996), 'Gender Perspectives and the Quality of Care in Underdeveloped Countries—Disease, Gender and Contextuality', *Social Science and Medicine*, Vol. 43, no. 5, 1996.

————— (1999), *The New Development Paradigm: Papers on Institutions, NGOs, Gender and Local Government,* Oxford University Press, Karachi.

Zaman, A. (1995), 'The Government's Present Agreement with the IMF: Misgovernment or Folly?' *Pakistan Journal of Applied Economics,* Vol. 11, no. 1 and 2, 1995.

INDEX

A

Abbas, DSP Syed Zafar, 241
Abbas, Syed Tajammal, 109
Afghan war, 74, 75, 77, 97, 112
Afghanistan, 74, 77, 93, 94, 111, 155
Africa, 25, 32, 37
Ahmad, R., 18
Ahmed, Babu Javed, 244
Ahmed, Constable Gulzar, 245
Ahmed, DIG Rana Maqbool, 243
Ahmed, Rana Saghir, 244
Ahmed, SI Sultan, 232, 233
Akbar, ASI Ali, 233
Ali, Rafaqat (Constable), 238
Ali, Raza, 109
Asia, 32, 39
Aurangzeb, Inspector, 239

B

Babar, Naseerullah, 128
Bajwa, DSP Yousaf, 241
Balochistan, 47, 74, 97–8, 188;
crimes scenario in, 113-14
Bangash, SP Muhammad Masood,
242, 246
Bangladesh, 51, 52, 74, 150
Becker, H., 62
Bernard, T., 60
Bhatti, SP HQ Khadim Hussain, 238,
247
Bhutto, Benazir, 151
Black Economy, size of, 201–203
Braithwaite, J., 58; on homicide, 58

Budget deficit, 196–201; non-
recovery of stuck-up loans, 198–
200; social cost of closure of
Karachi University, 200; sick
units, 201
Burgess, R., and Draper, P., 58; on
family violence, 58
Butt, Inspector Muhammad Saleem,
240

C

Census, 46
Chaudhry, IG Sardar Muhammad,
241, 243, 274, 275
China, 32, 34, 51
Chiniot incident, 108
Classical and Neo-Classical approach,
9–10
Clavey, T., 6
Committee on the Study of
Corruption, 81, 82, 83
Computable General Equilibrium
model (CGE), 148, 156;
autonomous political
developments and organic events,
149; values assigned to weights/
intensities of major events, 150–
51; of recurring events, 151; of the
composite index of law and order,
151–4; use of the Series on Index
of Law and Order in the context
of Modified CGE Model, 155–8;
and capital flows, 158; flight of
capital, 158–61